STUDIES IN SOVIET SOCIETY

VOLUME 1

Industry and Labour in the U.S.S.R.

Industry and Labour in the U.S.S.R.

Edited by G. V. OSIPOV

With an Introduction by
MAURICE HOOKHAM

Tavistock Publications
LONDON · SYDNEY · TORONTO · WELLINGTON

First Published in 1966
by Tavistock Publications Limited
11 New Fetter Lane, London E.C.4
Printed in Great Britain
in 10 on 12 point Monotype Times
by T. and A. Constable Limited, Edinburgh
© Tavistock Publications 1966
Prepared for publication by the
Novosti Press Agency (APN)

Contents

A NOTE ON TRANSLATION
AND TRANSLITERATION

The translation of the papers included in this volume was first prepared in Moscow by the Novosti Press Agency, but I have checked the translation against the original Russian texts and made considerable amendment in order to improve readability while maintaining the style and expression of the original. Transliteration of Russian technical terms and names has been kept as consistent as possible throughout, but place names have been transliterated according to the system employed in modern atlases wherever it appeared it would help the reader to locate them. The translation of occupations presented great difficulty owing to the differences in classification of occupations and the absence of agreed definitions of occupations in England. As a rule the nearest general English equivalent that would be intelligible to the reader has been used, although it may not convey exactly the technical distinctions made in the Russian.

Maurice Hookham

Introduction

MAURICE HOOKHAM

The papers published in this volume have been compiled by an editorial board composed of V. V. Denisov, F. V. Konstantinov, N. F. Naumova, and E. M. Rosental, under the general editorship of G. V. Osipov. About sixty papers, recently written by Soviet sociologists, social psychologists, demographers, and economists, on problems over a wide field of sociology, were selected by the board. The great majority had not previously been published either in the Soviet Union or abroad; reference is given in the Bibliography to those that have recently appeared in a Russian volume. They were translated in the Soviet Union under the supervision of the editorial board to make them available to the English reader. I have selected from these sixty papers those which fall broadly within the field of industrial sociology in the belief that they will be of the greatest immediate interest. From other papers of a more general nature, I have included in this introduction a brief statement of the theoretical foundations on which Soviet sociology rests, the categories of sociological problem that are being dealt with by Soviet sociologists, the methods they employ, and the institutional organization of their work.

At the Third, Fourth, and Fifth World Congresses of Sociologists, held in 1956, 1959, and 1962, Soviet sociologists presented papers and established contacts with sociologists from all over the world. P. N. Fedoseyev, Vice-President of the Academy of Sciences of the USSR, in the closing words of his paper at the Fourth World Congress, said 'Co-operation between Soviet sociologists and their foreign colleagues, an exchange of opinions concerning the problems and methods of research, will promote a further progress in sociological studies'.[1] The presentation of these papers is a further contribution to this purpose.

Thirty years ago, Dr J. F. Hecker published a work entitled *Russian Sociology*,[2] in which he traced the development of what he called 'the Marxo-Leninist theory of society'. In a foreword to this work, Sidney

Webb wrote 'The reader will not find in it any description of the social institutions of the USSR, in which so much "sociological thought and theory" has been embodied. Thought and theory about social institu-tions is a part, even an important part, of that embryonic science that is rightly termed sociology. But like any other branch of science, sociology must include also the objective study of the phenomena themselves of which it deals, the groupings of men which we call social institutions.' Many detailed sociological studies had in fact been made in the Soviet Union at the time when Sidney Webb wrote those words, though they had not been carried out by people who called themselves sociologists.[3] In the last ten years many more studies have been made and it is now possible to provide this long delayed reply to Sidney Webb's complaint.

Hecker traced the development of Marxist sociology in Russia back to the eighteenth century, when popular movements began to arise against the autocracy. The leaders of these movements 'sought to develop their programmes of action and give them rational justification by the aid of philosophy and the social sciences'.[4] He discusses the main schools of Russian sociological thought which arose and which had a strong influence on the development of modern sociology. They are the Slavophils, including Danilevsky; the Westernists, including Herzen and Chernishevsky; the Subjectivists, including Lavrov and Mikhailovsky; the Anarchists, including Kropotkin and Sorokin (who did much pioneering work on social mobility); the Marxists, including Plekhanov and Lenin; and the Revisionists including Struve, Tugan-Baronovsky, and Bogdanov. Hecker concludes his work with the words, 'Much of what is in vogue among sociologists today has been worked at by Russian sociologists. They were among the first to try to rid sociology of Darwinism and Spencerianism and to seek to establish it upon a sound scientific basis. But when all this is conceded them, we must also say that most of their good ideas have remained foreign to sociologists generally, and have since been wrought out independently by West European and American sociologists in a much more systematic way than by the earlier and unknown Russians. Of course, there are contributions made by such men as Kropotkin, Kovalevsky, Korkunov, Lenin, and others, that have now become the common possession of Western European and American students of social science. But there is, in addition, much ingenious sociological thought still buried in Russian periodical literature, or poorly edited in the collected works of many authors.'[5]

This was how it seemed to Hecker more than thirty years ago, and his work has remained the main source of information for the English reader. During the period of the cult of the personality of Stalin there was very little concrete sociological research done in the Soviet Union and consequently very little was published. The traditional exposition of the framework and individual propositions of historical materialism, in which some of the notions and categories developed by Marx, Engels, and Lenin were ignored, gave rise to the belief that Marxist sociology did not exist. When sociological research began again in the Soviet Union, from about 1954 (after the death of Stalin), it was understood by some Western sociologists that its roots connected with the names of Mikhailovsky, Lavrov, and Sorokin, but not with the names of Marx, Engels, and Lenin.

Some of the work of Soviet social scientists, which was also inspired by these earlier traditions, has now been made available to the West. A series of papers on Soviet psychology was published in 1957, edited by Brian Simon.[6] The introduction to these papers is relevant to an understanding of the work of Soviet sociologists. Herzen and Chernishevsky inspired I. M. Sechenov to start research into the physiology of the higher nervous system. This work was carried on by Pavlov on the materialist basis that 'mental phenomena are inseparably connected with the functioning of the brain and that they can be investigated by the same objective methods as are other phenomena of nature'.[7] Soviet psychologists have constructed on these foundations criticisms of mechanistic interpretations of the relations of mind and matter offered by empirical and behaviourist psychologists which underlie much of Western sociology.

Because they are dialectical materialists, Marxist psychologists have built on the materialist basis established by Sechenov and Pavlov in a way that has avoided the degeneration of materialism into mechanism. Simon argues that dialectical materialism differs from philosophical systems which provide a finished world-picture as a complex of ready-made things with fixed properties; it offers a view of the world as 'a complex of processes in which all things arise, have their existence and pass away; it insists that all phenomena must be studied in their movement and change and in inseparable connection with other phenomena . . . regards matter in motion as fundamental and inseparable from space and time. Finally it does not reduce all movement to mechanical motion, but conceives of a range of forms of movement of matter, from simple change of place to complex changes in the thought processes; within this range one form of movement derives from another one form of movement may be transformed into another, giving rise to new qualities of matter in motion – as the expression of differences in the form of motion. This permits of the conception of quantitative change being succeeded by qualitative change; a transition to a new level. The relevance of this conception to problems of the relation of body and mind, of the transition from sensation to thought, for instance, and to detailed questions concerning the relation of practical activity and mental processes is obvious.'[8]

Some Western sociologists have in recent years shown a great interest in the sociological writings of Marx and have made selections of his work more readily available to the English reader. They have not attempted to show either the current interpretations given to them by Soviet sociologists or the developments in sociological theory in the Soviet Union. Furthermore, they have argued that a great deal of Marx's work has been incorporated in Western sociology and that this entails the disappearance of a 'Marxist' sociology.[9]

Soviet sociologists, on the other hand, claim that they are Marxist sociologists. At the same time, there is in the Soviet Union by no means a uniformity of view about Marxist sociology. At a conference in October 1963, in Moscow, it was recognized that the extension of research in the social sciences had raised new methodological problems and that the nature of the subject sociology deserved serious consideration. A number of different views about Marxist sociology have been held by both Soviet and foreign Marxists. Some considered that Marxism as a whole is what is meant by sociology. Others connected Marxist sociology with the theory of scientific communism, and a third group held that there exists approximately the same distinction between historical materialism and Marxist sociology as there is between the theoretical and applied aspects of any branch of human knowledge. It was admitted that there were other points of view and that it was wrong to deny to the representatives of these different standpoints the right to defend their views. It was also pointed out that there was a natural tendency for further differentiation in the social sciences and that it was desirable to refrain from impatient attitudes to the opinions of others, the more so since, in each of the viewpoints mentioned, there is a rational kernel which it is not possible simply to reject.[10]

Soviet sociologists claim that Marx and Engels laid the foundations of Marxist sociology by a thorough analysis of actual societies, of actual social relations and social classes. They wrote in *The German Ideology*, 'Where speculation ends – in real life – there real, positive science begins; the representation of the practical activity, of the practical process of development of men.'[11] The essence of Marxist sociology is held to be the close study of the real process of life and the practical activity of men in each separate epoch, or each separate socio-economic formation. Socio-economic formations distinguished and studied by Engles, Marx, and Lenin (primitive communism, slave-owning and feudal societies, capitalism, and communism) were examined in their rise and development in the greatest detail. They also made a thorough analysis of the principal, and non-principal, social classes of modern society, the proletariat and the bourgeoisie, the peasantry and the big landowners, the petty and middle bourgeoisie, the lumpenproletariat, and various social strata.[12] In addition, between the 1840s and 1890s Marx and Engels analysed the social relations and specific conditions of the population in Britain, Ireland, France, Germany, Italy, Poland, Russia, India, and China.

From the extensive factual material they studied, they were able to define the general and specific features characterizing the development of each socio-economic formation and to formulate the basic laws governing the process of social development. The scientific theory of social development which they worked out is thus held by Soviet sociologists to be synonymous with sociology. In the broadest sense, it is a science concerned with the laws governing the rise, development, and change of socio-economic formations, manifest in concrete social conditions and relations. The latter are the products of human activity. They show, to a greater or less degree, the possibilities and necessities of social development in a particular historical epoch. They also actively influence the consciousness of men and, consequently, determine their social behaviour and activity.[13] In the narrower sense, sociology is a science concerned with the laws governing the development of the social structure and the interaction of its parts. Its field of study is the diverse elements of the social structure (classes, nations, social institutions, social values, etc.) in their organic relations both with one another and with the social relations of men as objects and subjects of social interaction.

Sociology is related to the other social sciences by the field of study, for example, economics deals with only one aspect of social life, whereas sociology deals with society as a whole; and by the nature of the conclusions, for example, history is a study in which one seeks to explain the course of historical events in all their concrete detail, whereas sociology has as its main task the discovery of general laws which govern concrete developments in particular societies. An example of a general sociological law is the law of interaction between the basis and the superstructure of a society. The basis of any society is its economic system; the political, legal, and other ideologica relations which are formed in the given society constitute the superstructure of the given economic basis. The superstructure not only is determined by its basis, and not only reflects its characteristic features; it also exerts an active reciprocal influence on it. In any particular socio-economic formation, at a particular stage in its development, a specific form of this law will operate. It can be discovered only by a study of that actual society. A study of the socialist society which developed in the Soviet Union, after the revolution in 1917, shows that the law of interaction between the basis and its superstructure operated in this society. The basis determined the superstructure, but the particular form of the law which operated then was one in which the superstructure played a specially active role. The special role played by the state in a socialist society is determined by economic causes, because of the nature of the economic system in which the means of production are socially owned.[14]

Soviet sociologists hold that concrete research is an essential method of Marxist sociology necessary for its development. Engels criticized attempts to divorce the materialist interpretation of history from concrete research. 'Our conception of history', he wrote, 'is above all a guide to study, not a lever for construction à la Hegelianism. . . .' Lenin wrote, 'Marxian dialectics requires a concrete analysis of each specific historical situation'. Against such a standpoint two antagonistic views are distinguished: scholasticism and empiricism. The scholasticist in sociology is seen to be one who deduces the facts of social life from a theory, or who attempts to fit new facts or phenomena into a predetermined theory. Dogmatism and scholasticism in the social sciences in the Soviet Union for a time replaced scientific research. Since the condemnation of this, in 1956, sociological research has revived in the Soviet Union. It is realized that concrete research into social problems is vitally necessary in a rapidly developing, new society. In this connection it is recognized that there is a danger of a descent into empiricism. While the study of 'stubborn' facts is held to be indispensable, it is denied that the study of the facts themselves will lead directly to a theory. The connection between empirical and theoretical knowledge is not one as simple or schematic as that held by the exponents of empiricism in sociology. The transition from concrete to abstract notions is complex. Marx wrote, 'Crass empiricism is transformed into false metaphysics, scholasticism, which toils painfully to deduce undeniably empirical phenomena by simple formal analysis from the general law, or to reason out a justification for them on the basis of that law'.[15]

The distinguishing features of Marxist sociology are defined by

Soviet sociologists as follows. First, its investigations are based on facts of objective social reality interpreted in the light of the theory that society is not a mechanical sum of individuals and social groups in isolation but a whole bound together by definite social relations characteristic of that society. These relations are seen to be in a state of motion and the task of sociology is seen to be the formulation of a scientific theory of social progress. Second, Soviet sociologists do not regard themselves as being merely confined to disclosing the general laws governing social development by means of empirical research. They accept as a major social function the role of contributing to purposeful change in accordance with the objective requirements of social development. It is not enough to know and understand the general laws of social development and their specific forms in particular societies. This makes it possible to define the trends of development. In order to exert a scientific influence on such development, it is above all necessary to know and understand the mechanism by which these laws work in given concrete conditions of place and time. The need for change and for the transformation of old social relations is accepted in Soviet society, and the sociologist is expected to contribute to the scientific planning of social change.

These distinguishing features may be illustrated by the examples of problems currently being investigated by Soviet sociologists, and by the methods they employ in such investigations. For example, the development of the educational system, whereby all young people will receive a basic eight years of education and the great majority of them higher education, makes it necessary not only to provide sufficient schools and institutions, grants for students, and arrangements for students in employment to be released for part-time education. It is also necessary to consider the effects of these developments on the family, along with the effects of the increased provision of nurseries and boarding schools, and of old age pensions, and the extension of public catering facilities. It is envisaged that the family will remain the basic nucleus of society, although it will undergo substantial changes. Soviet sociologists are called upon to play an active part in investigating these changes in the whole system of relations between people of different generations, and to make recommendations to the planning authorities.

The problems under investigation may be divided into three groups. First, those social problems connected with the creation of the material and technical bases of communism. Examples of these are the study of the laws governing the rise of labour productivity, technological

B

development, and the conversion of science into a direct productive force; working out new methods of training and re-training specialists in industry and agriculture to keep pace with technological progress; and the study of the social aspects of the comprehensive mechanization and automation of production. The second group consists of problems arising from the development of communist social relations. These include the study of concrete ways of transforming existing types of property ownership (state and collective farm or co-operative owner-ship) into a single form of communist ownership; means of overcoming the major differences between town and country life and between mental and physical labour; special problems connected with the position of women and young people; the development of the family and the extent to which the existing forms of work, wages, and legal regulation influence people's social relations. The third group is made up of prob-lems of individual development. These include the study of the best ways of bringing up people with a communist world-outlook and morality and of developing the scientific, artistic, and technological creativeness of working people; the study of the influence of the school, of the family, and of employment in the social psychology of working people; the study of the best means of organizing leisure; and the analysis of the causes of, and the working out of concrete means for eliminating, antisocial phenomena such as bureaucratic behaviour of officials towards members of the public, malingering, egoistic behaviour, and resort to bribery.

Problems of the methodology and techniques of sociological research are discussed at length in *The Practice and Methods of Concrete Socio-logical Research in the USSR*, which is based on research work carried out by sociologists in Moscow, Leningrad, Krasnoyarsk, Sverdlovsk, etc. This work involved the use of documentary material and records, regional and factory statistics, direct observation, interviews, and control and production experiments. A large-scale study of the effects of technological changes on workers in a number of workplaces in Gorky was based not only on a systematic analysis of the factory records but also on new techniques designed especially for the research. Particular attention was paid to the study of personal records, contain-ing details of the lives of individuals, which are regarded as especially important for the understanding of the socio-psychological development of the individual. The connection between a person's work and leisure-time activities is regarded as important. For example, the work of a control-panel operator depends on his ability to find the right measure of relaxation in his leisure-time activities. It has been found that many operators took part in amateur dramatics and studied in their leisure time. Observations and participant observation were carried out, particularly in relation to the development of young workers. About 1,000 interviews were recorded based on four questions and these were repeated a year later. Controlled experiments were conducted on two conveyor lines of a similar nature. Ninety-five per cent of the workers stated that they found the work monotonous and uninteresting. The work on one of the lines was then organized on a collective basis in which each worker was trained to perform an operation in addition to his original one, and given opportunities to use this wider skill to suggest and introduce improvements in the operation. When the inquiry was repeated, the workers on the control line stated, as before, that they found the work uninteresting but, on the reorganized line, they stated that the work had become interesting and varied.

A number of public opinion polls have been conducted. An institute was set up by the newspaper *Komsomolskaya Pravda* early in 1960. In a poll carried out in May 1960, young people were asked three questions: (i) Will mankind succeed in preventing war? (ii) What makes you sure? (iii) What should be done to strengthen peace? The results were reported in *Komsomolskaya Pravda*, 19 May 1960. A second poll was carried out in the same year to collect evidence on living standards. Early in 1961, there was an extensive poll of young people's views of their own generation. In August 1961, a poll was conducted among special work teams, which had volunteered to improve output, to collect evidence of the methods they had found to be most successful. In 1962, a poll was held on the question 'What do you think of young families?' Such polls are held to be valuable not only for the evidence that they produce but also because they help to form public opinion. The questions are usually framed in such a way as to preclude a simple 'yes' or 'no' answer. Those interviewed are invited to express their desires and opinions, or called upon to make proposals. The latter are regarded as especially valuable and, when analysed, form the basis of recommendations for implementation.

In investigations into living standards, statistical analysis is made of workers' budgets, using methods of the least squares, smoothing processes, regression analysis, and Engel curves.

In discussions of the methodology of sociological research, considerable importance is attached to logico-mathematical analysis and to the logic of scientific research. Attention is paid to problems of thought and language, the part played by formalization in logic, and to axiomatic, genetic, and hypothetico-deductive methods of formulating scientific theories. Although there are certain spheres of research in which wide use is made of formal logic, for example, in the analysis of social connections and social relations, dialectical logic is employed outside these limits. In large-scale research, theoretical conferences are held, usually in the field with the investigators and the investigated taking part, to discuss the results obtained. The reports of such conferences are published and used for further analysis.

The centre of sociological research in the Soviet Union is the Soviet Sociological Association, which was set up in 1958. There are more than fifty research institutes and social science departments engaged in sociological research. The Association's main tasks are to co-ordinate this research, to organize discussion of the results of the research and to assist in the organization of research by member institutions, and to maintain contacts with the International Sociological Association and with other national sociological associations. The Association has set up three standing committees to carry out these tasks: the committee for the co-ordination of sociological research, the committee for working out methods and techniques of sociological research; and the external relations committee. The Association holds annual conferences to examine the research carried out by various research organizations and to plan further work. It publishes a Sociological Yearbook (*Sotsiologicheskii Ezhegodnik*) which contains reports on the Association's activities, on conferences in the Soviet Union and abroad, and on the results of sociological research.

The main research centre in sociology is the Soviet Academy of Science and its various institutes (economic, philosophical, legal, ethnographic, etc.). Research is also carried out in the many social science departments of institutions of higher education, and by public organizations of all kinds, including trade unions. The work of the Institute of Philosophy of the Academy of Science provides some examples of the way in which the research is organized. The Institute has conducted research in collaboration with the Institute of Economics, the Institute of Law, and the Institute of World Economy and International Relations on the subject of the basic laws governing the transition from socialism to communism; with the Academies of Sciences of Turkmenia, Kazakhstan, and Kirgizia on the laws governing the transition of underdeveloped countries to socialism without passing through the capitalist stage of development; with the social science departments of Gorky University on technological progress and the working class; with the department of philosophy of the Moldavian Academy of Sciences and the Institute of Ethnography on the laws governing the cultural growth of the collective farm peasantry; with the Institute of Labour on social questions of labour and life; with the social problems section of the Academy of Construction and Architecture on social questions of housing construction; with the Institute of Economics on the problem of eliminating substantial disparities between mental and physical labour. Some of the other important sociological research centres in the Soviet Union which may be mentioned are the laboratories of sociological research at Leningrad State University, which is engaged in research on the conversion of labour into a prime vital requirement; at Sverdlovsk State University, which is examining the problem of raising the cultural and technical level of the working class and the peasantry during the transition to communism; at Moscow State University where the main problem being examined is the influence of automation on the change in working conditions and life of the working class; at Kiev State University, which is studying ways and means of the all-round development of the individual in life; and in the sociology section of the Institute of Economics and Organization of Production of the Academy of Sciences, which is working on the organization of the rational use of leisure time following the reduction in working hours.

The main journals which contain reports of this research are the fortnightly journal of the Communist Party (Kommunist), *Questions of Philosophy* (Voprosy Filosofii), *Philosophical Sciences* (Filosofskie Nauki), *Political Self-Education* (Politicheskoe Samoobrazovanie), the *Bulletin* of Leningrad State University, Economic, Philosophical and Law Series (Vestnik LGU), the *Bulletin* of the Moscow State University, Economic and Philosophical Series (Vestnik MGU), the *Bulletin* of the History of World Culture (Vestnik Istorii Mirovoi Kulturi), *Soviet State and Law* (Sovetskoe Gosudarstvo i Pravo). A further list of journals that contain occasional papers on sociological research is included in the bibliography.

Sociological research is financed from the State budget and by grants made by various public organizations. These funds also cover the cost of training sociologists, which is done mainly in the philosophy departments in the larger universities (Moscow, Leningrad, Kiev, and Tbilisi) as well as in post-graduate courses at most of the higher education institutions, research institutes, and at other centres. Courses of training may be divided into three stages: first, a basic course including the history of philosophy, and of sociology, modern Western sociology, Marxist sociology and philosophy, methods and techniques of sociological research, formal and mathematical logic, and logic of scientific cognition, the principles of higher mathematics, etc., as well as periods of practical scientific research at industrial or agricultural enterprises. The practical work is analysed and written up as a dissertation towards the diploma. The second stage is the training of highly qualified specialists, mainly in post-graduate courses. The main element of such a course is a piece of concrete sociological research, the purpose of which is to discover theoretical and practical solutions to current social problems. The results are published in dissertations. The third and highest stage is work leading to the doctorate in sociology, which also combines theoretical and practical problems. These include large-scale sociological surveys with practical objects and the results are embodied in doctoral theses and publicly presented. In all three stages emphasis is placed on the study of actual social situations, which is regarded as a necessary prerequisite for the successful study and development of sociological theory.

Recruitment to these courses is in the main from people directly engaged in industry and agriculture. Those who develop an interest in using their specialist knowledge or skill in application to sociological problems will be given opportunities to enter special post-graduate courses in sociology. In addition, hundreds of thousands of workers in industry and agriculture, together with the members and officials of public organizations, who show a special interest in the carrying out of large-scale research projects involving the distribution of questionnaires, conducting interviews, or collating and classifying the data obtained in surveys, both make an immediate contribution to sociological research and provide a source of recruitment for the training of specialists in sociology. The practical use made of the results of such research, by both Government and the Party, is valued as an important encouragement to the study of sociology.

NOTES AND REFERENCES

1. *Sociology in the USSR*, Report of the Fourth World Congress of Sociologists, Vol. I, pp. 177-8.

2. *Russian Sociology*, Julius F. Hecker, London, 1934, which was a revised edition of the work of the same title, first published in 1915 in New York as a doctoral dissertation at Columbia University.

3. See, for example, the annotated bibliography of Russian work on adolescents in *Psikhologia*, Vol. IV, section 3-4, 1931, pp. 401-20.

4. Hecker, op. cit., p. 6.

5. ibid., p. 299.

6. *Psychology in the Soviet Union*, edited with an introduction by Brian Simon, London, 1957; there is much of interest in *Educational Psychology in the USSR*, edited with an introduction by Brian and Joan Simon, London, 1963.

7. B. Simon, op. cit., p. 2.

8. ibid., pp. 4-5.

9. See, for example, *Karl Marx, Selected Writings in Sociology and Social Philosophy*, edited by T. B. Bottomore and Maximilien Rubel London, 1956, and Pelican Books, 1963.

'A great deal of Marx's work is a permanent acquisition of sociological thought: the definition of the field of study, the analysis of the economic structure and its relations with other parts of the social structure, the theory of social classes, and the theory of ideology. But this incorporation of Marx's ideas entails the disappearance of a "Marxist" sociology. Modern sociology is not the sociology of Marx, any more than it is the sociology of Durkheim, or Weber, or Hobhouse. It is a science which has advanced some way towards freeing itself from the various philosophical systems in which it originated, and with which its founders were still embroiled.' p. 63, Pelican edition.

Cf. also p. 40: 'The third theme, that of social revolution, has largely been neglected by sociologists and, for that matter, by other social scientists. Indeed, the whole problem of social change has received surprisingly little attention; only recently have sociologists, anthropologists and economists begun to study intensively one particular aspect of this problem, namely, the processes of social change in under-developed countries under the impact of Western technology. But it is curious, when one reflects upon the tremendous effects which revolutions have had upon human social organization, that no sociologist since Marx has thought it worth while either to analyse revolutionary movements or to attempt a comparative study of revolutions. The sociology of revolutions has so far only one major contribution to record, that of Marx himself.'

See also, *The Marxists*, C. Wright Mills, New York, 1962, and London, 1963, p. 13: 'However, there is today no "marxist social science" of any intellectual consequence. There is just – social science: without the work of Marx and other Marxists, it would not be what it is today; with their work alone, it would not nearly be as good as it happens to be. No one who does not come to grips with the ideas of Marxism can be an adequate social scientist; no one who believes that Marxism contains the last word can be one either. Is there any doubt about this after Max Weber, Thorstein Veblen, Karl Mannheim – to mention only three? We do now have ways – better than Marx's alone – of studying and understanding man, society and history, but the work of these three is quite unimaginable without his work.'

10. *Methodological Problems of Science*, Academy of Sciences, USSR, Moscow, 1964, chapters III, sections 4 and 10, IV, section 2. See also *Marxist and Bourgeois Sociology Today*, edited by F. V. Konstantinov, G. V. Osipov, and V. S. Semyonov, Academy of Sciences, USSR, Moscow, 1964.

11. *The German Ideology*, Marx and Engels, edited with an introduction by R. Pascal, New York, 1947, p. 15.

12. *The Eighteenth Brumaire of Louis Bonaparte*, Marx.

13. *Marx-Engels Selected Correspondence*, 1846-1895, London, 1934, letter from Marx to Kugelmann, 11 July 1868, pp. 246-7: 'even if there were no chapter on value in my book, the analysis of the real relationships which I give would contain the proof and demonstration of the real value relation. The nonsense about the necessity of proving the concept of value arises from complete ignorance both of the subject dealt with and of the method of science. Every child knows that a country which ceased to work, I will not say for a year, but for a few weeks, would die. Every child knows too that the mass of products corresponding to the different needs require different and quantitatively determined masses of the total labour of society. That this necessity of distributing social labour in definite proportions cannot be done away with by the *particular form* of social production, but can only change the *form it assumes*, is self evident. No natural laws can be done away with. What can

change, in changing historical circumstances, is the *form* in which these laws operate. And the form in which this proportional division of labour operates, in a state of society where the interconnection of social labour is manifested in the *private exchange* of the individual products of labour, is precisely the *exchange value* of these products. The science consists precisely in working out *how* the law of value operates. So that if one wanted at the very beginning to "explain" all the phenomena which apparently contradict that law, one would have to give the science *before* the science. It is precisely Ricardo's mistake that in his first chapter on value he takes as given all possible categories, which have still to be developed, in order to prove their conformity with the law of value. On the other hand, as you correctly assumed, *the history of the theory* certainly shows that the concept of the value relation has *always been the same*, whether more or less clear, hedged with illusions or scientifically precise. Since the thought process itself grows out of the conditions, is itself a *natural process*, thinking that really comprehends must always be the same, and can only vary gradually according to maturity of development, including that of the organ by which the thinking is done. Everything else is drivel. The vulgar economist has not the faintest idea that the actual everyday exchange relations need not be directly identical with the magnitudes of value. The point of bourgeois society consists precisely in this, that *a priori* there is no conscious, social regulation of production. The reasonable and the necessary in nature asserts itself only as a blindly working average. And then the vulgar economist thinks he has made a great discovery when, as against the disclosures of the inner connection, he proudly claims that in appearance things look different. In fact, he is boasting that he holds fast to the appearance and takes it for the last word. Why, then, any science at all? But the matter has also another background. When the inner connection is grasped all theoretical belief in the permanent necessity of existing conditions breaks down before their practical collapse.'

14. See *The Laws of Social Development*, G. Glezerman, Moscow, 1960, English edition.

15. In the paper referred to in Note 1 above, P. N. Fedoseyev distinguished in modern Western sociology two clearly discernible trends. Some of its representatives try to preserve its general theoretical character, but by abstracting sociology from the actual social processes turn it into a formal science, systematizing and classifying different social notions. The other more widespread trend in modern sociology is characterized by a descriptive approach to facts. Thus, sociological research is deprived of its general theoretical character. Some Western sociologists admit the danger of descriptive data prevailing over theoretical analysis and general conclusions from social phenomena. *The State of the Social Sciences*, edited by L. White, Chicago, 1956, p. 352, says: 'The fact gathering becomes so elaborate and monumental that the problem which initiated it disappears along with any possible conclusion'. In 1956, at the Amsterdam Congress, a number of speakers pointed out that sociology was being dissolved in statistics, had become a sociography of the various aspects of social life. Sociography of rural, urban, industrial, family, national life, etc., takes the place of sociology. In splitting sociology into individual independent descriptive sciences, an analysis of the main social processes becomes impossible. In some countries there have been recent attempts to combine the so-called empirical sociological studies with some general sociological conceptions. In evaluating them one must start from the fact to what extent general sociological notions correspond to actual facts, how typical and more or less comprehensive are the empirical data used by sociologists to prove certain theoretical statements.

Sociology in the USSR, Report of the Fourth World Congress of Sociologists, Vol. I, pp. 177-8.

1

The development of the productive forces in the Soviet Union

A. A. ZVORYKIN

AN ANALYSIS OF THE PRODUCTIVE FORCES

The cornerstone of general Marxist sociological theory is the analysis of the forces of production.[1] Their growth is the principal cause of change in social life. Their level, and the rate of their growth, are together the basic criteria of social progress. Marxist sociologists analyse productive forces into the following elements. First, there are the objects of labour, which include raw materials and semi-finished goods, i.e. everything on which man works. Second, there are the instruments of labour, or those objects with the help of which man operates on the objects of labour. Third, there are the means of labour, or the specific conditions necessary for the existence of the productive process which include, in the wider sense, roads and buildings. Fourth, there is the worker, necessary for carrying out the productive process, and, fifth, there are the experience, skill, and knowledge (technology and natural science) which are applied in the productive process.

These elements of production enter into various combinations. The significance of particular elements of production, and of their particular combination, is not uniform in the development of material social production. For example, however great the role played by objects of labour, they are not the determining element in production. The material technical basis on which production rests is of considerable importance for its development. Within the framework provided by this basis, the technique of production (the totality of the means and instruments of production including devices which help to increase the productivity of labour) serves as the most active, material element of production. The existence and functioning of the natural elements of production are brought about only by the activity of man, who sets them in motion and carries on the production process. The productive forces reveal the character of the relations between man and nature. They show how man operates on the objects of labour and carries on the production process with the help of the instruments and means of labour, utilizing their mechanical, physical, and chemical properties.

Definitions of the productive forces usually single out their 'constitutional' characteristics, the means of production and manpower, reflecting the objective laws that governed the development of the productive forces in the past, and will govern them in the future. In order to show the general trends in the development of the productive forces, however, we require a more detailed division of their elements, and of the factors influencing the growth of the productive force of human labour.

Marx said that the productive forces are determined by complex factors consisting of the average level of workers' skill, the level of the development of science and the extent of its application in technology, the social relations of the production process, the extent and efficiency of means of production, and, lastly, natural conditions. This scientific characterization of the elements of the productive forces is based on an analysis of the social production of Marx's day. The question arises whether all of these elements are equally important in all societies. In primitive society, the productive forces were largely determined by natural conditions. The instruments of labour were primitive, and their efficiency depended not so much on their design as on the material from which they were made. Slave-owning society increased man's importance as a productive force, although man was still only an elementary agent of production. He was mainly a source of energy and not a possessor of skill. The importance of tools grew steadily. Scientific discoveries began to be used in production for the first time.

In feudal society, man became the decisive factor in the productive forces. The growth of man's skill increased the importance of tools, and the development of various forms of co-operation increased the importance of the social relations of the production process.

Under capitalism the productive forces develop in conditions of an industrial revolution, during which there is a transition to machine production. The means of production become a much more important factor in the growth of productive forces. The other elements of the productive forces also continue to develop.

The productive forces of socialism differ basically from the productive forces of capitalism in their social form, although they have much in common with the latter from the material and technical standpoint. The new social system has opened up for them great additional possibilities and advantages: a planned and rational use of productive capacities, greater efficiency in the organization of production, balanced development, higher rates of economic growth, unlimited overall technical progress, new incentives for labour, and the creation of a new man.

In the present period of the transition from socialism to communism, the productive forces of the Soviet Union are developing in the following main directions:

(i) the electrification of the whole country, (ii) the consequent improvement of machinery, and (iii) of technology, (iv) a greater efficiency in the organization of social production in industry and agriculture, (v) the overall mechanization of production, (vi) the steadily increasing automation of production processes, (vii) the wide application of chemistry in the national economy, (viii) the thorough deveploment of new, economically effective industries, and new forms of power and materials, (ix) the thorough and rational utilization of natural resources, (x) the closer relations of science to production, (xi) the increase in the rate of scientific and technical progress, and (xii) the rise in the cultural and technical level of the people.

This characterization of the factors governing the expansion of the productive forces of communist society makes it possible to study concretely each one of them and to assess their importance for the development of the productive forces. It brings to light their influence and mutual dependence. This is important not only for theory but also, especially, for practice.

ELECTRIFICATION

Electrification occupies a place of special importance in the development of the productive forces of communism. In all its huge diversity and application, modern technology is based entirely on electric power. Electric power is transmitted over enormous distances, and is easily converted into other forms of energy (thermal, light, chemical, mechanical). It serves as the foundation for many new technological processes (e.g. electric smelting, electrolysis, electrothermy, electrochemistry, electric welding, and electric metal-working). Modern automation and control are based on the use of electric power. Electrification, therefore, is the mainspring of economic growth in the Soviet Union. A colossal increase in the output of electric power has been planned for 1961-1980. Towards the close of the second decade (1980), the Soviet Union will be generating 2,700,000-3,000,000 million kW a year, while in the first decade (1961-1970) the *per capita* consumption of power in industry will almost treble. Power-consuming industries will be swiftly expanded, and complete electrification will cover transport, agriculture, and urban and rural households.

In the course of the next twenty years the country's electrification will differ from present-day electrification, not only quantitatively, but also qualitatively. The Soviet Union is building ever bigger hydroelectric and thermal power stations like, for example, the 4,500,000 kW Bratsk and the 5,000,000 kW Krasnoyarsk stations. A 2,400,000 kW thermal power station is under construction at Krivoi Rog, and still bigger thermal power stations are being planned. Power engineering will develop through the use of various power resources including fuel (gas, liquid, and solid), water, nuclear and thermo-nuclear power. The amalgamation of all the power stations into a single grid for the Soviet Union, and its extension to include a number of other socialist countries, will be of very great importance.

PLANT AND MACHINERY

Plant and machinery, which are being developed in the system of social production, play a decisive role in the growth of the productive forces of communism. The discoveries that have been made in the sphere of atomic power have caused some specialists to advocate that atomic energy should be made the pivot of the development of the productive forces of communism. Others argue that the productive forces of future society will depend on the development of synthetic chemistry. No matter how important these new trends may be, it must be emphasized that it is not them but the means of labour, based on the use of electrical energy, which will determine the most important direction in the development of the productive forces of communism. The means of labour in particular will make possible the use of the opportunities provided by electrical energy and synthetic chemistry. At no other time has the long-term development of technology been so clear cut as it is under conditions of socialism. Electric power, electronics, new materials, and scientific discovery are making it possible to create means of labour for all of man's requirements. The capacity of machines is widening from a tiny fraction of one kilowatt to millions of kilowatts, and their speed and precision are also growing.

A fundamental change is taking place in the very character of modern machines. Marx distinguished three elements in individual machines and systems of machines. They are the working parts of the machine, the transmission, and the motor. Modern machines have acquired a fourth element. Automatic regulation, or a cybernetic apparatus, now permits automatic control, regulation, and operation in such a way as to allow the operating part to select the most effective kind of work at any given moment in conformity with the general conditions of production.

TECHNOLOGY

The importance of technology as one of the general trends in the development of the productive forces is sometimes underestimated. Technology forms a link between the instruments of labour and the objects of labour, and is the sum total of methods of operating on the objects of labour. It is frequently identified with tools and machinery, because, as some economists and sociologists argue, every technological process is formed within a definite system of technical means. This approach can be shown to be wrong. A technical task, like the working of metal, can be accomplished by various technological methods, such as cutting, stamping, or precision casting. Materials for identical purposes can be produced by means of mechanical or chemical treatment. Technological processes vary according to their degree of continuity and intensity. For example, an improvement in the technology of obtaining oil by flooding oil deposits has shortened the period of exploitation from 200-300 years to 25-30 years, and increased output by more than 60-70 per cent. The changeover from underground to open-cast mining increases labour productivity 5-6 times, and reduces the cost of coal 3-4 times. Hydraulic mining raises labour productivity 50-100 per cent and reduces the cost of coal by 25-30 per cent.

THE ORGANIZATION OF PRODUCTION

Labour productivity depends on the social combination of the production process, i.e. on how efficient this combination is both within the framework of one enterprise and also in the links between enterprises. Hence the great importance that is attached to the organization of social production. The economic laws of socialism allow production to be combined on a countrywide scale consciously and by plan. In recent years the Soviet Union has been paying greater attention to the thorough study and more rational use of various forms of the social combination of the production process. This includes the improvement of the organization of production within the framework of an individual enterprise, the choice of the most economical and efficient type of enterprise, and specialization and co-operation, which open up further additional resources for the development of the productive forces.

Some economists and sociologists have lately put forward the view that the development of modern techniques, based on electronics, automation, and remote control, makes the relatively small enterprise more economic. These assertions run counter to the actual trends in the development of science and technology. Although automation can raise the economic efficiency of small enterprises by sharply increasing their capacity, the concentration of production retains its advantages. The maximum size of an enterprise must conform with the level of development reached by science and technology, and with concrete economic conditions. As a rule, the establishment of large-scale enterprises, using highly productive equipment with well-organized scientific and design centres, gives reductions in overhead expenses. The stability of a socialist economy and the absence of the danger of production capacities being underloaded enable Soviet society to create the material and technical basis of communism, with the emphasis on ever bigger enterprise in all branches of production. The importance of combining and concentrating production in large-scale enterprises is growing. Combination acquires particular importance in the transition to the composite processing of raw, chiefly mineral, materials. The last, but in no way the least important, condition for promoting the Soviet Union's productive forces is the improvement in organizing social production at individual enterprises. The growth of capacities and the transition to continuous automation can only be effective where the production process is efficiently organized and proceeds smoothly, with precision. The highest stage of planned organization of the entire economy, and the most effective and rational use of mineral wealth and labour resources, will be achieved under communism in order to satisfy the growing requirements of human society. This applies to industry and agriculture in equal measure. In agriculture, the most effective social combination of the production process is achieved through a scientific distribution of production according to natural-economic zones and regions, greater and more thorough specialization, and the promotion of inter-collective-farm productive relations.

MECHANIZATION AND AUTOMATION

Universal mechanization is one of the general trends in the development of the productive forces. The advance of technology was linked up mainly with the improvement of machines in basic production. As a result, the number of workers engaged in this production decreased relatively faster than the number of workers engaged in auxiliary operations. In fact, the latter sometimes even increased. It was envisaged in the current Seven Year Plan that technical improvements should be made not only in individual enterprises and basic industries but also in the entire system for reception, storage, transportation, and distribution of raw materials, and for the transportation, storage, loading, and dispatch of semi-finished and finished products. In agriculture, as well, overall mechanization has been made the foundation for increasing the productivity of farm labour.

Universal mechanization is inseparably linked with automation. Automation of production is a new stage that had been made possible by the joint development of science and technology, and, mainly, by putting production on an electric power basis and by the use of electronics and new improved technical means. Automation leads to the creation of the new productive apparatus of communist society. As the building of communism progresses, automatic machine systems will increasingly become the general form of production, They will radically change man's role in production, and provide the material basis for eliminating the essential differences between physical and mental labour.

Priority of importance is attached to the development of machine-building, to the utmost expansion of the output of automatic systems and machines, remote control systems, electronics and precision instruments, in order that, within the next twenty years, automation will reach a mass scale and the transition can be made to automatic workshops and factories. Such workshops and factories already exist (e.g. a ball-bearing department, in Moscow's First State Ball-Bearing Plant, where within the next few years 80 per cent of the output will come from automatic production lines), but their number is small. However, in the near future enterprises of this kind will determine the character and level of the country's entire industry.

Specialists have already tried to produce standard designs for fully automated engineering plants. At these plants all operations are controlled from a single panel, consisting of instruments and television communications that permit observation of the production process in any part of the plant. The output is directed round the circumference and the supply fans out radially from the centre. The central control panel is at the heart of the entire system; pocket transmitters, working on individual wavelengths, permit the operator to tune in on the selector in the central control room. The production processes are carried out with the help of control programmes using tape-recordings of the task. Electronic computers and regulators select the best work schedules for the equipment perform all the necessary computations, and draw up all the records.

These automatic plants are a matter of the future, but individual elements of these plants are already in being. For example, in 1960, the mechanization department of the State Institute for Designing Metallurgical Plants worked out approximate designs for an automatic iron and steel plant. These included technological processes and units that best lend themselves to automation, automated transport, and cybernetic means of automated measurement, control, and regulation of individual sectors, departments, and the plant as a whole. An economic analysis of these approximate designs shows that, compared with present-day requirements, the floor space can be reduced by 25-40 per cent, and capital investment for transport by one and a half or two times. In transport, labour productivity can, during the first stage, be increased 5-8 times, and, when the plant is fully automated, it can be increased 10-15 times. On the whole, compared with a conventional factory, an automated plant will cost 20-25 per cent less, the cost of adaptation can be lowered to 40 per cent, and the plant will require less than one-third of the workers.

METALLURGY AND ORGANIC CHEMICAL SYNTHESIS

Modern technology makes heavy demands on materials for production. These demands can be satisfied by metallurgy in concert with the chemistry of organic synthesis. Some specialists consider that, for high temperatures and speeds, the most promising materials from the modern technological point of view are metals, their carbides, and ceramic materials. The physics of solids, which is a new and rapidly developing branch of physics, shows that the strength of metals can be considerably increased. Metallurgists believe that the strength of most metals can be roughly doubled in the course of 25 years, even by using those methods that have already been developed or are in the process of development.

A new technology, known as vacuum metallurgy, is already being used to produce higher quality, heat-resistant, structural, instrumental, and building steels. Metallurgy is called upon to create light-weight, heat-, frost-, and water-resistant, and easily worked structural materials. These materials must be usable at very low and very high temperatures. They must resist corrosion and stresses. Materials are also needed with magnetic, electrical, and semi-conductor properties for electronic equipment, and with the capacity to resist atomic radiation and cosmic rays.

Other specialists hold that these new demands made on materials will be met by chemistry, through the improvement of plastics. Plastic materials and their derivatives resist oxidation and reduction, have excellent heat-insulating properties, withstand shocks, and are easily made by various methods and in different sizes. They can operate either permanently at temperatures of up to 290°C, or for thousands of hours at temperatures of 10,000-11,000°C. Other types of plastics are suitable for low temperatures. The use of plastics, reinforced with glass fibre, has opened up remarkable new possibilities. Heat-resistant plastic insulation has become decisive in a number of new fields, beginning with computing devices and ending with guided missiles. These new plastic materials will revolutionize technology. They will, of course, develop side by side, and in close interrelation with, metals and their alloys, for which ever new possibilities are also being opened up by science.

The chemistry of organic synthesis is causing a far-reaching revolution in the production of synthetic fibres, various types of polythene and other materials for industrial and domestic consumption. Under the current Seven Year Plan, the output of chemical fibres is to be increased 3·8-4 times, and of the most versatile synthetic fibres 12-14 times.

Modern science and technology are bringing about profound changes in production, not only by opening up new possibilities for old industries but also by preparing the ground for, and developing, new industries to satisfy man's requirements with the utmost economy and efficiency. Possibilities are arising of creating new branches of technology on fundamentally new principles, as perhaps will be the case with the further development of atomic and thermonuclear power stations.

The setting up of new chemical industries is giving rise to tremendous possibilities. Depending on the extent to which the sowing and harvesting of cotton is mechanized, the number of man-days required to produce a

C

ton of fibre ranges from 175 to 240. Of this labour, 97-98 per cent is
spent on growing cotton and 2-3 per cent at ginneries. It takes 460-470
man-days to produce a ton of flax-fibre. On the other hand, only 56
man-days are required to produce a ton of artificial viscose staple fibre,
which can be used for the same purpose.

NATURAL RESOURCES

In listing the factors on which the productive force of labour depends,
Marx laid stress on natural conditions. Today, man's possibilities of
penetrating into the depths of the earth and making thorough surveys
of natural wealth have increased many times over, and the more
systematic use of natural resources can accelerate the growth of the
productive forces of labour at an unheard-of rate. To hasten the process,
priority will be given to the use of natural resources that can be rapidly
developed and yield the greatest economic benefit. This will determine
the geographical changes in the distribution of industry. For example,
the incalculable natural wealth of the area east of the Urals is speeding
up the industrial development of that area. New power facilities using
deposits of cheap coal will be created. The hydro-power resources of
the Angara and the Yenisei in Siberia are being harnessed. The country's
third metallurgical base is being set up. Man is opening up further
possibilities for expanding the productive forces by actively remaking
natural conditions, and not simply adapting himself to them.

SCIENCE: A DIRECT PRODUCTIVE FORCE

As science develops and is applied in industry, it becomes a direct productive force. Four major trends have taken shape in the development
of science in the Soviet Union: (i) research aimed at promoting and
improving power engineering, beginning with the power and fuel
balance sheet and ending with such problems as the discovery of new
sources of energy, the direct transformation of various forms of energy
into electricity, and the solution of problems connected with the
control of thermo-nuclear reactions; (ii) research aimed at creating
new machines, automatic and telemechanical systems, radioelectronics,
the improvement of computing, regulating, and information machines,
i.e. devices that bring about far-reaching, fundamental changes not only
in production but also in all aspects of human life; (iii) the study of

chemical processes, the development of new technological methods, the creation of artificial and synthetic substitutes for natural materials and also new materials not available in natural form; and (iv) the improvement of existing methods of prospecting for minerals and of the composite utilization of raw materials, and also the development of new and more efficient methods.

HUMAN LABOUR

No matter how deep the changes that automation and the use of cybernetic devices will make in man's activity, he will retain the leading role in all spheres of social production. No matter how effective the machine, the limits of its uses and the ways of improving them will depend wholly on man. The creation of the productive forces of communism lead, not to the disappearance of labour, but to its profound development and transformation. The entire development of social life, the expansion of its material and technical basis and, in particular, the progress of science and technology, are preparing the ground for an organic merging of mental and physical labour in the productive activity of people. All of this can in no way be interpreted as freeing man from labour. Communist society, which is based on highly organized production and developed technology, changes the character of labour, but does not free the members of society from it. It will by no means be a society of anarchy and idleness. Every member of society will take part in social labour and help to ensure the uninterrupted growth of its material and cultural life. Labour for the well-being of society becomes a vital requirement, and a conscious need. The ability of every person will be applied with the greatest benefit to society. Man's growing role as the bearer of the productive forces is a reflection of his greater experience, of his knowledge and ability, and of the power over nature that science is placing in his hands.

NOTE

1. The terminology employed in this paper is more fully defined, and illustrated, in *Political Economy – a Textbook*, produced by the Institute of Economics of the Academy of Sciences, published in a fourth edition in Moscow, in 1962. An English translation of the second edition of this textbook was published by Lawrence and Wishart in London, in 1957. The opening passage of this paper is more fully dealt with in Chapter 1 of the fourth edition and the later passages in chapters 34 to 36.

2

The rate of growth of the Soviet working class and changes in its composition with respect to occupation and skill

G. L. SMIRNOV

CHANGES IN THE STRUCTURE OF THE WORKING CLASS

The continuous growth of industrial production in the Soviet Union has given rise to constant changes in the social structure and to an increase in the proportion of the working class in the population of the country. The following data (*Table 1*) taken from the last two censuses,[1] show the percentage composition of the country's population by social groups:

Table 1. Breakdown of population by occupation (in percentages)

Social group	1939	1959
Total population	100·0	100·0
Workers and office employees	50·2	68·3
Collective farmers	47·2	31·4
Individual farmers and handicraftsmen, not belonging to co-operatives	2·6	0·3

From these data it may be seen that the proportion of workers and office employees in the country's population rose by 18·1 per cent over twenty years. In 1959, their number had reached 142,700,000, including family dependants. Academician V. S. Nemchinov has estimated that the working class taken separately, along with family dependants, increased in percentage from 14·6 in 1928 to 44·2 in 1959.[2]

In 1913, some 8,600,000 workers and handicraftsmen (including seasonal hands) were occupied in large-scale and small-scale industry on the territory of former tsarist Russia, or approximately 7,700,000 on that territory of the Soviet Union up to 17 September 1939. A calculation of the mean annual number of workers and handicraftsmen shows that there were 5,400,000 of them, in 1913, within that territory, of which some 3,500,000 constituted the average annual number of wage workers.[3] According to Rashin's calculations, the approximate total of wage workers in Russia in 1913, including household 'servants', amounted to 17,800,000.[4]

In 1959, the number of workers in the Soviet Union amounted to 46,146,000, or 46·5 per cent of the occupied population.[4a] The distribution of workers in the various sectors of the national economy and, consequently, the industrial structure of the working class are shown in *Table 2.*

Table 2. The industrial structure of the working class in 1959

Sectors of the national economy	Total number occupied persons	Total number of workers	Workers as percentage of occupied persons
Totals	99,130,212	46,146,573	100
Engaged in material production sectors	80,862,676	38,912,229	84·3
including:			
industry, building, transport and communications	36,575,187	29,987,991	65·0
agriculture	38,425,967	5,918,418	12·0
trade, restaurants, agricultural procurements, supply of materials and machinery	5,170,665	2,533,992	5·5
engaged in non-productive sectors (education, science, art, health, housing and utilities, consumer goods supply, administration, finance, and banking)	14,453,128	5,328,317	11·5
including:			
education, science, art, and health services	9,793,040	3,289,580	7·1
armed services	3,623,000	1,822,850	4·0
place of work unknown or insufficiently known	191,408	83,177	0·2

In 1964, the number of workers and employees amounted to 73,200,000.[4b]

It is possible to calculate the total number of workers in the Soviet Union from the census data and statistical yearbooks of the Central Board of Statistics.

The total personnel in industrial production amounted to 24,297,000 in 1962, as against 8,000,000 in 1932. The corresponding figures for workers alone were 20,176,000 and 6,007,000, respectively. A general picture of the growth in the number of workers in industry is given in *Table 3*:[5]

Table 3. *Average annual number of industrial workers in the Soviet Union ('000)*

Branches of industry	1913	1940	1963
Industry as a whole	3,536	8,290	20,760
Engineering and metalworking	510	2,395	6,938
Coalmining	196	436	986
Oil extraction and refining	51	45	150
Ferrous metals (including ore-mining)	274	332	979
Light industry	—	1,489	3,550
Food processing	725	1,029	1,919

The table shows that the growth in the number of industrial workers was much faster in heavy industry than in all other branches. Whereas the total number of industrial workers increased by more than 2·5 times in the period from 1940 to 1963, the corresponding increases were 2·4 times in light industry, 1·8 times in food processing, more than 2·8 times for engineering and metalworking, nearly 2·3 times for the coal industry, over 3·3 times for oil, and over 2·8 times for ferrous metals. These figures indicate that the growth in the number of the working class occurred primarily in its most skilled and highly organized sections.

The builders, who form the next biggest group of the working class, numbered 5,731,000 in 1963.[6] According to Rashin's data, there were only 1,500,000 builders in Russia in 1913.[7] Subsequently, their number grew from 646,000 in 1928 and 1,935,000 in 1940, to 4,430,000 in 1956 and 5,365,000 in 1959.

Transport personnel occupy third place. In 1963, there were about 2,000,000 railway workers in the country, 166,000 persons in water transport, and more than 1,419,600 in motor freight transport. Other transport occupations (including carters, cabdrivers, haulagemen, carriers, loaders, and longshoremen) totalled to 2,721,900 in 1959. There was a total of 8,025,400 persons employed mainly in physical work, in transport, both freight and passenger (according to the census in 1959). This is a nearly twofold increase as compared with 1939, when there were 4,615,000 workers of this category.[8] The growth took place primarily through an increase in the number of workers employed by motor transport and municipal electric transport, and also by railway transport.

Socialist transformation of the countryside has resulted in the complete disappearance of the rural proletariat – the hired farm labourer, of whom there were 4,500,000 in 1913, according to A. Rashin's data.[9] A new worker – the state-farm worker – has appeared in the countryside in steadily growing numbers. In the period from 1940 to 1963, state-farm production personnel grew in number from 1,186,000 to 7,426,000.[10]

The general picture of the growth in number of the working class shows the steady increase in importance of its labour in the national economy. This may also be seen in the data on the growth of the country's fixed assets. Whereas total productive fixed assets in 1963 increased over 10 times as compared with 1929, industrial productive fixed assets grew over 50 times. Over that same period, the productive assets of agriculture (not counting livestock) increased 9·4 times.[11]

A characteristic feature of production in the Soviet Union is the concentration of the main mass of industrial workers in large-scale enterprises, as can be seen from *Table 4*:

Table 4. Large-scale manufacturing enterprises grouped with respect to number of workers (as percentage of total)[12]

Size of group	Number of enterprises			Number of workers		
	1913	1950	1958	1913	1950	1958
Large-scale manufacturing industry as a whole	100	100	100	100	100	100
Enterprises employing:						
under 500	91·6	91·1	85·2	41·1	30·4	25·4
from 500 to 1,000	4·5	4·4	7·4	15·2	13·1	13·4
from 1,001 to 3,000	–	3·3	5·3	–	23·6	23·5
from 3,001 to 10,000	3·9	1·0	1·8	43·7	22·0	23·4
over 10,000	–	0·2	0·3	–	10·9	14·3

Whereas in tsarist Russia 58·9 per cent of all workers in the manufacturing industry were engaged at establishments employing more than 500, in the Soviet Union the percentage is now 74·6. Thirty-three per cent of the workers in the United States were concentrated at establishments employing over 1,000, according to data for 1952; the corresponding percentage for the Soviet Union was 56·5 in 1950 and 61·2 in 1958. Public ownership of the means of production provides conditions for the highest concentration of production in the world.

In 1963, the percentage of workers in undertakings employing up to 200 annual average was 9·9; 201 to 1,000—32·5; 1,001 to 3,000—25·3; 3,001 to 10,000—21·2; and 10,001 or over—11·1.[12a]

THE RATE OF GROWTH OF THE NUMBER OF
WOMEN WORKERS

The formation and development of the Soviet working class cannot be properly understood without examining the part played by women in this process. In 1963 the number of women workers and office employees exceeded 34,300,000, which was 49 per cent of the country's total.[12b] Women of the nationalities inhabiting the outlying parts of tsarist Russia are taking an ever more active part in production. The increase in the number of women workers and office employees, over the period from 1933 to 1961, was 2,100,000 or 8·1 times in Central Asia and Kazakhstan, and 700,000 or 4·7 times in the Transcaucasus.[13]

In tsarist Russia, according to the 1897 census data, 55 per cent of the women wage-workers were house servants, and 25 per cent were labourers employed by kulaks (rich peasants) and landowners, whereas only 13 per cent were employed in industrial establishments or on building jobs, and 4 per cent in education and public health institutions. In the Soviet Union, 39 per cent of the total number of women occupied in the national economy in 1961 were employed in industry and construction, and 24 per cent in education and public health. Whereas, in 1913, women made up 24·5 per cent of the total industrial labour force by 1961 the percentage had risen to 45. *Tables 5* and *6* give an idea of how the percentage of women among total industrial workers has increased in the Soviet Union.[14]

Table 5. Growth in the proportion of women among total industrial workers (percentages)

Branch of industry	1913 (mean for the year)	1928 (mean for the year)	1940 (as of 1 Nov.)	1961 (as of 1 Jan.)
Percentage of women workers in industry as a whole	24·5	28·6	42·9	45·6
Of which:				
in engineering and metal-working	4·2	8·9	31·5	38·9
in the textile and clothing industries	55·7	61·2	72·0	72·9
in food processing	22·0	26·4	48·6	54·4

In 1913, about two-thirds of the total number of women industrial workers in tsarist Russia were employed at textile and clothing factories, and only 2·4 per cent in engineering and metal-working. Today the corresponding figures for the Soviet Union are 25·3 and 27·5 per cent, respectively. Women also make up a considerable part of the workers employed in such branches of industry as food, fur and leather, rubber, footwear, paper, and oil-refining, among others.[15]

Table 6. Percentage of the total number of women industrial workers engaged in individual branches

Branch of industry	1913 (mean for the year)	1928 (mean for the year)	1940 (as of 1 Nov.	1962 (as of 1 Jan.)
In industry as a whole	100	100	100	100
Of which:				
in engineering and metal-working	2·4	5·5	23·5	27·5
in the textile and clothing industries	63·1	64·5	29·5	25·3
in food processing	12·8	7·2	13·4	10·5

According to the data of the population census, the number of women employed at power stations increased more than fourfold between 1939 and 1959; during this period the percentage of women among the total workers in these stations increased from 23 to 32. The numbers of women turners, milling machine operators, and other machine-tool workers increased during this period more than twofold, though the proportion of workers in these occupations remained constant at 28 per cent. Women working at pressing and stamping machines made up 64 per cent of the total, an increase of 2·8 times, chemical workers 57 per cent, an increase of 2·4 times, compositors 78 per cent, an increase of 1·8 times, and drivers of trams, trolleybuses, and underground trains 57 per cent, a threefold increase.[16]

CHANGES IN THE NATIONAL COMPOSITION
OF THE WORKING CLASS

A very important distinguishing feature of the Soviet working class is its multi-national composition. The growth in number of the working class of the national republics has been especially rapid. In many of the Union republics there had formerly been hardly any industrial working class. It has made its appearance during the period of Soviet government. From 1926, when the restoration of the pre-revolutionary level of the economy was coming to an end, the numbers of workers and office employees engaged in the national economy increased sixfold for the country as a whole and tenfold for Central Asia and Kazakhstan.

An increase in the percentage of the working class in the country's total population is an index of its progress. It measures the industrialization of the country's economy, the consolidation and development of the socialist mode of production, and the inclusion of ever wider sections of the population in active participation in key branches of the national economy.

CHANGES IN TRADES AND SKILLS

The numerical growth in the working class has been accompanied by profound and varied qualitative changes in its structural make-up in regard to trade and skill. This is brought about, first of all, by the steady increase in mechanization of the productive processes. Greater mechanization of production is accompanied by an increase in the number and proportion of skilled workers.

During the period from 1948 to 1962 there was an increase in the employment in industry of rolling-mill operators from 14,000 to 25,000, of galvanizers from 23,000 (in 1954) to 50,000, of welders from 66,000 (in 1948) to 283,000, blacksmiths operating hammers, press, and stamping machines, from 23,000 to 48,000, laboratory assistants from 43,000 to 136,000, machinists and mechanics from 290,000 to 1,063,000, machine and instrument setters, from 76,000 to 219,000, fitters from 710,000 to 2,022,000, metal machines from 505,000 to 1,222,000, tractor drivers from 15,000 to 77,000, truck drivers from 182,000 to 276,000, machine stampers and pressers from 40,000 to 114,000, electricians from 343,000 (in 1959) to 465,000 in 1962[17].

As a result of the mechanization of production and of the increase in skill of the workers, and also of other measures, the average annual labour productivity of industrial workers increased approximately 12·6 times in the period from 1940 to 1964 (in spite of a reduction in the length of the working-day). In manufacturing industry it increased 3·6 times, in construction 3·4 times, and railway transport 2·8 times.[17a]

All the measures enumerated above will release considerable labour power for further growth in the volume of industry. The main effect is that automation and universal mechanization will essentially transform the character of the worker's labour. For example, the trade of stoker at a modern thermal electric station has nothing in common with what it was 20 years ago. Today the stoker at a major thermal electric station operates the boiler unit from a control desk. Not once throughout his shift does he take up a poker or shovel, because most of the processes at the big stations have been completely mechanized and automated. As a rule he is a person with a secondary technical education, and frequently he is a student at a correspondence or evening college. The prospects for automation are that engineers and technicians will replace the worker at the automatic machine tool, automated unit, or automatic production line, to run complex production processes. With automation, the labour process qualitatively changes; its conditions become healthier; and the process of abolishing the existing differences between physical and mental labour continues.

Automation and universal mechanization present the working class with the need to raise its professional and general educational level. The following figures show what has been done to prepare workers with diverse skills in the period from 1940 to 1963: 14,000,000 persons were trained at technical secondary and vocational schools for industry, construction, transport, and agriculture.[18] In addition, some three million persons now annually acquire new trades and skills (3,150,000 in 1963) and more than five million annually raise their skill (6,119,000 in 1963) in enterprises, institutions, and organizations.[19]

However important may be the raising of the production skill of workers, it is only one aspect of their development. Another side of the matter is the raising of their general cultural level and, in particular, their general educational level. Whereas, in 1918, 36 per cent of industrial labourers were illiterate, today illiteracy among workers has been wiped out completely. More than that, 38·6 per cent of them have a secondary and even a higher education, as against only 8·2 per cent in 1939. The cultural and technical level of the working class has been rising especially rapidly during the past few years owing to the influx of young people with a junior-secondary or secondary education. Not only individual work teams but even entire plants and factories have appeared in the country staffed almost entirely by young people who have reached a high general education level. There are whole branches of industry in which more than half of the workers have a higher or secondary education. For example, 53·5 per cent of iron, steel, and metal workers, 51·4 per cent of chemists, 64 per cent of printers, 55·3 per cent of weavers, 55·5 per cent of spinners, 53 per cent of knitters, 56·5 per cent of clothing workers, 40·8 per cent of railway workers, 42·7 per cent of truck drivers, and 69·1 per cent of tram, trolley-bus, and underground drivers have a secondary or higher education.[19a]

At the beginning of 1964, 32 per cent of the total population had higher or secondary (complete or incomplete) education. Half the employed population had had such an education, including 44 per cent of the workers, 26 per cent of the collective farmers, and 92 per cent of the white-collar workers and specialists.[19b]

So many now wish to study that a new problem has arisen, namely, how to keep production going during the periods of entrance and term examinations. In some enterprises most of the workers have to go off to schools and colleges at these times. The rules and regulations for admission to correspondence and evening colleges have now been modified to provide for a more extended entrance examination period and college directors have been instructed to extend the regular term examination periods as well. Those studying after working-hours have a shorter working-day and receive, among other privileges, time off to take examinations in addition to their regular vacation.

It is interesting to note in this connection that a movement was started to encourage every worker to acquire engineering knowledge. It was launched at the initiative of Communist Labour Teams in Volgograd, Kharkov, and a number of other regions and has spread far and wide. The craving for knowledge called forth by technical progress, the general rise in cultural level in the country, and the educational work of the state, are all factors of great importance. They in turn affect both the development of engineering and technology and the general development of the individual. In this respect two sides of the matter may be mentioned which show the importance of raising the general educational level of the workers.

First, a rise in the general educational level leads to higher labour efficiency. According to S. Strumilin, the labour productivity of workers who have graduated from junior secondary school increased, on average, by 67 per cent as compared with workers of the same age and length of service, but without secondary education, other conditions being equal.[20] The rise in general educational level promotes more active participation in rationalizing production and invention. The data[21] for 1956 on the educational background of promoters of production efficiency in Shop No. 5 of the Pervouralsk New Pipe Plant are very interesting in this respect (*Table 7*).

Table 7. Educational background in relation to participation in rationalization of production

Type of education of worker	Rationalizers of production		
	N	N	%
Incomplete secondary	742	120	16·6
Technical secondary	75	33	44
Higher	20	16	90

The level of the creative activity of workers in the country as a whole, during the past few years, can be seen from the following data: whereas, in 1952, 834,000 proposals for promoting production efficiency were introduced in the national economy and gave a total saving of 434,000,000 roubles, in 1964 the corresponding figures were 2,761,000 and 1,774,000,000 roubles, respectively.[22] The development among workers of rationalization of production and invention on a mass scale introduces a new phenomenon in the life of society. Amateur talent is how being fruitfully applied in the sciences just as it traditionally have been in the arts.

With a rise in their general educational level, workers are attempting the mastery of additional trades, which is also a big source of reserves for raising labour productivity. Furthermore, the ability to switch from one operation to another promotes the all-round development of workers, makes their labour more creative, and is conducive to a critical attitude to the production norms and techniques in force. The striving to master more than one trade is especially characteristic of Communist Labour Teams. In the city of Samarkand we made the acquaintance of ten teams who are competing for the title of Communist Labour Team. All the members of five of them could cope with all the jobs involved. In the other five, they all had mastered two of three related trades.

Second, a rise in the general educational level of the workers leads to the widening of their horizons and the extension of their cultural interests. They are drawn more fully into various kinds of public activity. With young junior-secondary and secondary school graduates forming the bulk of the working-class recruits, the desire to raise cultural standards has become noticeably stronger. This striving of working youth for culture is expressed, for example, in the fact that a large number of them attend the 'universities of culture', as they are called. In conjunction with the change in character of labour as a result of the mechanization and automation of production, a rise in the cultural level of the workers ensures both the gradual removal of the dividing line between mental and physical labour, and the gradual elevation of the cultural and technical level of the workers to that of engineering and technical personnel.

As technology in enterprises develops and becomes more complex, workers who have received technical or engineering diplomas will be increasingly engaged full time with machine tools and automatic production lines. The complex machinery of our times makes ever greater demands on the worker in terms of technical training. A secondary and higher specialized education will become the rule and will no longer be the dividing line distinguishing engineering and technical personnel from workers. Any differences which remains between the worker and the foreman, and the foreman and the manager, will be connected with the different functions they have to perform in the co-ordination of the productive process.

REFERENCES

1. *The Soviet Census, 1959* (Itogi Vsesoyuznoi Perepisi Naseleniya 1959 goda), Moscow, 1962, p. 92.
2. *The World Historical Significance of the Great October Socialist Revolution,* Moscow, 1957, p. 65.
3. *The National Economy of the Soviet Union in 1959,* Moscow, 1960, p. 138.
4. A. G. Rashin, *Formation of the Russian Working Class,* Moscow, 1958, p. 171.
4a. *The Soviet Census, 1959,* p. 104.
4b. *USSR in Figures in 1964,* p. 117.
5. *The National Economy of the Soviet Union in 1959,* p. 139, and *The National Economy of the Soviet Union in 1963,* p. 122.
6. ibid., p. 468.
7. A. G. Rashin, *Formation of the Russian Working Class,* p. 171.
8. *Statistical Gazette* (Vestnik Statistiki), No. 12, 1960, pp. 10-11.
9. A. G. Rashin, op. cit., p. 171.
10. *The National Economy of the Soviet Union in 1963,* p. 369.
11. *The National Economy of the Soviet Union in 1963,* p. 55.
12. ibid., 1959, p. 140.
12a. *The National Economy of the Soviet Union in 1963,* p. 129.
12b. ibid., p. 490.
13. *Women and Children in the Soviet Union, a Statistical Handbook,* Moscow, 1963, p. 105.
14. ibid., p. 104.
15. ibid., p. 108.
16. ibid., pp. 94-7.
17. *The National Economy of the Soviet Union in 1962,* p. 460.
17a. *USSR in Figures in 1964,* p. 24.
18. *The National Economy of the Soviet Union in 1963,* p. 494.
19. ibid., p. 497.
19a. *The Soviet Census, 1959,* pp. 177-180.
19b. *The National Economy of the Soviet Union in 1963,* p. 29.
20. *Problems of Philosophy* (Voprosy Filosofii), No. 3, 1954, p. 50.
21. *Philosophical Sciences* (Filosofskie Nauki), No. 3, 1959, p. 6. (The table was compiled by E. Pysina, an instructor in political economy at the Urals State University.)
22. These, and subsequent figures, are given in terms of new roubles, as revalued in January 1961. Ten 'old' roubles = one 'new' rouble. A rough guide to the exchange value of the rouble is $2\frac{1}{2}$ roubles = £1.

3

Redistribution of labour and changes in its occupational composition

A. P. OSIPOV

INTRODUCTION

The transition to automatic systems of production changes the character and content of labour. It gives rise to new occupations, which can be termed wide-range occupations to distinguish them from the multi-purpose and narrow-range occupations prevailing before. Multi-purpose and narrow-range occupations correspond to the operation of particular machines. Each new machine, or even new tool, brings into being a new occupation. Wide-range occupations correspond to the operation of systems of machines, such as automatic lines.

With the progress of automation, the operations requiring lengthy occupational training are gradually taken over by machines. The worker retains merely the direction and control of them. The elements of craft and manual training in wide-range occupations decrease and technological knowledge becomes more important. This does not mean that physical labour will be completely abolished. It will still remain in totally automated production, though in a modified form. Techno-logical progress lightens physical labour, eliminates its depressing monotony, and makes it richer and more creative. The worker's labour becomes simpler as far as manual skill is concerned, but it becomes much more complicated as regards knowledge. Such work increasingly calls for engineer-technicians. For example, operations involving mental activity already predominate in steel making. In the steel maker's working-day, control of production accounts for 50 per cent of the time, the technological process itself for 20 per cent, analysis for 3 per cent, setting up the operation for 7 per cent, actual operation for 15 per cent, and keeping records for 5 per cent.

Wide-range occupations include different forms of labour, combine high skill and extensive knowledge, and unite physical and mental activities in a single process of labour. Such occupations can be regarded as a transitional stage to that type of production in which labour will become a means of developing all of man's abilities, including his mental and physical abilities. In other words, they are the transitional stage in the development of the working man of the future communist society. Mechanization and automation require ever higher technical standards and skills. This arises principally from the growing complexity of equipment. Another factor is the development of automatic control devices and electronic equipment. Finally, automation decreases the number of operators, and the fewer they are, the more versatile their skills and knowledge must be. The traditional concept of a 'highly skilled worker' changes in the process. Manual skill and narrow specialized craft, acquired by dint of many years of experience and recognized in elaborate skill ratings, are no longer required in conditions of automation. Other qualities are now required in the worker, including a wide education, technical knowledge, an intelligent grasp of the process of production as a whole, with an ability to direct and control machinery.

Mechanization and automation are based on the application to production of mathematics, physics, mechanics, chemistry, and other sciences. These provide common principles for the design and operation of different systems of machines and for many other elements of production. They also provide the basis for general education and specialized knowledge, as well as for operating and maintenance skills. They make it possible to train operators in the fundamentals of science and technology, so that they are able to work in various branches of production. This does not, however, exclude specialized skill in the operation of one or another kind of equipment. This can be quickly acquired or modified, since an operator familiar with the fundamentals of science and technology can switch over, after a short period of retraining, to work in another branch of production.

GROWTH IN VOLUME AND DISTRIBUTION OF LABOUR POWER

A rapid growth in the volume of manpower is characteristic of the development of Soviet society. The rate of growth rose sharply after 1930, following the elimination of unemployment. The total labour force increased from 12,900,000 in 1913 (within the present-day frontiers) to 70,500,000 in 1963, or 5·5 times. Such a high rate of growth shows the favourable conditions for population growth and full employment.

At present four-fifths of the able-bodied population are gainfully employed.

Essential changes have occurred during these years in the distribution of manpower over the branches of the national economy, as may be seen in *Table 1*.

Table 1. *Distribution of gainfully employed population (in percentages)*

Occupation	1913	1963
Total (minus students and servicemen)	100	100
Inclusive of:		
Industry and construction	9	34
Agriculture and forestry (incl. personal household plots)	75	34
Transport and communications	2	8
Trade, public catering, procurement and supply of materials and equipment	9	6
Education and health	1	13
State administration, co-operative and social organizations, banks, and insurance establishments	} 4	2
Other sectors of the national economy (municipal services, etc.)		3

The most conspicuous change is the redistribution of manpower between industry and agriculture. As a result of industrialization, the proportion of workers in industry and construction, among the total gainfully employed, increased from 9 per cent in 1913 to 34 per cent in 1963. At the same time, the collectivization and mechanization of farming have considerably raised the productivity of labour, and hence the proportion of manpower in agriculture decreased from 75 per cent in 1913 to 34 per cent in 1963.

In the first Five Year Plan period (1928-1932), 8,500,000 out of the 12,500,000 new employees in industry were former peasants. Up to World War II, the main source for the organized enlistment of manpower was the countryside. Despite a considerable decrease in rural manpower, its proportion is still high. Large-scale measures in progress to mechanize agricultural production will release more manpower now engaged in farming.

Table 1 indicates another major trend in the distribution of gainfully employed population during the period of Soviet power: in 1913, health and education accounted for 1 per cent of the gainfully employed population, while the figure for 1963 is 13 per cent. According to the

D

national census of 1959, 47 per 1,000 worked in health, education, and science (27 in 1939).

The changes in the distribution of manpower, and in the growth of the gainfully employed population, have been especially substantial (see *Table 2*) since the late 1920s, when the Soviet people had restored the war-devastated economy and started the full-scale construction of socialism.

Table 2. Distribution of employees by sectors of the national economy

Sector of national economy	Number of employees by sector (annual averages '000)		Ratio of 1963 figure to 1928 figure
	1928	1963	
Total for the national economy	10,790	70,500	6·5
Inclusive of:			
1. Industry	3,773	24,950	6·6
2. Construction	723	5,170	7·2
3. State farms and subsidiary enterprises	345	7,930	23·0
4. Transport	1,270	6,858	5·4
5. Communications	95	880	9·2
6. Trade, public catering, procurement and supply of materials and equipment	587	5,490	9·3
7. Municipal services	147	2,210	15·0
8. Health	399	3,935	9·9
9. Education	725	5,815	8·0
10. Science and scientific services	82	2,395	29·2
11. Banks and insurance establishments	95	290	3·1
12. State administration, economic management, co-operative and social organizations	1,010	1,310	1·3
13. Others	1,539	2,357	1·5

Source: Annual statistical abstract *Narodnoe Khozyaistvo SSSR v 1958 g.* Gospolitizdat, 1959, p. 658; and *SSSR v tsifrakh v 1962 godu*, a short survey of statistics, Gospolitizdat, 1963, pp. 266-8.

From *Table 2* it is clear that, from 1928 to 1963, about three-quarters of the total increase of gainfully employed population went into industry, construction, state farms and subsidiary enterprises, transportation and communications. i.e. the key branches of the national economy. Such changes in the social distribution of labour are progressive. Between 1928 and 1962, the number of employees in industry increased 6·4 times, in construction 7·1 times, and on the state farms and subsidiary enterprises 22·5 times, with an overall increase of gainfully employed population of 6·3 times. A high rate of increase in manpower in these branches is an important factor in the growth of national wealth. Rapid increases in the number of employees are shown by trade, public catering (9 times), and municipal services (14·4 times), i.e. various forms of services. Scientific manpower shows an especially striking increase: 27·3 times. The figure points to the increasing use of scientific manpower in production and to the rapid pace of the cultural revolution in the country.

Technological progress, and especially mechanization and automation in recent years, have enhanced the role, and broadened the range of employment, of technical engineering workers. Their proportion has increased both in the total number of the gainfully employed population in general, and in the number of industrial workers in particular.

The number of specialists with a higher-school and secondary-school education, employed in the national economy, was 190,000 in 1913, 521,000 in 1928, and 10,598,000 by the end of 1963, i.e. it had increased nearly 55-fold as compared with 1913. From 1928 to 1963, the number of engineers who had a higher-school education increased 28-fold (from 47,000 to 1,325,000) engineers with a secondary-school education, 45-fold (from 51,000 to 2,293,000), of agronomists, zootechnicians, and veterinary experts more than 11-fold (from 59,000 to 665,000). According to the 1939 and 1959 censuses, the number of engineers with a higher or secondary education increased in the interim 2·5 times, and that of agronomists, zootechnicians, and veterinary experts 1·6 times, with the total number of brain workers increasing 48 per cent. Specialists with a higher or secondary education accounted for 5 per cent in 1932, and for 9 per cent in 1961 in the total number of industrial personnel.

The high proportion of manpower in material production is a significant result of the redistribution of manpower. In 1963, the production of goods, plus transportation of goods, with industrial communications and trade, accounted for 80·8 per cent of the gainfully employed population, while the non-material sections accounted for 19·2 per cent, including 13·0 per cent in education and health. With the total increase of manpower in the national economy by 6·3 times, the number of employees in public health increased 9·6 times and in education 7·6 times, which is an indication of the higher level of social and cultural services.

The technical re-equipment of the national economy entailed the redistribution of manpower not only between different sectors but also within each sector. The process is shown in *Table 3*.

Table 3. Average annual number of employees in major industries of the USSR ('000)

Industry	1913	1940	1962
All industries	3,536	8,290	20,176
Inclusive of:			
Machine-building and metal-working	510	2,395	6,584
Coal-mining	196	436	996
Oil extraction	51	45	150
Iron and steel	307	405	947
Light industry	1,133	1,489	3,543
Food	735	1,049	1,884
Building materials	–	252	1,383

From the table it is evident that, between 1913 and 1962, the number of employees in machine-building and metal-working industries increased 12·2 times, with a total increase of industrial employees of 5·5 times. In 1961, there were 1,375,000 workers in the building materials industry, which did not exist as an independent industry in 1913, and employed only 252,000 in 1940. From 1959, coal-mining shows a decrease in the annual averages of employees. It employed 1,074,000 in 1959; 1,031,000 in 1960; and 996,000 in 1962. These decreases arose from changes in the country's fuel sources.

Changes in the distribution of manpower in agriculture are shown in *Table 4*.

Table 4. Number of employees on collective farms, state farms, and state subsidiary enterprises (annual averages, '000,000)

Farming sector	1940	1961	1962
Total for all sectors	31·3	28·1	27·7
Inclusive of:			
Collective farms (socially owned sectors)	29·0	20·7	20·0
State farms and subsidiary enterprises	1·8	7·36	7·7
Machine, tractor, and machine-maintenance stations	0·5	0·003	—

The distribution of manpower in agriculture was influenced by the transformation of some collective farms into state farms in 1957-1961, the reorganization of machine and tractor stations in 1958, and of machine-maintenance stations in 1961. The new principles of farming are converting agricultural work into a variety of industrial production.

Primitive agricultural implements were used in Russia before the 1917 Revolution. According to the 1910 census, the peasant farms used 10,000,000 wooden ploughs, 4,200,000 iron ploughs, and 17,700,000 wooden barrows. At the beginning of 1964, there were 2,600,000 tractors (in terms of 15-h.p. units), 916,000 lorries, and hundreds of thousands of other machines. In the pre-revolutionary countryside, draft cattle were practically the only source of traction, and machinery accounted for less than 1 per cent. By 1964, mechanical tractors accounted for 98·0 per cent of the total power capacity employed in agriculture.

The redistribution of manpower between the various branches of the national economy, and within them, indicates the progressive changes which have occurred in the socialist social division of labour. First, there has been an increase in the gainfully employed population. Second, there is better distribution of manpower between the material and non-material spheres. Third, there has been an increase in proportion and in absolute numbers of industrial workers. The total number of industrial workers has increased at a high rate, especially so in heavy industry, and machine-building in particular. With technical progress in agriculture, the proportion of machine operators has also increased. Fourth, there has been a high rate of growth in the number of brain workers, particularly specialists and research workers, with higher and secondary school education. Finally, the redistribution of manpower between, and within, the sections of the national economy indicates the wider employment of skilled labour. The number of workers has increased in those branches of the national economy which employ highly skilled labour, and decreased in those which employ semi-skilled labour.

OCCUPATIONS

A more detailed description of the redistribution of manpower in the national economy, and of the occupational changes involved in the process, is furnished by the data on the numbers employed by occupations. These data warrant the conclusion that machines tend to remove the differences between different kinds of labour and to oust manual operations. The substitution of machines for manual labour eliminates occupations involving arduous physical labour, and increases the number of occupations involving the maintenance of machines. This point is illustrated by *Table 5*, which lists the comparative data on the number of workers by occupations for machine-building and coal-mining in 1925, 1954, and 1959.

Table 5. *Numbers of workers in selected trades ('000)*

Trades	1925	1954	1959
Machine-building and metal-working industries			
Power truck operators and electric welders	none	5·6	14·2
Electroplaters	0·4	17·8	30·4
Machine operators	5·1	83·3	128·7
Machine-tool setters	1·2	53·0	77·7
Pyrometer testers	none	5·3	6·1
Fitters	41·0	512·5	896·2
Automatic machine-tool operators	none	13·5	14·7
Metal lathe operators	18·4	224·8	412·9
Milling machine operators	3·3	74·9	129·0
Electricians	2·7	115·1	128·5
Coal-mining (underground workers)			
Combine operators	none	2·7	5·3
Combine assistant operators	none	2·3	4·8
Cutting machine operators and their assistants	0·3	5·4	6·4
Cutter-loader operators and their assistants	none	0·1	0·2
Electric drill operators	} 1·6	{ 4·4	5·6
Manual drillers		0·05	none
Electric-tram drivers	none	17·9	28·4
Conveyer operators	none	17·9	20·8
Haulage men	9·0	8·2	none
Sled handlers	6·4	none	none
Horse-tram drivers	2·9	0·6	none

It is clear from *Table 5* that occupations involving arduous manual labour have been eliminated especially rapidly in coal-mining. The cutter-loader has relieved coal-drillers of hard manual work, the conveyer put an end to sled handling, and the electric-tram operators replaced the horse-tram drivers. The operation of coal combines, electric haulage, and conveyer belts has produced a range of new occupations, which did not exist in 1925.

In the machine-building and metal-working industries power truck operators had taken over the heavy physical labour of hauliers and porters by 1954. Extensive introduction of standardized, mass-produced automatic, and semi-automatic machine tools, considerably increased the number of fitters from 1,200 in 1925 to 77,000 in 1959. Automatic machine-tool operators came into being as a new occupation. Between 1951 and 1959, the number of automatic machine-tool setters increased 1·5 times, of electric welders 2·8 times, operators of presses for plastics 2·3 times, and conveyor operators 3·3 times. Setters of automatic machines, electricians in charge of the maintenance and adjustment of control devices and instruments, computer machine operators, electronic equipment technicians, and many other highly skilled specialists came into being during the years under review.

The same trend is observed in building, which used to be a seasonal craft occupation, but has now become an advanced, highly mechanized branch of the national economy during the Soviet régime. By 1962, builders had 62,000 travelling cranes, more than 43,000 excavators, more than 47,000 bulldozers, 13,000 scrapers, tens of thousands of tractors, and high-capacity tip lorries, etc. Earth-moving was 91 per cent mechanized, concrete work 74·1 per cent, and the assembly of concrete and reinforced concrete structures 91 per cent. Plastering and painting were mechanized 58·2 per cent, and 64·1 per cent, respectively.

Changes in the technology and organization of building have altered the occupational structure of the building industry. Excavator, crane, bulldozer, and dredger operators have replaced porters and navvies. The mechanization of concrete work has led to the replacement of crushers, mixers, rammers, and wheelbarrow men by rock-crusher, screen, concrete mixer, transporter, and conveyer operators. Concrete assembly is becoming a major occupation in building with the development of prefabricated construction. Electric- and petrol-saw operators are now doing the hard work previously done by carpenters. Tractor, winch, and crane operators have replaced carters and hauliers.

The number of machine operators in agriculture has grown considerably. The mechanization of the major kinds of cultivation can be described by the following data for 1960 (as a percentage of the total for a given kind of work):

Ploughing for spring crops by tractor-drawn ploughs	98
Sowing of spring cereals by tractor-drawn sowers	97
Harvesting of cereals by tractor-drawn and self-propelled machines	94

The technical re-equipment of agriculture has been accompanied by a steady increase in the number of machine-operators, of whom there were 2,800,000 in 1963 (1,400,000 in 1940), though the overall number of these engaged in farming decreased. The number of specialists, with a higher or secondary school education, employed at collective farms, state farms, and state subsidiary enterprises, was 416,000 at the beginning of 1963 (50,000 in 1941). The mechanization of agricultural processes on collective farms, state farms, machine-tractor and machine-maintenance stations, increased the number of tractor and combine operators 1·5 times (from 1,237,000 to 1,878,000) between 1940 and 1963. In 1925, there were no such occupations in agriculture, since the level of mechanization was very low. By the end of 1928, there were only 18,000 tractors (in terms of 15-h.p. units) and 2 combine harvesters.

In ten years (from 1948 to 1959), the number of employees engaged in mechanized processes increased by roughly 3·3 times, and in automated processes 4·3 times, in the machine-building industry as a whole. At present, more than 70 per cent of all workers in machine-building are engaged in automated and mechanized processes.

The extensive introduction of machines in all branches of the national economy increases the number of employees engaged in the service and maintenance of machinery. It is clear from *Table 5* that, between 1925 and 1959, the numbers of fitters in the machine-building and metal-working industries increased nearly 22 times, and that of electricians nearly 64 times. The development of engineering and the extensive introduction of machinery not only change the occupational structure but also give rise to occupations which are to be found in common in many different branches of industry. As an approximate estimate, the proportion of these recurrent occupations in industry, construction, and transport, amounts to about one-third of the total of different occupations, and covers over 60 per cent of the total number of employees.

The large proportion of these employees has made it necessary to have a single reference table for such occupations in order to provide a common system of calculation of the work performed and skill ratings at any enterprise regardless of the branch of industry or its organization. The common principles underlying the construction and operation of machines call for a common category of knowledge and skill in similar occupations. The Labour and Wages Committee, under the Council of Ministers of the Soviet Union, examined the work of more than 5,000 narrow-range occupations and recognized that it was expedient to widen, in step with the requirements of production, the range of knowledge and skills of workers in most occupations. As a result, no more than 314 recurrent occupations were listed in the place of several thousand occupations previously in use. The list for machine-building, for example, included only 158 recurrent occupations instead of 2,960. The reference tables for recurrent occupations list only 10 fitter's trades whereas, in 1937, a fitter's trade was subdivided into more than 150 occupations.

Thus, technological progress leads to certain trends in the occupational structure; with the development of mechanization and automation, wide-range occupations replace narrow-range trades. These occupations are based not on direct manual operations (which are taken over by machines), but on the control of machines. The proportion of functions like setting, maintenance, and operation increases sharply in these occupations.

From the point of view of training, the above changes in the occupational composition of personnel warrant the following conclusions. First, changes in specialized occupations eliminate many of the old occupations, in particular those involving arduous physical labour, and increase rapidly the new occupations combining elements of manual and mental activity. Second, uniformity of scientific and technical principles in the operator's knowledge, experience, and skill are characteristic of the newer occupations, which leads to the use of common basic principles in their occupational training. Third, the extension of the breadth of occupations in socialist production becomes a distinctive feature of occupational specialization to an increasing extent. The operator's work depends more and more on modern equipment, which will demand ever higher skills and educational standards from the worker, until highly skilled labour becomes the only kind of labour in communist society.

4

Development of the communist socio-economic structure and social progress

S. G. STRUMILIN

HISTORICAL BACKGROUND: CAPITALISM AND SOCIALISM

The decisive driving force of history is the mode of production of material wealth and, above all, the development of the productive forces. First place among these is held by the people themselves, the population of the country, and its power resources. All the other conditions of development, such as a more or less favourable climate, the natural fertility of the soil, and the water, timber, and mineral resources, are of less significance. Moreover, natural wealth is not always found and tapped by man at once and it can lie dormant for thousands of years before being developed by man's reason and labour. The possibilities of tapping the natural wealth grow as man becomes better equipped with scientific knowledge and with power resources.

We are living in a world of peaceful competition between different economic systems. The people alone judge the relative efficiency of these systems and the forces which are shaping their future. Is it possible to predict this judgement by analysing, with sufficient certainty, not only the prospects of growth but also the major structural changes in the composition of the world's population for at least 20 years ahead?

In ten years (from 1950 to 1960) the population of the world rose, approximately, from 2,500 million to 3,000 million, i.e. by 500 million or 20 per cent. If we assume that, in future there will be an increase of 20 per cent each decade, in 1980, 20 years later, there would be a maximum population of 4,200 million. If we take into account a probable slowing down of this rate, and add 500 million for each decade, there would be a population of 4,000 million in 1980. The increase in 20 years would thus range between 140 and 144 per cent. The probable margin of error is not considerable.

Similar calculations for each of the competing systems are of much greater interest. Recent data show that the population of the Western countries totalled about 600 million people in 1960, and that its annual natural rate of increase does not exceed 1 per cent. The population of the socialist countries exceeded 1,050 million in 1960, and its annual increase, about 25 million, is 2·4 per cent. The absolute increase of the latter was at least four times greater than that of the Western countries. The population of all other countries, which adhere to the Bandung principles, and which are mainly politically neutral, amounted to about 1,350 million in the same year, with an annual increase of up to 19 million, i.e. 1·4 per cent on the average.

With different rates of population growth in these three groups of countries, even if we assume that each of them preserves all its members, their share in the total population clearly will be different in 20 years from now. The share of the socialist countries will considerably rise. Their population grows steadily, not only by virtue of the natural population increase, but also because many more new countries and peoples, in the course of their internal development, become ripe for socialism and set out to create socialist societies. They are attracted to the socialist community first of all by the great successes of the socialist system and of its planned economy, which have been demonstrated during many years of experience in the Soviet Union. This experience is especially attractive for the underdeveloped countries today, when the colonial system is disintegrating.

It is a fact that dozens of such underdeveloped countries are beginning to make use of methods of industrialization which have yielded amazing results. It is difficult to determine how many of these countries will join the socialist community in the next 10-20 years, but we can confidently expect that their movement in this direction will grow, and not diminish, with each passing year. After World War II, the population of the socialist community, through the influx of new members, reached not less than 830 million by 1960. This figure includes about 80 million in countries liberated from Nazism, and about 750 million people in the underdeveloped countries, or up to 36 per cent of the total population in these countries. We can expect that this process will continue at about the same rate in future.

Let us be very conservative, and assume that, in the next 20 years, not more than 30 per cent of the population in the neutral countries, and not more than 10 per cent of the population in the Western countries, will take the socialist road and that in the first ten years, by 1970, only half of this rate will be attained. In that case the changes in the world's population will be as shown in *Table 1*.

Table 1. Changes in world population

Groups of countries	Population, millions						Increase per cent	
	1960		1970		1980			
	Total	%	Total	%	Total	%	In 10 years	In 20 years
First variant								
1. Socialist countries	1,050	35	1,331	37	1,687	40	26·8	60·7
2. Capitalist countries	600	20	664	19	733	18	10·6	22·1
3. Other countries*	1,350	45	1,551	44	1,783	42	14·9	32·1
Total	3,000	100	3,546	100	4,203	100	18·2	40·1
Second variant								
1. Socialist countries	1,050	35	1,597	45	2,295	54	52·1	118·6
2. Capitalist countries	600	20	631	18	660	16	5·2	10·0
3. Other countries*	1,350	45	1,318	37	1,248	30	−2·4	−7·6

* In this group we include countries which have been liberated from colonial rule or are fighting for their liberation.

In the first variant, only the natural increase of the population in each group has been taken into account, according to sufficiently reliable statistics; this gives the least probable population growth in the socialist countries. In the second variant, an attempt has been made to calculate the increase in the population of these countries based on the most probable transition of a number of countries to socialism. This higher level will probably be nearer to the truth. The population of the socialist community in 20 years will thus include not less than half of the world's population.

THE SOCIO-ECONOMIC STRUCTURE OF COMMUNISM

Communism means above all a highly organized society of free and intelligent people. At the same time, it is a classless society in which the productive forces reach a level in which all sources of social wealth flow in a full stream, and the great principle of 'From each according to his ability, to each according to his needs' is realized. Last, but not least, it is a social system in which all the creative abilities and talents, all the finest moral traits of the free man, his spiritual wealth, moral purity, and physical perfection will be developed and displayed to the full.

The building of communism presupposes a number of material, social, and ideological prerequisites. The cardinal precondition for the transition to communism is the building up of a powerful material and technical basis. The creation of such a basis presupposes a high rate of growth in the power and engineering industries, and development of science and technology, such as would ensure technical progress and production of life's necessities and comforts on an unprecedented scale. Some pertinent figures are given in *Table 2*.

Table 2. Economic growth

	1950	1960	1970	1980
1. Electric power production, million kWh	91,000	292,000	up to 1,000,000	up to 3,000,000
as a percentage of 1960	31	100	342	1,027
2. Industrial output				
as a percentage of 1950	100	303	758	1,818
as a percentage of 1960	33	100	250	600
3. National income				
as a percentage of 1960	37·5	100	250	500

These rates seem amazing to critics and some of them have already declared them to be Utopian. Yet, these rates are even somewhat lower than the actual achievements of the Soviet Union in the preceding ten years, and leave the people of our country the chance to overfulfil, through their own initiative, the assignments of their Party and their Government. It is instructive, for example, that the West German power expert, Fritz Baade,[1] in his latest estimate of the development of the world power industry, proceeds from world growth rates of not more than 60 per cent in ten years; American experts on the governmental Power Commission[2] calculate that this increase, even for the United States, will not be higher than 53 per cent in ten years, whereas in the Soviet Union electric power production is approximately trebled every ten years.

According to American forecasts,[3] generation of electric power in the United States will range from 1,866,000 million to 2,013,000 million kWh in 1980. This means that, in this key sector of the economy, the Soviet Union will overcome the existing lag behind the United States in that year. It will be much easier to do the same in engineering and other industries. In the United States, the output of the engineering industry in the last ten years has increased by not more than 56 per cent, while in the Soviet Union it has risen 5 times. With such a correlation, the Soviet engineering industry will draw level with the United States by the end of 1965. In 1980, the Soviet engineering industry will exceed American industry more than five times over in volume of output.

The Soviet Union at present lags behind the United States in total industrial output. Even according to the most conservative estimates, in 1960, Soviet industrial output was 60 per cent of the American. In 1970, the Soviet Union will exceed this level (105 per cent) and, in 1980, it will be at least 170 per cent of the American level (taking into account the present growth rates in that country). American economists admit that these rates will inevitably slow down. Consequently, the lag of the United States behind the Soviet Union will be even greater.

Proceeding from the share of world industrial output in different countries, and from growth rates in the last ten years, we can give a probable picture of future trends for the next 10-20 years. These changes in the share of world industrial output of the competing economic systems, according to our estimates, will be as set out in *Table 3*.

Table 3. World industrial output

| | Percentage of world total | | | |
	1950	1960	1970	1980
1. Socialist countries	18	33	51	60
2. Capitalist countries	77	56	37	29
3. Other countries	5	11	12	11
Total	100	100	100	100
Growth (as percentage of 1960)				
1. Socialist countries	28	100	342	832
2. Capitalist countries	68	100	146	234
3. Other countries	24	100	154	445
Average	50	100	222	452

The growth rates of the less developed countries in the socialist community are especially high because they are being helped by the more advanced countries, primarily the Soviet Union. By 1970, the socialist countries will produce more than half, and, in 1980, at least 60 per cent, of world industrial output. At the same time, the share of the Western countries will be cut by half. These figures do not take into account the inevitable slowing down of growth rates in the Western countries, nor of the entire additional output of the socialist community as a result of its extension. If these factors are taken into account, the share of the world socialist system will be still higher.

Similar calculations of the entire national income for the different systems are in our opinion even more favourable for the socialist community. The gross national product of the United States in the last ten years (1951-1960), in stable prices, rose by only 38-39 per cent and the national income even less, by 35 per cent. The Paley Commission[4] has officially estimated that the gross national product is to rise another 45 per cent in the next 15 years, by 1975. In five years, this will be an increase of not more than 13 per cent, and in ten years, up to 28 per cent. In the Soviet Union, the national income in the next ten years will rise by 150 per cent. In 1960, it was still only about 60 per cent of the American level. The national income of the United States in Soviet currency amounted to 244,000 million roubles. In 1970, the Soviet national income will be greater than that of the United States, at least by 54,000 million roubles, or by 17 per cent. In 1980, this will amount to 334,000 million roubles, or 84 per cent.

These results will be achieved simultaneously with the introduction of the shortest working-day in the world, the provision of an abundance of material and cultural goods and services, and the achievement of the highest living standard. The rise in labour productivity will be the decisive factor. In the last ten years, labour productivity in Soviet industry has almost doubled. By 1970, it is to be doubled once again, and in 20 years, by 1981, it will rise 4-4·5 times as compared with the present level. The United States expects to raise labour productivity by 2·5 per cent annually, or up to 27 per cent in ten years. From a comparison of such a correlation of these growth rates it may be seen that the Soviet Union has every possibility of greatly outstripping the United States in labour productivity as well.

CONSUMPTION UNDER COMMUNISM

Creation of the material and technical basis of communism will bring the Soviet Union close to applying the principle of distribution according to needs. There will be a reduction of the working-day to 5-6 hours in the next 10 years. Real wages of factory and office workers (taking into account the payments from public funds) will nearly double in 10 years, on the average, and increase 3-3·5 times in 20 years (1961-1980). The incomes of collective farmers will rise even higher, more than 4 times. Each family will have a well-appointed flat. Moreover, starting in 1970, houses will gradually become rent-free, and also all the services of public utilities and urban transport will be free for all citizens. In

10-15 years improved and cheaper public catering will predominate over home cooking. Free dinners to all persons employed in factories, offices, and collective farms will gradually be introduced in the 1970s.

Free accommodation in nurseries, kindergartens, and children's summer camps will be provided in town and country. Boarding schools, with free maintenance of the children, will be organized on a large scale. All schools will serve free lunches; the children will be able to stay there to the end of the day and receive free dinners. Clothing and textbooks will also be free. Each family will be able to maintain its children free in children's institutions. A network of well-appointed homes for the aged and for invalids, capable of providing free accommodation to all who desire it, will be set up in town and country.

Public consumption funds satisfy the various social and cultural needs of the population in the form of free services, free or subsidized supplies, and supplies for direct payment. Pensions, allowances, and grants are made from these funds. They also cover payments for holidays, free medical services, and the education of young people. They will continue to rise. In 1980, they will make up about half of the total real income of the population, that is, as much as the individual wages received by all the working people.

In 20 years, much progress will be made in other spheres of communist construction, above all in the communist education and polytechnical instruction of the new generations. The Soviet educational system is based on social upbringing of the children, and on close ties with life and productive labour. Boarding schools and other cultural and educational establishments will be built on a vast scale. All schools will have instructional workshops, and chemistry, physics, and other laboratories; in rural areas farming plots will be organized near the schools. Large factories will have special instructional production shops for school-children and many of them will offer their workers facilities for higher education. All schools will have facilities for physical and aesthetic education, for the study of music, painting, and sculpture.

Science will play an increasing role in communist construction, and will become a direct productive force in full measure. The material and moral stimulation of inventions and of innovations in production will become of prime importance. The development of such a movement on a mass scale will be the more important because the organic fusion of science and production is the best guarantee of the rapid development of science itself.

The ties with science are no less important and beneficial to labour. Labour will become more fruitful in step with the application of scientific achievements in the development of automatic productive processes and their control by cybernetics. Labour becomes easier, more interesting, and attractive. It ceases to be merely a means of gaining a livelihood and turns into genuine creative endeavour.

We can confidently say that the leisure which the workers will increasingly enjoy, as the working-day is cut, will not be spent in idleness. The people will, more and more, devote their leisure to public activities, to cultural interests, mental and physical development, and artistic creation. Manual and mental labour will increasingly merge. The proportion of technicians and engineers will rise; experimental and research work will assume a wider scale and the ties of industry with scientific institutes will be strengthened. The workers will take a much greater part in the management of production, and communist forms of labour will spread. Communist construction presupposes the development of democratic principles in management and the improvement of the centralized guidance of the national economy. There will be a further extension, within the framework of the single national economic plan, of the economic independence of local bodies and of initiative from as low as the individual enterprise. In future the principle that all leading personnel, in all spheres of the country's life, are elected, replaceable, and accountable to their electors will be universally introduced. The aim is to get the masses of the people to master the skills of management, so that managerial work would cease to be a special profession.

In the course of the further development of socialist democracy the organs of the state, which are concerned with planning and managing the economy and cultural affairs, are gradually being converted into organs of public self-government.

At the same time, the transition to communism implies the fullest development of the personality and the rights of citizens. Equal rights for all are exercised in the free choice of an occupation, and in the enjoyment of all other civil liberties to the greatest extent. There will be no limits on these other than the rules of the communist way of life which will be spontaneously and habitually observed by all people.

In the course of 20 years, communist society will be built in the Soviet Union in the main by the all-out effort of the people. It will come about as a result of economic and cultural achievements, of the gradual merging of state and co-operative forms of property into one form of property belonging to the entire people, and of the gradual transition to the ever fuller application of the great principle 'from each according to his ability, to each according to his needs'. This will not be full

E

communism, for the completion of which more time and effort will be required. But the results achieved will open up a new era of social changes and the regeneration of the whole world.

REFERENCES

1. F. Baade, *World Energetics Production*, Moscow, 1960, and F. Baade, *Competition by the year 2000*, Moscow, 1962.
2. *Resources for Freedom*, A Report to the President by the President's Materials Policy Commission, Washington, 1952, Vol. III, *The Outlook for Energy Sources*.
3. N. Galochkin, Forecasts for the development of US. energy sources, *Planovoe Khoziaistvo*, 1961, No. 7, pp. 83-9.
4. See Note 2, above.

5

Social changes in working-class families over a period of nine years

F. YU. ALESHINA

INTRODUCTION

In March 1959, the Labour Institute[1] made a special study of the budgets of a sample group of families, which had been used in an earlier investigation. Out of all the families previously investigated by the All-Union Council of Trade Unions, a number of families were selected in three cities – Moscow, Gorky, and Ivanovo – and the budget study was limited to 100 families. For purely technical reasons, budgets were studied for March 1959 only. The authors of the study were able to locate in Moscow, Gorky, and Ivanovo the families that had been investigated in 1951-1956, including 41 families in Moscow, 28 in Gorky, and 34 in Ivanovo. All these families, already experienced in keeping accounts, kept them for March 1959 in the same form as in 1951-1956.[2] The selection of families was not based on any preconceived notions. No proportions were predetermined as to the number of families in each city or in various industries, or as to the size of each family or its aggregate income. The families investigated are not representative of any other family groups. However, it is evident that even such a small number of family budgets does graphically reflect, subject to some variations, the fundamental trends characterizing the development of Soviet society as a whole.

The budgets of these families were grouped and analysed for the sole purposes of establishing the specific features of these 100 families and of presenting a dynamic picture of their changes. In order to draw clear-cut conclusions from a detailed study of budgets, the families of old-age pensioners and single individuals were, in most cases, excluded from the study, since their budgets naturally differ from those of married workers.

In order to provide comparable data, the budgets included covered only the months of March in 1951, 1956, 1959, and 1961. The materials were limited to one month in each year, which of course is subject to the effects of accidental fluctuations, but no information was available for the rest of the year 1959, and comparability of information for 1951, 1956, 1959, and 1961 was the primary concern.

After excluding the old-age pensioners and single individuals, there remained 92 budgets, out of 103, which were grouped as follows:

1. by cities (Moscow, Gorky, and Ivanovo);
2. by industries (iron and steel, engineering, chemical, and textile industries);
3. according to the average monthly income per member of the family (up to 40 roubles, 40·1 to 70, and over 70 roubles).[3]

There were two varieties of the third group: the income per member of the family was based on March 1959, and the budget grouping for 1956 and 1951 corresponded to that of March 1959. The same grouping was also used independently for each year, in order to study the shifts of families from one group to another and to analyze the structure of incomes and expenses in each group.

CHANGES IN THE COMPOSITION AND STRUCTURE OF FAMILIES

Since this section is concerned only with changes in the composition and structure of families, the material for 1951, 1959, and 1961 was examined on the basis of different family samples (94 families in 1951, 98 families in 1959, and 100 families in 1961). This is due to the fact that some persons registered as being single in 1951 had in the meantime got married. Wherever reference is made to the entire sample (both married and individual persons), 103 families are examined.

Table 1. Distribution of families by size

No. of people per family	1951		1959	
	No.	%	No.	%
One	9	8·7	5	4·8
Two	9	8·7	21	20·4
Three	22	21·4	21	20·4
Four	24	23·3	30	29·1
Five	15	14·6	15	14·6
Six	14	13·6	4	3·9
Seven	10	9·7	7	6·8
Total	103	100·0	103	100·0

The distribution of families according to their size is set out in *Table 1*.

It may be seen from *Table 1* that, during the period from 1951 to 1959, there was a sharp increase in the number of families with two members. This is attributable to the fact that young people are getting married and adult children are leaving their families to work at other towns. The number of families with three members has remained practically unchanged. There was a certain increase in the percentage of families of four. At the same time there was a considerable decrease in the number of families of six and more members, as well as in the number of single individuals. The average size of a family investigated in 1951 was 4·30, and in 1959, 3·86; a decrease of 10·2 per cent. In addition to some changes in the average size of a family, the number of wage-earners in each family is growing, while the number of dependants per wage-earner (less single individuals) is declining.

Table 2. Numbers of wage-earners and dependants

Industries	1951		1956		1959	
	No. of wage-earners	No. of dependants per wage-earner	No. of wage-earners	No. of dependants per wage-earner	No. of wage-earners	No. of dependants per wage-earner
Engineering	1·51	1·96	1·91	1·26	2·05	0·91
Iron and steel	1·56	2·08	1·68	1·66	1·31	1·95
Textile and clothing	1·72	1·29	2·05	0·70	2·08	0·58
Chemicals	1·50	1·53	1·55	1·50	1·70	0·88

It may be seen from *Table 2* that in 1951-1959, the number of wage-earners decreased only in the families of workers employed in the iron and steel industry. The number of wage-earners declined from 1·56 in 1951 to 1·31 in 1959, while the number of dependants decreased in 1956 and went up again in 1959. The reason is that the head of a family employed in the iron and steel industry is paid more highly than a person employed in other industries and, therefore, the families of iron and steel workers do not need supplementary incomes.

The number of wage-earners in the families of textile and clothing workers is steadily rising. Whereas, in 1951, there was an average of 1·72 wage-earners and 1·29 dependants per wage-earner in each family of a textile or clothing worker, in 1959 each family averaged as many as 2·08 wage-earners and only 0·58 dependants. It should be borne in mind that the wages in the textile and clothing industries are, as a rule, somewhat lower than those in the engineering, iron and steel, or chemical

industries. Therefore the families of textile and clothing workers sometimes need supplementary incomes.

The study also demonstrated that, in addition to the general growth of
employment in each family, there is an increase in the employment of
women and a decrease in the number of housewives. Whereas, in 1951,
out of 103 families investigated, women aged between 18 and 64 were
not gainfully employed in 31 families (30 per cent of all the families,
primarily the families of iron and steel and engineering workers), in
1959 the number of families where women are housewives fell off
considerably. Out of 103 families investigated, there are housewives in
only 18 (17·4 per cent of all the families), and out of this number 17 are
families of iron and steel, engineering, and chemical workers, and only
one is a textile worker's family.

During the period from 1951 to 1959, the composition of families
changed as well. In 1951, the average family of 4·30 comprised 1·56 wage-
earners, 2·63 dependants, 0·06 old-age pensioners, and 0·05 recipients
of scholarships and grants. In 1959, the average size of a family declined
to 3·86, while the wage-earners accounted for 1·91 and the number of
dependants decreased to 1·72; there were as many as 0·16 old-age
pensioners and 0·07 recipients of scholarships and grants. Another
striking feature is that, in 1959, the proportion of old-age pensioners
considerably increased as compared to 1951. This is mainly the result
of the enactment of a new pension law.

The families may be grouped as follows in terms of the aggregate
monthly income per member in 1959:

up to 40 roubles	16·5 per cent
from 40·1 to 70	60·2 per cent
over 70	23·3 per cent

The data for 1961, which were derived from 100 family budgets including the 92 families investgated in 1959, show the following distribution
of income per head:

up to 40 roubles	8 per cent
from 40·1 to 70	62 per cent
over 70	30 per cent

The changes between the groups in 1961 compared with the groups in
1959 show that there has been a considerable increase in the third group
(over 70 roubles per head) from 23·3 per cent to 30 per cent, and a sharp
reduction in the group of the lowest incomes from 16·5 per cent to 8 per
cent, a reduction of more than 50 per cent. A comparison of the data

for 1961, based on the budgets of 100 families, with those for 1951 shows the changes more graphically. There is a reduction of the group with the lowest incomes from 45 per cent to 8 per cent, an increase in the second group (incomes of from 40·1 to 70 roubles per head) from 43 to 62 per cent, and of the third group from 12 to 30 per cent. The rise in the level of well-being of the workers' families during recent years is clearly evident.

The distribution of families in terms of the number of children relative to different average incomes per member (less single individuals) was as shown in *Table 3*.

Table 3. Income and family size

Per capita income group (at current prices of respective years)	1951			1959		
	Total no. of families	Average size	No. of children per family	Total no. of families	Average size	No. of children per family
Up to 40 roubles	41	5·06	2·75	19	4·79	2·42
From 40·1 to 70	48	3·79	1·62	58	3·81	1·06
Over 70	5	3·00	0·40	21	3·19	0·47
Total	94	4·30	2·04	98	3·86	1·19

As a rule, the larger the family, the more children it has, and the lower is its average *per capita* income. Thus, in a family with a *per capita* income of up to 40 roubles, there is an average of 2·42 children, whereas the families with higher *per capita* incomes (over 70 roubles) have only 0·47 children, i.e. an average of one child per two families. The natural changes of population and other demographic data are largely determined by the age composition of the population. There were certain changes in the distribution of family members according to their sex and age (including single individuals) during the period from 1951 to 1959. Thus, in 1951, children under 13 accounted for 40·5 per cent including: children under 1, 1·9 per cent, between 1 and 2, 4·3 per cent, between 3 and 6, 14·3 per cent, and between 7 and 13, 20·1 per cent. In 1959, children under 13 accounted only for 24·7 per cent including: no children under 1, between 1 and 2, 1·8 per cent, between 3 and 6, 2·8 per cent, between 7 and 13, 20·1 per cent. The decrease in the average number of younger children was due to the natural process of family 'ageing' in 1951-1959. By 1961, this 'ageing' became, naturally, even greater.

It should be noted that in the families under study the number of women under pensionable age is much higher than that of men. Thus, in 1951, there were 74 men aged between 18 and 59 against 110 women aged between 18 and 54, while in 1959 there were 99 men against 136 women. As to the various industries involved, we find that, in the families of iron and steel workers, there is an equal number of men and women, while in the families of textile and clothing workers, in 1951, there were twice as many women under pensionable age as men. This is due to the specific nature of this industry which has long been regarded as a woman's domain.

LIVING AND CULTURAL STANDARDS

The main conclusion that arises from an analysis of selected budgets of working-class families for March 1951, 1956, 1959, and 1961 is the steady rise of their living and cultural standards. The incomes of these families are growing year by year. There has been an increase of wages earned by the head of the family and by its members. A considerable and ever-growing proportion of family incomes is also derived from scholarships and benefits, as well as from social services provided by the government, public organizations, and trade unions free of charge or at a discount. Since it is difficult to assess these services for the past years, or to glean them from budget records, they were not taken into account in analysing the budgets. Therefore the incomes of working-class families incorporated into the budgets under study are actually considerably underestimated. This fact should be constantly borne in mind while examining the following data.

The most typical feature characterizing the growing well-being of the families investigated is the rise of cash earnings per family. These earnings are increasing at a rapid pace. The average cash earnings per family increased from 158·5 roubles in March 1951, to 177·2 roubles in March 1956, i.e. by 11·8 per cent during 5 years. In March 1959, they reached 206·3 roubles, thus registering a 30·2 per cent increase as against March 1951, and a 16·5 per cent increase for three years (1956-1959). In 1961, the average money income of a family reached 211 roubles (according to the budgets of 100 families) and had increased in comparison with 1951 (according to the budgets of 92 families) by 33·75 per cent. The increase during the five years from 1956 to 1961 was more than 19 per cent. The rate of income growth has been obviously accelerated during the past few years. In 1951-1956 the yearly increment of incomes amounted to 2·3 per cent, and from 1956 to 1961 it was 3·8 per cent. In other words, during the recent period the rate of increment increased by two-thirds. As the state prices of consumer goods remain stable or go down, the growth of incomes in the families under study is a very essential factor in the improvement of their living standards.

The cash earnings per member of a family showed a still more pronounced upward trend. The point is that the families whose heads were middle-aged in 1951 decreased in size owing to the marriage of grown-up children. This affected the average size of families, which in 1951 was 4·14 members, in 1956, 4·09 members, and in 1959 only 3·87 members. As a result, the average income of each member increased from 38·3 roubles in 1951 to 43·3 roubles in 1956, 53·3 roubles in 1959, and, according to the data for 100 families in 1961, it had grown to 59 roubles. In other words, the average income per member rose by 13·1 per cent between 1951 and 1956, or at an average of 3·3 per cent each year, while, between 1956 and 1961, there was a total increase of 36·5 per cent and an average increase of 7·3 per cent a year.

The total of average monthly wages received in March each year increased year after year and rose by 41·8 per cent from 1951 to 1959, or 47·5 per cent by 1961. It is noteworthy that, even though the average earnings of the head of the family increased substantially (by 22·4 per cent from 1951 to 1959), they were considerably outpaced by the rise in the wages of the other members, which rose by 92·8 per cent, and the total rise of wages earned by all the members. The share of the other members of the family (apart from the main breadwinner) in the aggregate wages of all the family increased from 27·5 per cent in March 1951 to 37·5 per cent in March 1959, and rose from one-quarter of the total family income to one-third. As to the share of the earnings of the head of the family in the average aggregate income, it was slowly but steadily declining and by March 1959 accounted for less than one-half of the entire income of the family.

This follows from an increase in the number of wage-earners in each family and the improvement of their skills resulting in the growth of their aggregate wages. It should be noted that the natural process of family 'ageing' makes itself felt since the grown-up children and house-wives relieved of child-care are gainfully employed in industry and augment the aggregate family income by their earnings. It is obvious that in 8 years the 'ageing' of a family could not result in the doubling of wages earned by the other members. It is evident that the main factor that contributed to the increase of wages earned by the other members was the improvement of living conditions. This enabled more housewives to undertake some gainful employment.

Wages constitute the main, the growing, but by no means the only source of income in the families investigated. The structure of incomes in the families under study is set out in *Table 4*.

Table 4. The proportion of incomes from different sources in the aggregate income of 92 families under study (in percentages)

Types of income	March 1951	March 1956	March 1959
Earnings of the head of the family	52·7	50·9	49·6
Earnings of the other members	20·0	28·3	29·7
Total wages	72·7	79·2	79·3
Additional bonuses	1·0	1·5	0·9
Social security, pensions, scholarships, and other benefits	5·8	4·8	6·6
Proceeds from individual farms	3·5	2·4	1·8
Miscellaneous (loans, debts repaid, etc.)	17·0	12·1	11·4
Total income	100·0	100·0	100·0

No allowance is made for the services (such as annual holidays) received from the state free of charge or at a discount.

The proportion of wages as the main source of income is growing in the families investigated year after year: from 72·7 per cent of the total income in March 1951 to 79·3 per cent in March 1959. Prior to 1956, when the new pension law was enacted, the total amount of pensions and other benefits was somewhat lagging behind the general growth of family incomes. This led to a decrease in the proportion of social security benefits, pensions, etc., in the aggregate income of the families under study (from 5·8 per cent in 1951 to 4·8 per cent in 1956). By March 1959, this lag had been more than offset, and the share of this type of income had reached 6·2 per cent of the aggregate income, i.e. became relatively larger than in March 1951, despite a considerable growth of the aggregate family income.

The share of profits from individual farms declined from 3·5 per cent in March 1951 to 1·8 per cent in March 1959. The improvement of the efficiency of state shops and the increasing employment of family members at state enterprises make individual farming too burdensome and less profitable.

The families under study differ as to the skills, trades, and spheres of employment of their heads and other members. The wages of family members and the aggregate family incomes differ accordingly. The steps taken in the Soviet Union to level wages, to raise the wages of low-paid workers, and to eliminate low wages, as well as the expansion of services offered free of charge and at a discount, tend to level family incomes. The growth of family incomes (per member between 1951and1959) and the levelling of these incomes may be seen from *Table 5.*

Table 5. Distribution of 92 families on the basis of the average income per member in March 1951, 1956, and 1959

Average income per member in March of each year (actual earnings)	Number of families			Percentage		
	March 1951	March 1956	March 1959	March 1951	March 1956	March 1959
Up to 40 roubles	46	40	15	50·0	43·5	16·3
40·1 to 70 roubles	35	37	57	38·1	40·2	62·0
Over 70 roubles	11	15	20	11·9	16·3	21·7
Total	92	92	92	100	100	100

We assume that the families with a monthly income of less than 40 roubles per member are relatively low-paid (but only *relatively* since an average income of 30-40 roubles per member is by no means small). The families with an average monthly income of 40-70 roubles *per capita* constitute the middle-income group, and those with an average income of more than 70 roubles per member to the high-income group.

The growth of family incomes between 1951 and 1959 finds its expression, first and foremost, in the large-scale movement of families from the low-income group to the middle-income group, and from the latter into the high-income group. The relative proportion of families with an average *per capita* income of less than 40 roubles constituted 50 per cent in March 1951, and by March 1959 they had been reduced to a third of the original number. The share of the group with a *per capita* income of 40·1 to 70 roubles rose in the meantime by more than a half, and is now predominant. The relative share of the group of families with an average *per capita* income of more than 70 roubles noticeably increased and moved from third place to second. These shifts graphically illustrate changes in the living standards of the families investigated.

The levelling of family incomes is primarily shown by the fact that 62 per cent of all the families, i.e. the vast majority, belong to the middle-income group. It is significant that the expansion of the middle-income group resulted solely from the shrinkage of the low-income group without any decrease in the high-income group. Between 1951 and 1959, there was an increase in the incomes of all three groups.

The total of family expenses is rising almost as fast as the amount of incomes. Between 1956 and 1959, the general growth of family incomes was accompanied by radical changes in the volume and distribution of expenses, which testify to the improvement of living standards in the families under study.

Table 6. Changes in expenditure: average percentage
for each family (March 1951 = 100)

Total expenditure per family	March 1956	March 1959
Total	111·8	130·2
Including:		
Rent, fuel, public utilities	102·2	132·4
Food	109·0	133·0
Manufactured goods, including furniture and household utensils	111·6	154·9
Cultural and educational needs (newspapers, books, magazines, cinema, and theatre)	159·4	209·2
Hygiene and toilet	115·1	137·7

The conclusions are also wholly supported by the data from the investigation of 100 families in 1961, which show the following growth of incomes and their levelling (*Table 7*):

Table 7. Growth and levelling of incomes
of 100 families

Income per family member, in roubles	Number of families 1951	Number of families 1961
Up to 40	45	8
40·1 to 70	43	62
Over 70	12	30

We shall now examine further details of the structure of family expenses and analyse changes in their most essential aspects. The structure reveals qualitative changes in the living standards of the families under study.

During the eight-year period, the proportion of rent in relation to total expenditure remained stable and constituted 4·0 to 4·4 per cent of all cash expenditures. An analysis of food expenses is very significant. As compared to March 1951, these expenses showed, in 1959, an average increase of 33·0 per cent per family. This growth is due to an increase in the volume of food consumed, and simultaneous improvement of its quality, as a result of the consumption of more nutritious food, par-

Table 8. The structure of expenditure in 92 families investigated for 1951-1959 (in percentages)

Items	March 1951	March 1956	March 1959
Rent, fuel, public utilities (less repairs and construction)	4·4	4·0	4·4
Food, including meals at public catering establishments, kindergartens, and crèches	51·8	50·7	49·1
Clothing, underwear, footwear, furniture, and household utensils	18·0	17·9	21·9
Cultural and educational needs	1·5	2·2	2·5
Hygiene and toilet	2·2	2·2	2·3
Cigarettes and tobacco	0·9	0·9	0·9
Membership dues to public organizations	1·3	1·0	1·0
Taxes	6·1	6·7	6·3
Miscellaneous	13·8	14·4	11·6
Total	100	100	100

ticularly animal products. At the same time the share of food expenses decreased by 1·7 per cent in eight years. The main factor in a relatively moderate growth of expenditure on food is that these expenses, in many of the families investigated, have reached a level where they ensure physiologically adequate nutrition (particularly as regards such foodstuffs as sugar, fats, and fish). As a result, the families are able to use their growing incomes to increase the purchases of manufactured goods, particularly durable goods, and to satisfy more fully their ever-growing requirements.

The improvement of living standards is characterized particularly by an increase in expenses incurred in the purchase of manufactured goods. People are better-dressed, better-shod, and buy good quality furniture and a wide variety of household utensils for their flats. These expenses have shown a particularly marked increase since 1956. Expenses incurred in purchasing manufactured goods, which in March 1956 were a mere 11·6 per cent higher than in March 1959, had, by March 1959, exceeded the level of March 1951 by 54·9 per cent, showing a far greater increment than food expenses (+33 per cent as against March 1951). Thus the income increment was used, in the main, to buy more manufactured goods. Likewise significant is a spurt in expenses to meet cultural needs: an increase by two-thirds over 1951-1959. Expenses under hygiene and toilet rose by 15 per cent in March 1956, and by 37·7 per cent by March 1959 (as against 1951). These include primarily expenses incurred in purchasing perfumes, in the payment of laundry bills, as well as in paying for the services of barbers and hairdressers.

The above statistics clearly demonstrate the trend of the improvement of the living and cultural standards of the population. An increase in the purchase of more and better clothes, footwear, furniture, and educational facilities, accompanied by a reduction or stabilization in the proportion of such expenses as are no longer given top priority (for instance, food) are the specific features characterizing the expenses incurred by the families investigated.

It is only natural that the growth of various expenses differs from family to family, depending on its income level. The dynamics of the growth of various expenses in family income groups are tabulated below.

Table 9. Changes in the expenditure of 92 families as of March 1959 (1951 = 100)

Items	up to 40·0 March 1959	40·1-70·0 March 1959	Over 70·1 March 1959
Food, including meals at public catering establishments, kindergartens, and crèches	119·0	125·4	132·0
Underwear, footwear, furniture, and household utensils	107·3	116·6	209·0
Cultural requirements	441·3	240·2	131·6
Hygiene and toilet	165·9	141·3	115·4

That families that come within the middle- and high-income groups increased, to a far greater extent than had low-income families, the purchases of manufactured goods, such as clothing, footwear, underwear, headgear, furniture, etc. At the same time, one should constantly bear in mind the above-mentioned large-scale movement of a great number of families into higher-income groups, as well as the marked decrease in the proportion of low-income families. It is evident that the increment of food expenses of families with an average *per capita* income of up to 40 roubles (+19 per cent) considerably exceeded the increment of purchases of manufactured goods (+7 per cent), and these families mainly improved their diet. As to the group with a *per capita* income of 40·1 to 70 roubles, the increment of food expenses for 1951-1959, equal to 25 per cent, differed but little from the increment of expenses on manufactured goods, equal to 32 per cent. The levelling of wages, and the abolition of taxes, have undoubtedly resulted in a marked increase in the purchasing of manufactured goods by relatively low-paid family groups (it should be recalled that the present study dates back to 1959).

HOUSING CONDITIONS

A comparison of housing conditions in the families investigated in 1959 with the conditions of 1951 goes to show that fewer families live in hostels or rent private flats, while more had moved into comfortable factory-owned and municipal houses. During this period, the number of families occupying two rooms increased almost by one-third. There was a marked increase in the average floor-space per family as well as in *per capita* housing available. *Per capita* housing floor-space rose by an average of 29 per cent. Particularly noticeable was the improvement of housing conditions in the families of engineering workers in Moscow (an average improvement of 35 per cent) and the families of chemical workers in Gorky (34·5 per cent). In 1951-1959, 27 families out of 103 received new flats. The total floor-space in newly built blocks of flats rose by 63 per cent as againt the floor-space occupied by them in 1951. It should be noted that single-room and two-room flats account for 30 per cent of the floor-space recently received by working-class families.

Housing conditions in working-class families vary considerably from city to city. In Moscow, almost all the workers live in factory-owned and municipal houses. In Gorky, most of the families investigated (71 per cent) live in factory-owned houses, whereas in Ivanovo only half of the families live in factory-owned and municipal houses. The rest live in private houses of their own. In Moscow and Gorky, where most of the workers live in factory-owned houses, the improvement of their housing conditions is more striking than in Ivanovo.

In March 1959, rent and payment for public utilities, including electricity, gas, and fuel, averaged in the city of Moscow eight roubles per family, which constitutes approximately 3·5 per cent of total expenses. Since Muscovites are better provided with gas and central heating, their fuel expenses are very low, on average about 0·4 roubles a month per family. In Gorky, the housing expenses of the families investigated are roughly the same as in Moscow, 8·2 roubles in March 1959, but the structure of expenses in that city is different. Heating expenses are higher amounting to 1·5 roubles. There is no doubt that an increase in gas resources available in Gorky will change the situation. In March 1959, rent and heating expenses averaged 4·1 per cent of total family expenses in the Gorky families.

Relatively higher expenditure in the families of Ivanovo workers is due to greater heating costs, which account for approximately two-thirds of total housing expenses. More than half of the families investigated occupy private houses of their own, which are relatively expensive to heat in winter-time. It is precisely the large proportion of private houses in the city of Ivanovo that results in a relatively lower rent, since the owners of private houses are free from such expenses. *Table 10* contains an analysis of the structure of housing expenditure.

Table 10. Expenditure on housing

	Moscow March		Gorky March		Ivanovo March	
	1951	1959	1951	1959	1951	1959
Rent and public utilities in roubles	8·22	8·01	4·33	8·18	7·16	11·3
Percentage of total monthly expenditure	4·8	3·6	3·2	4·1	4·4	5·7
Including: Rent in roubles	3·17	3·16	1·1	2·42	2·45	1·13
Percentage of total expenditure	1·9	1·4	0·8	1·2	1·5	0·6
Public utilities	2·82	4·43	2·14	4·22	2·08	2·82
Percentage of total expenditure	1·6	2·0	1·6	2·1	1·3	1·4
Fuel expenditure	2·21	0·42	1·09	1·54	2·63	7·35
Per cent	1·3	0·2	0·8	0·8	1·6	3·7
In addition: Maintenance, repair, and construction costs (for private housing), taxes and insurance	—	0·13	—	0·93	1·08	15·12*

* A considerable increase in these expenses is due to the investment of a large sum in the construction of a private house by one of the families in Ivanovo.

The results of the study demonstrate that it is more expensive to have one's own private house than a flat in a factory-owned or municipal house. An attempt was made to compare the housing expenses of Ivanovo textile workers living in a factory-owned house with the expenses incurred by those living in houses of their own (see *Table 11*). The family income is almost the same, but the families living in factory-owned houses spend 8·96 roubles a month on housing, including repairs and insurance, which constitutes 5·5 per cent of their incomes. As for the families occupying houses of their own, their housing expenses constitute 16·7 roubles, or 10·4 per cent of income, of which

7·0 roubles go to pay taxes, insurance, and cover other housing costs. Repair costs in private houses also exceed considerably similar expenses in a factory-owned house; in the present example the repair costs averaged 2·4 roubles per month in private houses as against 0·16 roubles in a factory-owned house. This goes to show that the families living in factory-owned houses enjoy considerable privileges granted by the factories and the state. The families occupying private houses have a somewhat greater opportunity of keeping individual garden plots which provide them with an additional income, and to a certain extent compensate them for extra expenses incurred in maintaining their own houses. The data of the study show that the families occupying private houses have a net return of approximately 7·8 roubles per month from their individual garden plots.

The most noticeable improvement of housing conditions took place in the first group (an average income of up to 40 roubles *per capita*). Between 1951 and 1959, an average increase in floor-space per family amounted to 36 per cent, with an average increase per member of 42 per cent. A considerable increase was registered in the proportion of flats with all modern conveniences. Nevertheless, the housing expenses, including public utilities and heating, do not exceed 4·4 per cent of the total expenses of this group as of 1959.

In the second group (with an average *per capita* income of 40·1 to 70 roubles), which includes most of the families investigated, there was a similarly marked improvement in housing conditions. There was more than a twofold increase in the number of families provided with gas and half of the families had moved into flats provided with baths and telephones. The improvement of housing conditions did not have any tangible effect on the rents of these families. If the average housing expenses, including rent, public utilities, and heating, amounted to 6·78 roubles, or 4·5 per cent of total expenses, in 1951, in 1959 this sum increased to 7·1 roubles and accounted for 4·9 per cent of total expenses.

In the highly paid group the housing conditions in 1951-1959 did not show such a striking improvement as in the two former groups but in this group there was also a marked improvement in some amenities.

Great changes had occurred in 1961 in the housing conditions and amenities of the 100 families under review. The total extent of the housing space occupied by them increased during this period from 1835·4 square metres in 1951 to 2280·6 square metres in 1961. Housing provision per head rose from 4·5 square metres in 1951 to 6·3 square metres in 1961. The total housing space per member of the 100 families investigated came to more than 10 square metres. In spite of such a considerable

F

Table 11. *Comparison of expenditure on factory-owned and private houses*

| | Average monthly expenses per family, total | | Average monthly housing expenses, total | | Including | | | | | | | | | | | |
| | | | | | Rent | | Public utilities – electricity, water, sewage etc. | | Firewood and paraffin | | Total | | Major repairs, taxes, insurance, etc. | | Current repairs | |
	No.	%	No.	%	No.	%	No.	%	No.	%	No.	%	No.	%	No.	%
Residents of factory-owned houses	162·77	100	8·95	5·5	2·9	1·8	3·72	2·3	1·54	0·9	8·16	5·0	0·63	0·4	0·16	0·1
Residents of private houses	161·58	100	16·79	10·4	–	–	2·12	1·3	5·23	3·2	7·35	4·5	7·05	4·4	2·39	1·5

improvement in housing conditions, the outlay on rent and communal services increased by only 14 per cent for all the families investigated.

FOOD CONSUMPTION

The total sum of food expenses incurred by the families investigated increased by 33 per cent, while the proportion of these expenses in total expenditures was reduced from 52 per cent in March 1951 to 49 per cent in March 1959. The data of the 92 budgets bear out the fact that the higher the *per capita* income of the family, the lower is the proportion of its food expenses. Thus, in families with an average income of more than 70·0 roubles *per capita*, the food expenses amount to 40 per cent of all expenses.

Table 12. Increase in food consumption per adult member in 92 families (1951 = 100 per cent)

Foodstuffs	1959	1961*
Rye bread and flour converted into its bread equivalent	69·9	63·2
Wheat bread and flour converted into its bread equivalent	111·2	85·9
Potatoes	88·8	90·6
Cabbage and other vegetables	132·3	127·0
Fresh fruit	441·2	468·2
Milk and dairy products converted into their milk equivalent (less butter)	140·6	202·4
Butter	179·5	—
Vegetable oil and margarine	159·8	—
Meat	149·7	173·3
Sausages and smoked provisions	187·1	231·4
Fish	191·8	215·4
Sugar and confectionery	138·6	166·8

* Figures for 100 families (including the 92). Figures for consumption of butter and vegetable oil are not available.

It may be seen from this table that all the families under review reduced their consumption of rye bread and increased their consumption of milk, butter, meat, meat products, fish, and fresh fruit.

In spite of the rapid growth of food consumption in the families investigated in all the three cities, the budget materials demonstrate that there still remains some disparity in the diets of the families residing in Moscow, Gorky, and Ivanovo. The Moscow families consume more meat, meat products, butter, fruit, and sugar than the families investigated in Gorky and Ivanovo, while the latter consume more bread and potatoes. However, it should be noted that difference in the consumption of staples by the families investigated in Moscow, on the one hand, and in the cities of Gorky and Ivanovo, had considerably decreased in 1951-1959. As regards milk, this difference had practically disappeared. In fact, if the daily consumption per adult consumer in Moscow is estimated at 100, we shall receive the following indices for the families investigated in Gorky and Ivanovo:

Table 13. *Consumption ratio per adult consumer in families investigated in Moscow, Gorky, and Ivanovo (March 1951 and March 1959)*

Type of food	Year	Moscow families	Gorky families	Ivanovo families
Meat	1951	100	76·9	71·8
	1959	100	78·4	76·2
Fresh fruit	1951	100	27·5	34·9
	1959	100	40·4	93·9
Fish	1951	100	76·0	102·9*
	1959	100	84·4	97·3
Milk	1951	100	64·8	113·9
	1959	100	93·8	139·9
Wheat bread	1951	100	91·3	68·9
	1959	100	142·8	110·3

* Fish consumption in Ivanovo was somewhat higher than in 1951 as a result of herring consumption.

Apart from geographical differences, it is interesting to note differences in consumption in families with different *per capita* incomes. The consumption per adult member differs considerably, depending on the average *per capita* income of the family. The materials of the study demonstrate that the difference in food consumption between families with an average *per capita* income of over 70 roubles and the families with a *per capita* income of 40·1-70 roubles is smaller than the difference between those with an income of 40·1-70 roubles and those whose average *per capita* income is lower than 40 roubles. For instance, as regards such an important staple as meat, there is practically no difference in consumption between the groups with *per capita* incomes of 40·1-70 and over 70 roubles. However, the group with an average *per capita* income of over 70 roubles consumes a far greater amount of dairy products: 20 per cent more butter and 33 per cent more of other dairy products, primarily cheese, sour cream, and curds. This group consumes twice the amount of fruit consumed by the group with a *per capita* income of 40·1-70 roubles and 36 per cent more vegetables.

An estimate was made of the chemical composition of food consumed by the families investigated and of its calorific value. The improvement of food quality between 1951 and 1961 affected the chemical composition of food consumed. An increase was registered, in March 1959 as against March 1951, in the amount of nutritious elements contained in the daily ration of each member of the families investigated (per adult member): proteins increased by 10·5 per cent including animal proteins by 60 per cent, fats by 45·9 per cent including animal fats by 75·3 per cent.

The data from the investigation of the 100 families in 1961 confirm the fact that there has been an improvement in the quality of the foodstuffs consumed. In 1961, in comparison with 1951, the quantity of food per adult member per day increased as follows: albumen by 16 per cent, including animal products by 70 per cent, and fats by 51 per cent, including animal products by 80 per cent. The total calorific value of foodstuffs consumed rose from 3,324 to 3,716 calories a day for an adult, and 3,324 per head including children; and the proportion of calories obtained from animal products grew by almost one and a half times. The increased consumption of calories arose from the fact that during the period under consideration many of the children in the families investigated had become adults.

The total calorific value of the foodstuffs consumed by the families investigated has practically reached the physiological norm. The proportion of animal fats in total food consumption even exceeds the physiological norm but, at the same time, the consumption of proteins is inadequate by the standards of the Institute of Nutrition of the Academy of Medical Sciences.

The daily food consumption per head of each adult member of the families investigated contained the following amounts of foodstuffs and calories:

Table 14. Daily food consumption

	1961	*Physiological norm calculated per adult member of the families*
Albumen	86·7	103·9
Fats	89·11	106·0
Carbohydrates	520·0	436·7
Calories	3317·81	3202·2

The analysis of the budgets studied demonstrates that the growth of family incomes is accompanied by a considerable improvement in their diets. Thus, in the families with an average *per capita* income up to 40 roubles the total calorific value constitutes 2,800 calories. In the families with an average *per capita* income of 40·1 to 70 roubles, it exceeds the physiological norm and amounts to 3,132 calories, while in the group with an income exceeding 70 roubles it is more than 3,500 calories. The cash value of each calorie consumed depends on the average *per capita* income. It amounts to 2·3 kopeks in the group with an average *per capita* income of up to 40 roubles, to 2·7 kopeks in the group with a *per capita* income of 40·1 to 70 roubles, and to 3·2 kopeks in the group whose average *per capita* income exceeds 70 roubles.

The diet structure has changed considerably since 1951. Most of the foodstuffs were purchased in state shops (up to 70 per cent, or 86·8 per cent including public catering). In all the families investigated, the structure of food purchases in state and co-operative shops in March 1951, 1956, and 1959 (at 1959 prices) was as shown in *Table 15*.

Table 15. Food purchases (in percentages)

	1951	1956	1959
Bread and flour	28·7	27·5	18·0
Cereals and macaroni	7·0	5·5	4·5
Potatoes	3·1	1·3	1·4
Vegetables	5·0	2·5	3·0*
Fresh fruit	1·0	1·3	3·2
Milk	2·6	5·1	6·7
Dairy products (less butter)	1·8	3·1	3·2
Butter	5·5	7·4	7·9
Eggs	3·9	1·2	2·7
Vegetable oil	3·6	3·6	3·0
Meat and lard	8·1	8·4	10·6
Sausages and smoked provisions	5·4	6·7	7·8
Fish	4·2	5·0	5·2
Sugar	11·8	15·2	11·5
Confectionery	5·2	5·4	5·9
The remainder	3·1	3·8	5·4
Total	100	100	100

* Out of all the vegetables consumed in 1959 more than half were purchased at collective farm markets or grown on individual farms. The above figure includes only the vegetables purchased in state shops.

During the period under review, the proportion of bread and flour purchases declined by one-third. The proportion of purchases of cereals macaroni, and potatoes decreased as well. A marked upward trend was registered in the proportion of purchases of nutritious meat and dairy products: milk purchases increased 2·5 times, dairy products (less butter) almost twice, butter by one-half, meat and lard by approximately one-third, sausages and smoked provisions by one-half. The proportion of fresh fruit trebled. All these data testify to the continuous improvement in quality of food consumed by the families investigated.

It is necessary to know the source of the foodstuffs. The foodstuffs purchased in state shops cost much less than those purchased at collective-farm markets. The proportion of food purchased in state shops, by the 92 families investigated during 1951-1959 increased from 65·7 per cent in March 1951 to 75·1 per cent in March 1959. At the same time, the improvement of food stocks in state shops greatly affected the volume and cost of purchases at collective-farm markets. A decrease was registered in the market purchases of foodstuffs by working-class families from 13·6 per cent of food expenses in 1951 to 9·6 per cent in 1959. There was a similar decline in the consumption of foodstuffs grown on individual plots in the 92 families investigated from 7·7 per cent to 3·6 per cent.

The improvement in living standards is accompanied by changes in consumption structure: the range of goods is expanding and their quality is improving. An ever greater proportion of consumption is assumed by manufactured and high-quality goods and particularly, by durable goods, such as furniture, sewing-machines, TV and radio sets, etc. During 1951-1959, the working-class families under study increased their expenditure on manufactured goods, as is shown by the following data (*Table 16*).

Table 16. Expenditure on manufactured goods

	Average monthly expenditure on manufactured goods per family (in roubles)		Percentage of total family expenditure	
	1951	1959	1951	1959
For all the families investigated	28·5	43·2	18·0	21·9
Including:				
Moscow	26·69	46·16	15·6	21·9
Gorky	28·87	43·84	21·7	22·1
Ivanovo	30·49	38·85	18·8	19·7

It may be seen from this table that, on the whole, in all the families investigated, the proportion of expenses incurred in purchasing textiles, clothing, underwear, footwear, etc., rose from 18 per cent in March 1951 to 21·9 per cent in March 1959. The absolute sum spent on manufactured goods in 92 families increased during this period by more than one-half, i.e. by 51·6 per cent. It should be noted that, during 1951-1959, the expenses on manufactured goods showed a particularly marked increase of 73 per cent in the families investigated in Moscow, a somewhat small increase of 51·9 per cent was registered in the Gorky families, and an increase of 27·4 per cent in the families of Ivanovo.

The budget analysis shows that the growth of the *per capita* family income is accompanied by an increase in the proportion of expenditure on manufactured goods. Thus, in the family group with a *per capita* income of up to 40 roubles, the proportion of expenditure on clothing, underwear, textiles, footwear, haberdashery, etc., constitutes 13 per cent of total family expenditure, in the group with a *per capita* income of 40·1 to 70 roubles, 20·3 per cent, and in the families with a *per capita* income over 70 roubles, 25·3 per cent.

A comparison of the consumption of cloth from 1951 to 1961 shows that, whereas in 1951 the 100 families bought 349·7 metres of cloth, in 1961 they purchased 365·1 metres. This is a total increase of 4 per cent. The purchase of silk increased by 18 per cent, amounting to 25·5 metres as against 21·6 metres. The consumption of woollen cloth increased even faster; 31·1 metres as against the former 19 metres. Cotton cloth purchases were lower; 253·5 as against 280·6 metres. A comparison of the data for 1951 with 1961 gives the following picture: five ready-made coats were bought on average per month in 1951 and eleven per month in 1961, and the corresponding figures for suits were 9 and 14, and dresses 9 and 12. The monthly purchases of leather footwear increased from 50 pairs to 55 pairs and of rubber footwear decreased from 43 pairs to 24. Thus the purchases of manufactured goods showed the same tendencies as occurred in the purchase of foodstuffs. People were dressing better and were buying higher-value goods in clothing and footwear. The total purchases of cloth for the whole country increased during this period by 34 per cent, and of footwear by 74 per cent. There was an increase in consumption by the population of goods which improved the material well being of the Soviet people.

CULTURAL AND EDUCATIONAL EXPENDITURE

Expenditure to meet cultural requirements is growing year by year.

Table 17. Expenditure to meet cultural and educational needs (average per family)

	Number of families	Average annual expenditure per family (in roubles)		1959, as percentage of 1951
		1951	1959	
All families investigated	92	28·92	60·58	214·1
Including:				
Moscow	39	64·78	61·78	95·4
Gorky	22	15·60	57·01	365·5
Ivanovo	31	35·09	61·56	175·7

Whereas, in 1951, the average expenditure for cultural requirements of the 92 families investigated was at an annual level of 28·9 roubles, in 1953 this sum increased to 60·5 roubles, or more than double. As to Gorky, this expenditure increased in 1959 more than 3·5 times as compared to 1951, whereas in Ivanovo an increase of 75·7 per cent was registered. The main reason for a certain reduction in Moscow is that about half of the families investigated had purchased TV sets by 1959 and somewhat reduced their spending on the cinema and theatre. The proportion of expenditure to meet cultural and educational needs in the total family budget is growing year after year. In 1959, the share of this expenditure compared with 1951 increased 2·4 times in Gorky, almost by one-third in Ivanovo, and approximately by two-thirds as regards all 92 families investigated.

Let us now examine the growth of expenditure to meet cultural and educational requirements in 1951-1959 in the families with different *per capita* incomes. (The expenditure in March 1951 and 1959 was likewise based on the annual level.)

Table 18. Expenditure to meet cultural and educational requirements in families with different per capita incomes

Per capita income (in roubles)	Number of families	Annual expenditure per family (in roubles)		1959, as percentage of 1951
		1951	1959	
Up to 40·0	15	13·1	57·7	440·0
40·1-70·0	57	23·6	56·8	240·3
Over 70·0	20	55·7	73·2	131·5

As may be seen from this table, expenditure on cultural and educational requirements in the families under study showed a particularly marked increase in the up to 40 roubles income group and the smallest increase in the group whose *per capita* income exceeds 70 roubles. In fact, in the first group the annual sum of cultural and educational expenses in 1959 increased by 44·2 roubles as against 1951, in the 40·1-70 rouble income group, by 33·2 roubles, and in the highest income group by 17·5 roubles. The proportion of expenditure on cultural needs in the total family budget is likewise going up to the greatest extent in the families with a relatively small *per capita* income. In the up to 40 rouble income group, it rose four times in 1959 as compared to 1951, and in the 40·1-70 rouble income group it increased twofold.

Information on the rate of attendances at the cinema, theatre, museums, lectures, and meetings gives some notion of the extent to which the families investigated satisfy their cultural and educational needs.

Table 19. Rate of attendance at the cinema, theatre, lectures, etc., in March 1959 as against March 1956 (per 100 families)

| | 1956=100 | | |
	Cinema	*Theatre and concerts*	*Lectures, meetings and other educational programmes*
Total for all families	137·6	131·8	179·7
Including:			
Moscow	102·9	91·0	154·0
Gorky	150·0	292·9	140·0
Ivanovo	184·6	148·0	301·6
For family groups with an average *per capita* income (in roubles) of			
Up to 40·0	260·3	100·0	300·0
40·1-70·0	120·1	154·3	254·3
Over 70·0	119·2	110·0	156·0

It may be seen from *Table 19* that the frequency of visits to the cinema increased by 37·6 per cent in March 1959, while visits to theatres and concerts increased by 31·8 per cent. However, in Moscow, cinema visits by members of the families investigated showed an increase of only

·9 per cent, whereas theatre attendance even slightly declined, no doubt owing to the development of television. In Gorky, there was an obvious ncrease in theatre-going, whereas in Ivanovo cinema attendance showed an upward trend.

Whereas in March 1951, cinema visits by members of the second and hird groups were more than double those by members of the first group, by March 1959 this disparity had almost disappeared with an overall ncrease in cinema attendances. Between March 1956 and March 1959, cinema attendance in the first family group rose by 160 per cent, in the second group by 20 per cent, and in the third group by 19 per cent. The rate of theatre and concert attendance during the same period increased by 54 per cent in the second group, and by 10 per cent in the third.

The cultural standards of the 92 families investigated are, to a certain extent, characterized by the existence of family libraries and the number of books in them.

Table 20. Family libraries

Cities and average per capita income groups as of 1959	Year	No. of family libraries	Total number of books in families	Average number of books in a family library
Total for all families	1951	42	1,359	32
	1959	65	3,596	55
Including:				
Moscow	1951	14	497	36
	1959	29	1,749	60
Gorky	1951	8	191	24
	1959	14	564	40
Ivanovo	1951	20	671	34
	1959	22	1,263	58
For family groups with an average *per capita* income (in roubles) of				
Up to 40	1951	11	208	19
	1959	11	338	31
40·1 to 70	1951	26	978	38
	1959	40	2,380	60
Over 70	1951	5	109	22
	1959	17	790	46

Most of the families investigated systematically purchase new books and gradually increase their home libraries. The number of families having libraries of their own is steadily growing. Thus, in 1951, 46 per cent of all families had home libraries, and the number of books in those

libraries averaged 32, while in 1959 the number of families having hom
libraries increased by 25 per cent and constituted 71 per cent of all th
families, whereas the average number of books per library increased t
55 books. In Moscow the average number of families having hom
libraries increased in 1951-1959 by 38 per cent, while the averag
number of books went up by 24. During the same period, in Gorky, th
number of families having libraries of their own increased by 27 pe
cent, and the average number of books per library by 16; in Ivanovo
the number of families having libraries increased by 7 per cent, and th
average number of books by 24. If in 1951, there were only 19 book
per family in the up to 40 rouble income group, in 1959 there wer
as many as 31. In the 40·1-70 rouble group the number of books pe
family increased in 1951-1959 from 36 to 60.

Information on newspaper and magazine subscriptions gives som
notion of the improvement of cultural standards in the families in
vestigated (*Table 21*).

*Table 21. Newspaper and magazine subscriptions in 92 families investi
gated (as of March)*

Average per capita income group (*in roubles*)	Year	No. of families	No. of families subscribing to newspapers and magazines	No. of newspapers and magazines subscribed to	Proportion o, newspaper and magazine subscribers
Up to 40	1956	15	6	6	40·0
	1959	15	10	10	66·6
40·1-70	1956	57	39	56	68·4
	1959	57	46	77	80·7
Over 70	1956	20	11	14	55·0
	1959	20	15	34	75·0
Total for all families	1956	92	56	76	60·9
	1959	92	71	121	77·2

In 1956, 60 per cent of all the families subscribed to newspapers and
magazines, while in 1959 this number went up to 77. The first group
showed an increase of 27 per cent, the second group of 12 per cent, and
the third group of 20 per cent. The group with an average *per capita*
income of more than 70 roubles ranked first in the number of subscribers
for newspapers and magazines. In this group, there was an average of
more than two newspapers and more than two magazines per family in
1959. But the greatest increase in newspaper and magazine subscriptions

was registered in the up to 40 rouble income group. By 1959, this group had nearly overtaken the other two as to the percentage of subscribers.

The data provided by the investigation of these families in 1961 shows that expenditure on cultural and educational objects increased during the eleven years by two and a half times and the proportion of expenditure on cultural objects out of total expenditure grew from 1·5 per cent to 3.4 per cent. In analysing these expenditures, however, it must be noted that the monthly figures do not accurately reflect the total level of expenses. For example, out of the 100 families investigated, 70 subscribed to 125 different newspapers and 32 families subscribed to 45 different journals. Subscriptions to newspapers, however, are usually made in the months of November and December and, therefore, in March, when the investigations were made, these expenditures did not feature.

Many members of the families investigated regularly borrow books from public libraries. An increase in the use of public libraries, in addition to family libraries, is another significant indication of cultural development. We have gleaned the following relevant information from budget records.

Table 22. Books borrowed from public libraries

	Year	Members borrowing library books	Percentage of library borrowers
Total for 92 families	1956	60	17·6
	1959	101	29·8
Including:			
Moscow	1956	28	17·8
	1959	43	29·1
Gorky	1956	12	14·3
	1959	12	13·8
Ivanovo	1956	20	20·0
	1959	46	44·2
Average *per capita* income group (in roubles)			
Up to 40	1956	6	8·5
	1959	10	13·5
40·1-70	1956	38	18·3
	1959	67	32·8
Over 70	1956	16	26·2
	1959	24	39·3

Whereas, in 1956, only about 18 per cent of family members (in cluding school-age children) borrowed books from libraries, in 195 the number of families using libraries increased by 11·3 per cent i Moscow and 24·2 per cent in Ivanovo. It is significant that even thoug in the high- and medium-income groups 85 per cent of the families ha home libraries in 1959, 40 per cent of the members of these familie borrowed books from public libraries.

The cultural standards of the families investigated are to a certai extent characterized by the availability of such cultural and educationa facilities as radio and TV sets and musical instruments. In 1959, 8 families investigated (i.e. those that furnished data on radios) showe an increase of 40 per cent in possession of radio sets, while in the cit of Moscow the number increased almost 6 times.

In 1951, none of the families investigated had a television set, refrigerator, or a washing-machine; in 1959, 24 of the families ha purchased a television set and, in 1961, 42 families had one, 10 familie had a refrigerator, and 5 had a washing-machine. There were 60 radio as against 15, and 82 sewing-machines as against the former 30. Mor than three-quarters of all the families investigated in 1959 had a sewing-machine. Half of the families with incomes up to 40 roubles per head and a quarter with incomes of 40·1 to 70 roubles and more per head had a bicycle in the family. There was a noticeable increase during the years 1956 to 1959 of the number of musical instruments; in the families with an average income per head of up to 40 roubles and over 70 roubles the increase was one and a half times, and in families with an average income of between 40·1 and 70 roubles two and a half times.

In addition to these facts there is some evidence about the satisfaction of cultural needs in the data on visits to the cinema, theatre, museums, and lectures. The average figures for each of the 100 families during the month in 1961 were 5·4 visits to cinemas, 1·2 visits to theatres, concerts, and amateur performances.

The facts quoted in this paper show convincingly that during the decade great advances were made in raising the material and cultural levels of the working people and there was a noticeable improvement in the material well being of the Soviet people.

NOTES

1. The Institute of Labour is a research institute set up by the Council of Ministers of the Soviet Union to investigate questions of labour and wages.

2. At the beginning of 1964, a group of staff members of the department concerned with the study of the standard of living at the Institute of Labour (including V. Acharkan, V. Vasilyeva, V. Dyachenko, and N. Kuznetsova) published 'One hundred family budgets' (*The Economic Gazette*, 4 January 1964), which contains full details of the 92 family budgets discussed in the present paper. The data for 1961 are taken from this publication, and were inserted into this paper by R. Ya. Chicherova, a member of the staff of the Institute of Philosophy of the Soviet Academy of Science.

3. 'New' roubles; see p. 36, note 22.

6

Social mobility and choice of occupation

V. N. SHUBKIN

INTRODUCTION

The establishment of the social relations of socialism led to most important changes in Soviet society and to its extremely high level of social mobility. This process is still actively under way. The high rate of economic growth, technical progress, the tremendous increasing demands of the national economy for skilled workers, the enhancement of the role of science, and the high degree of social homogeneity have all created the basis for a free choice of profession according to inclination, given young people confidence in the morrow, and made possible the selection of new vocations not traditional in the particular family.

When investigating the correlation of the occupations of fathers and children, the following factors must always be distinguished: (1) the material form of the division of labour, i.e. the social division of labour as a form of development of the productive forces which causes a definite, although mobile, relation between the occupations of fathers and children; (2) the correlation of the generations caused by the transmission, within the family, of technical and occupational experience, working habits, inclinations, and antipathies, which leads to a certain continuity of various forms of occupational division of labour; and (3) the correlation of the generations which arises from social restrictions, and from caste, economic, or political privileges.

Socialism does not remove the material basis for the social division of labour. Interconnection between the generations is also preserved, to a certain extent, as a result of the transmission of occupational and technical experience in the family. At the same time, those interconnections which arose from property and political privileges, wealth, title, economic and social inequality gradually disappear.

The eradication of class distinctions, and the attainment of increasing social homogeneity, have a number of bases in Soviet societies. These include the growth of labour productivity and the transition to communist forms of production and distribution, the disappearance of the differences in the socio-economic, cultural, and living standards of town and countryside, and of the distinctions between intellectual and manual work, the reduction of the gap between the incomes of workers and peasants, and of the higher- and lower-paid groups of workers. They are also promoted by the movement of a part of the collective farmers, chiefly young people, into the ranks of the working class, and the movement of workers and peasants into the ranks of the intelligentsia. These transitions, regarded as one of the manifestations of the general laws governing the development of Soviet society, deserve a thorough analysis.

CORRELATION OF OCCUPATIONS OF PARENTS AND CHILDREN

The connections between the occupations of fathers, the professional inclinations of the children, and their choice of a profession is shown in a statistical analysis of the data of an experimental investigation carried out among young people leaving secondary schools in the town and region of Novosibirsk, in 1962, by a group of sociologists from the Institute of Economics of the Siberian branch of the Soviet Academy of Sciences. An analogous investigation was carried out in the town of Kyzyl (Tuva Autonomous Region).

A word must first be said about the general attitudes of social tone of the generation now embarking on life. One of the questions in an anonymous questionnaire distributed among the youth was: 'Are you sure that you will be able to find work in your chosen profession?' Out of 289 pupils questioned in general schools in Novosibirsk Region and in the town of Kyzyl, only 19, i.e. 6 per cent, answered 'no'. The overwhelming majority of the young people were confident that they would be able to work in their chosen profession. Thus the first thing that strikes one when analysing this data is the social optimism of our youth.

Which professions are most popular with young people? What correlation is there between the occupations of the fathers and those that the children would like to enter?

An occupational inclination arises at school as a demand for a certain type of work. It first appears in the attitude of the pupil to school sub-

G

Table 1. Occupations of the fathers and inclinations of the children

Fathers' occupations require knowledge of science	As percentage of total			
Children choose professions requiring knowledge of science	Physico-mathematical	Natural science	Humanities	Total
Physico-mathematical	54	22	23	100*
Natural science	57	32	11	100
Humanities	53	17	27	100*
Sons				
Physico-mathematical	84	8	8	100
Natural science	80	20	—	100
Humanities	88	12	—	100
Daughters				
Physico-mathematical	35	32	33	100
Natural science	31	46	23	100
Humanities	8	23	61	100*

* Discrepancy due to small percentage who chose occupations not subsumed under these categories.

jects. The questionnaire made it possible to discover (and assess quantitatively) the young people's attitude to different subjects. Unfortunately, the whole of this information cannot be given within the limits of this paper. It must be mentioned in passing that literature and mathematics proved to be the favourites. Boys and girls said: 'We like both poetry and physics!' When the question of their future work is raised the situation changes. The occupations which they want to take up are often far removed from the traditional ones in their own families. First, let us consider the correlation between the occupations of the fathers and the professional inclinations of the children in terms of 'horizontal' mobility. This does not mean movement towards more creative, attractive or highly paid work, but simply the choice by the children of different occupations from those of their fathers. For this purpose, all vocations mentioned during the investigation (and they numbered more than 100) were grouped as follows: the first group included professions demanding primarily technical and physico-mathematical training, the second, a knowledge of natural science, and the third, the humanities.

An analysis shows that the greatest continuity is observed in the first group, where 50 per cent of the children, whose fathers' occupations required technical and physico-mathematical knowledge, wished to choose the same professions. Of this number, 84 per cent are boys and 35 per cent girls. The majority of the children (57 per cent) whose

athers were connected with the natural sciences wished to choose pro-
essions of the first group. Thirty-two per cent of them wished to
ontinue in the vocations of their fathers, and, among these, two-thirds
.re girls and one-third boys. In other words, in the natural sciences the
ontinuity is mainly kept up by the daughters. Of all groups, the children of
.atural scientists show the least leaning for the humanities: 0·11 per cent.

Finally, the children of fathers working in the humanities also show
he greatest desire (53 per cent) for work connected with mathematics,
physics, and engineering. This refers in particular to the sons, who
onstitute the greatest number (88 per cent) of those desiring to choose
professions of the first group. On the other hand, the majority of the
laughters (61 per cent) are faithful to their fathers' professions. Employment requiring physico-mathematical training is least popular
.mong the daughters. In short, only 27 per cent of the sons and daugh-
ers whose parents were trained in the humanities want to continue in
his line.

The general picture is as follows: 54 per cent of the children of engin-
ers, 32 per cent of the children of natural scientists, and 27 per cent
of the children of those trained in the humanities want to continue their
parents' professions.

Occupations requiring a knowledge of mathematics, physics, and
ngineering are, on the whole, most popular with the young. This does
.ot mean that all children of the first group want to keep to their fathers'
vocations. Many children from the natural science and humanities
groups also show a desire for employments in the first group. In this
:ase it is mainly the sons, as there is a direct contrast between the wishes
of boys and girls. This tendency is all the more cogent because differences in the level of instruction, practical training, and professional
orientation do not arise in this case, since the boys and girls attend the
;ame classes at schools.

Technical progress and the great successes in the physico-mathematical sciences in recent years apparently have a very strong influence
on the formation of professional inclinations, and result in great
mobility in the aspirations of different groups of young people. At the
;ame time, these influences, which have a great effect on boys, tell less
with girls, who wish to specialize in the humanities and natural sciences
.s a rule.

The effect of these factors on the formation of professional leanings
.n boys and girls cannot be ignored. On the one hand, as society strives
.o provide work and education for each according to his inclination, it
.nust take them into account when deploying both industrial and

educational establishments. The grouping together, in a given district
or city, of enterprises and educational establishments with a physico
mathematical bias will evidently promote the employment of young men
in keeping with their inclinations, and provide them with appropriate
further education. It will not be easy for girls leaving school in such areas
to find work to their liking. As a result, a district with sufficient labour
resources may find itself short of workers and some young people who
are obliged to work in occupations not to their taste, may move from
one enterprise to another, and from one educational establishment to
another, i.e. a high degree of fluctuation and migration of labour power
may occur. Finally, the situation may arise in which, despite the large
number of young people who want to continue their education, the
enrolment at educational establishments will be below standard. On
the other hand, the differences in the professional leanings of boys and
girls must be taken into account when guiding the young people's
choice of a profession.

Finally, the fact that, even in this relatively small sample, none of the
sons of families in the humanities and natural science groups wished to
take up the humanities cannot be overlooked. There are a number of
reasons for this. But we should not remain indifferent to the fact that
the humanities and natural sciences are falling more and more to the
share of women, while men choose professions demanding physico-
mathematical training. The prospect of such a division of labour
according to sex is hardly satisfactory. An interest in the humanities
and natural sciences evidently must be aroused among boys and a
liking for physico-mathematical subjects developed in girls.

VERTICAL MOBILITY

The question of the correlation of fathers and children in terms of
'vertical mobility' is an interesting one. In the West, this expression is
usually applied to the movement of members of the lower classes up
an hierarchical ladder. Such an interpretation has no value in Soviet
sociology, for the very conception of prestige, as of all human values,
has changed radically for Soviet people. In reply to one of the questions
in the questionnaire – 'What attracts you to the occupation you have
chosen?' – only 2 per cent of the young people replied 'high wages',
while 25 per cent wrote 'its importance for the national economy, and
45 per cent 'the creative nature of the work'.

The investigation showed that the overwhelming majority of Soviet youth assess an occupation by the scope which it provides for creative work. Therefore, while not claiming that this was a final solution of the question, the scale of popularity of occupations was constructed on this principle. But, as there does not exist a classification of occupations from this point of view, the authors of the questionnaire had to resort to expert opinions. The experts classified all occupations mentioned in our questionnaires according to a 10-point system, based on the opportunities for creative work which they provide under normal conditions of social production. From this classification, an average was deduced for every occupation, and the scale of occupations constructed. As a result, the less creative vocations, which received from one to four points, formed the first group, occupations receiving four to eight points, the second, and the most creative occupations, which were given eight to ten points, the third (see *Table 2*).

*Table 2. Occupations of the fathers and
inclinations of the children*

Classification of occupations according to opportunities provided for creative work			
Fathers' occupations	As percentage of total		
Professions chosen by children	Group 1	Group 2	Group 3	Total
Intending to go to work immediately on leaving school			
Group I	41	59	–	100
Group II	65	33	2	100
Group III	70	30	–	100
Intending to go to work on leaving college			
Group I	3	71	26	100
Group II	1	51	48	100
Group III	–	40	60	100

Nearly all pupils leaving school name a vocation which gives little or average scope for creative work. Moreover, the majority of the children (70 per cent) whose fathers have the most creative professions are prepared to take up vocations of the first group. And vice versa, the majority of the children (59 per cent) of the first group want callings of the second group. In other words, here we find a fairly stable inverse ratio between the occupations of the fathers and the professional aspirations of the children on leaving school.

It would be premature to accept this as final, for the picture changes radically when we analyse the occupations which the young people choose on leaving a college or technical school. In this case, 60 per cent of the children of families in the third group wish to continue in the callings of their fathers, while none of them want to choose an occupation in the first group; and 71 per cent of the children of the first group want vocations providing average opportunities for creative work (second group). Finally, the majority of the children of the second group want to follow in the footsteps of their fathers, although many of them (48 per cent) would like to transfer to occupations in the third group.

The question arises, how are we to account for the fact that children of the third group on leaving school are prepared to work in trades of the first group, and later hope to acquire occupations in the third group? It might be assumed that the authors were dealing with a group of young people who themselves did not know exactly what they wanted from life, and that this was the explanation of the movement from the first group to the third.

In reality this is not so. The children of third-group families have quite definite aspirations to follow in the footsteps of their fathers. Where to work immediately on leaving school is a question for this group of young people which is not fully decided, but only provisionally. On the other hand, children from families of the first group also have very definite aspirations: the majority of them want to change over immediately from the trades of their fathers to occupations offering average scope for creative work.

The whole of this analysis suggests, first of all, that the greater the scope for creative work provided in any occupation, the greater the continuity between the occupations of the parents and children. Second, the aspirations of the children show a definite sequence of stages: the majority of the first group want to pass on to the second, half of the second to the third, while the majority of the third group want to remain in it, although a considerable number (40 per cent) intend to choose occupations of the second group.

The conclusion to be drawn from this is that scientific and technical progress, mechanization and automation, the disappearance of non-creative trades and, hence, the rise in the proportion of more creative occupations will evidently lead to conditions in which a free choice of occupation will be possible, and in which a variation of work will regularly occur. That, however, will not mean that the continuity between the occupations of fathers and children will be broken. On the contrary, the more creative nature of work will make this continuity still more stable in a number of cases. This close correlation of the occupations of fathers and children is based on community of creative demands and interests. It has nothing in common with the social pre-destination in the type of society in which private property and in-equality prevail.

SOCIAL STATUS OF FATHERS AND OCCUPATIONAL CHOICES OF CHILDREN

In a certain sense, occupational inclinations can be classified as social inclinations, or an aspiration to remain in one social group or move on to another. In this connection, an attempt was made to trace the correla-tion between the fathers' social status and the children's inclinations.

Four social groups were chosen for this purpose: industrial and building workers, agricultural workers and collective farmers, workers in the public services, and the intelligentsia. In the first stage, i.e. when analysing the data of the experimental investigation, the authors deemed it possible to limit themselves to these groups, although they were convinced that, when making sociological investigations, in particular when investigating factors determining the choice of an occupation and, moreover, when definite proposals have to be drawn up, it is necessary to pick out more differentiated social groups. Here, not only do the forms of property count, but also the position in the system of production, and in the system of the social division of labour, i.e. the occupation and the level of skill, including education, and, evidently the amount of income, although the first and the second determine the third to a considerable extent.

Table 3. Fathers' social status and children's inclinations

Groups to which parents belong	Children want to become (as percentages of total)				
	Industrial and building workers	*Agricultural workers and collective farmers*	*Public service workers*	*Intelli-gentsia*	*Total*
Industrial and building workers	35	–	5	60	100
Agricultural workers and collective farmers	87	12	–	–	100
Public service workers	56	4	4	36	100
Intelligentsia	25	1	3	71	100

As *Table 3* shows, the smallest percentage of the children want to work in the public services after leaving school. Here we find only 5 per cent of the children of industrial workers, four per cent of the children of public service workers, and three per cent of the children of intellectuals. Intellectual professions are the most popular: 71 per cent of the children of intellectuals, 60 per cent of the children of industrial workers, and 36 per cent of the children of public service workers want to join this group. The popularity and the prestige of the intelligentsia are particularly noticeable when we consider the occupations which the pupils want to choose on finishing their education. One hundred per cent of the children of intellectuals and of workers in industry and the public services, and 87 per cent of the children of collective farmers and agricultural workers want to enter an intellectual profession. At the same time, this also points to the shortcomings which still exist in arousing respect among schoolchildren for production work.

Practice is the criterion of the authenticity of any investigation. It is important to study not only aspirations, wishes, and interests, but also their intensity and close connection with real actions and decisions. In our analysis, this necessitates a comparison of occupational leanings with the employment actually entered by young people after leaving school.

For this purpose, data were collected on the type of work and study chosen by the young men and girls. Here, additional difficulties arose in connection with the fact that the questionnaires were anonymous. Therefore, the authors were deprived of the possibility of establishing the vocation chosen by each of the young people in question. They were obliged to limit themselves to a general analysis. Nevertheless, the data obtained make it possible to judge the connection between the father's occupations and the inclinations and choices of occupations by the children.

Let us deal first of all with the correlation between the fathers' occupations and the work taken up by the children on leaving school.

As may be seen from *Table 4*, the pattern of occupations chosen by the daughters sharply differs from that of the fathers' occupations. The greatest continuity is observed in the case of daughters whose fathers were connected with the humanities and natural sciences. On the other hand, one-half of the daughters whose fathers worked in professions requiring technical and physico-mathematical training did not follow in their footsteps.

A different pattern is presented by the sons. Here, three-quarters of them chose work demanding engineering or physico-mathematical

Table 4. Fathers' occupations and choice of employment

Occupations requiring a knowledge of science	Ratio of fathers' occupations (as percentage of total)	Ratio of children's employment (as percentage of total)
Sons		
Physico-mathematical	70	75
Natural science	15	25
Humanities	15	–
Total	100	100
Daughters		
Physico-mathematical	81	42
Natural science	8	44
Humanities	11	14
Total	100	100

training. On the whole, this is in keeping with their occupational leanings. One-quarter took up natural sciences, and in no case did the sons of fathers working in the humanities follow in their footsteps. This also confirms the close relationship between occupational leanings and the choice of employment.

A comparison of *Tables 2* and *3* shows, in the first place, the close connection between the occupational inclinations and the actual choice of employment. The regularities revealed in the analysis of occupational inclinations are confirmed, as a rule, in the actual choice of employment. This shows that the objective social conditions favour a genuinely free choice of employment by a considerable number of young people in accordance with their inclinations. Thus we see that a study of occupational inclinations is highly relevant for an understanding of the motives guiding the actual choice of work.

Considerable interest also attaches to a comparison of the fathers' occupations with the children's inclinations and the actual employment of young people on leaving school, when classifying vocations according to their creative potential.

Table 5 shows that the young people more than realized the 'minimum programme' which they set themselves before leaving school. The vocations actually entered by the young people have a higher rating than their initial intentions. This applies in all cases, except that of village girls who were employed in more creative work than that of their parents, although less creative than they had hoped for on leaving school. As for the occupations which the young men and girls wanted to take up on completing their education, these cannot be judged as yet,

Table 5. Fathers' occupations and choice of employment

	Classification of vocations according to creative potential		
	Fathers' occupations	Occupational inclinations of children		Vocations actually entered by school-leavers
		on leaving school	on completion of higher education	
General schools (as a whole) Including:	5·00	4·20	7·30	5·30
1. Boys	5·10	3·82	7·35	5·23
2. Girls	4·80	4·50	7·26	5·30
Urban general schools Including:	5·27	4·20	7·60	5·55
1. Boys	5·31	3·81	7·70	5·43
2. Girls	5·21	4·50	7·47	5·70
Rural general schools Including:	3·80	4·20	6·03	4·30
1. Boys	4·27	3·84	5·62	4·48
2. Girls	3·32	4·48	6·36	4·1

because many of the boys and girls went to work straight from school planning to continue their education and move on to more highly, qualified work in the future.

The classification of vocations also shows that on leaving school both urban and rural youth wanted work offering equal scope for creative initiative (as a whole: 4·2; boys: 3·81 and 3·84; girls: 4·50 and 4·48). However, the points assigned to the actual vocations entered on leaving school vary considerably: from 5·55 to 4·30 (as a whole), and 5·43 to 4·48 for boys, and 5·7 to 4·1 for girls. The highest creative potential was offered by the vocations taken up by urban youth. Lowest in the scale were village girls.

Behind these differences there lies the very important and not yet finally solved problem of the equality of town and countryside in the spheres of socio-economic, cultural, and living conditions. The gradual eradication of these differences creates more equal opportunities for entering the more creative occupations in both town and countryside.

Finally, the changes in the social structure after leaving school are shown in *Table 6*:

Table 6. Change in the social structure arising from the choice of occupation

Social groups	Social status			
	Fathers	children		
		both sexes	sons	daughters
	%	%	%	%
Industrial workers	10	18	22	13
Agricultural workers and collective farmers	17	1	2	—
Workers in public services	11	8	8	8
Intelligentsia	62	73	68	79
Total	100	100	100	100

As *Table 6* shows, the structural changes are connected with the growth in the number of industrial workers, primarily due to the influx of boys, and in the number of intellectuals, due to the influx of girls. The drop in the proportion of those engaged in agricultural production is an inevitable occurrence arising from the growth of the productive forces. Such a sharp drop, if not controlled, may lead to labour shortage in agriculture.

The drop in the number of workers in the public services also, to a certain extent, contradicts the tendencies in the general development of the economy, for the proportion of such workers in the Soviet Union is small.

CONCLUSIONS

The results of our investigation show that technical progress gives rise to a fairly high 'horizontal' mobility towards occupations connected with mathematics, physics, and engineering. This is not a 'vogue' but a real and stable trend, particularly characteristic of the majority of the young men, where there are diametrically opposed aspirations on the part of girls.

The analysis reveals great 'vertical' mobility too, in the sense of the desire to move up to more creative occupations. This desire is closely correlated with the actual choice of work. Both urban and rural youth have already obtained more creative work than they had hoped for on leaving school. At the same time, it must be clearly understood that young people have greater opportunities in towns than in the country. This is evidently one of the reasons for the migration of the young people to the towns. Within certain limits this process in inevitable, but, under the specific conditions of Siberia, it may give rise to some difficulties in securing sufficient workers for agriculture.

The intellectual professions prove to be very popular. This arises from the desire of young people to advance their cultural standards and technical knowledge. The elimination of the distinctions between intellectual and physical work occurs in the Soviet Union as a result both of a rise in the cultural standards and technical knowledge of the parents, and of a shift of children of workers and peasants to more creative occupations.

The analysis shows that the occupational inclinations and the actual choice of employment are closely correlated, and if this correlation is not fully revealed among school-leavers, these young people later attempt to fulfil their unrealized aspirations. That is why it is so important to study systematically and to guide wisely the occupational choices of the younger generation. More favourable conditions for a free choice of employment result from scientific and technical progress, the creation of the material and technical bases of communism, the abolition of the distinctions between town and countryside and between mental and physical work, and from growing material well-being. At the same time, there will be a firmer correlation between the occupations of fathers and children, based on a community of creative requirements, and there will be greater opportunities for the development of individual abilities and a rounded personality.

7

Effect of vocational distinctions on the attitude to work

A. G. ZDRAVOMYSLOV and V. A. YADOV

INTRODUCTION

This paper was compiled by a research team at the Leningrad University Laboratory of Sociological Studies, consisting of V. V. Vodzinskaya and M. M. Grigoryan, both junior research associates, and A. A. Kissel, G. I. Saganenko, and A. S. Shaev, members of the laboratory staff, under the direction of the authors. It is divided into two parts. First, we analyse the main features characterizing attitudes to work and attempt to classify the main types of worker on the basis of their attitude to work, with proposals for some methods of assessing the differences arising from various factors in the attitude to work. Second, we discuss the effects on the attitude to work of vocational distinctions caused by differences in the nature and content of work. Finally, we formulate a number of conclusions.

A classification of the basic types of young worker according to their attitude to work is important both in practice and in theory. Any concrete approach to the task of educating young workers is unthinkable without it, because different types of worker should be set different objectives. The theoretical significance lies in the fact that a classification of this kind is essential for an analysis of the basic objective and subjective factors which condition the process of moulding a communist attitude to work.

The worker's attitude to, or interest in, the job he does incorporates a series of objective and subjective elements and is intricately associated with his other interests. Attitude to work is basic in determining all human activity and defines the worker's personality. In practice there are no two people who have absolutely identical attitudes to work. There are, however, common features and our task is to distinguish them.

THE MAIN FEATURES CHARACTERIZING
ATTITUDES TO WORK

The Laboratory of Sociological Studies at Leningrad University, in an attempt to classify the main types of young workers, recorded the performances of a group of workers on the job. The record included data to show the degree of conscientiousness of the workers in terms of how well they carried out the production task set, and also a general index of their initiative and discipline. The degree to which the worker fulfilled his output quota was first recorded as a measure of his conscientiousness. This was assessed in relative terms so that comparisons could be drawn between different workers. These terms ignored how the rates were fixed and the concrete conditions of production. Second, the quality of the work done was noted. Third, information was recorded to indicate the worker's sense of responsibility. Initiative was assessed under three heads: participation in rationalization, submission of proposals for improved organization of labour, and participation in movements of advanced workers (groups of volunteers pledged to achieve high output). This information was recorded for a basic sample of 2,665 workers employed in 25 factories in Leningrad. They were selected at random from within the area but account was taken of the nature and the content of their work.

We were able to produce a preliminary assessment of attitudes to work, as shown in *Table 1*.

Table 1. Performance by workers at 25 Leningrad factories

	Workers
Quota fulfilment	
(255 of the workers interviewed were paid by the hour)	
1. High overfulfilment	266
2. Overfulfilment	1,132
3. Fulfilment	915
4. Underfulfilment	102
Quality of work done	
1. Good	1,643
2. Average	992
3. Poor	29
Could be given responsible work	
1. Yes	1.904
2. No	766
Took part in movements of advanced workers	
1. Yes	535
2. No	2,135

Took part in rationalization
1. Yes   320
2. No   2,346

Made proposals to improve organization of labour
1. Yes   683
2. No   1,987

Table 1 shows that the overwhelming majority of young workers viewed their work with a sense of responsibility, most of them did work of a high quality and overfulfilled their quotas. One-third made proposals for the improvement of the organization of labour and thereby showed an interest in making conditions better for everyone; one-quarter took part in movements of advanced workers, and one-seventh made rationalization suggestions. Negative features of the attitude to work, such as poor quality and underfulfilment of quotas, were rather rare, occurring in under 5 per cent of the sample. It must be noted that underfulfilment of quota is not always due to the worker himself and is not the basic measure of his attitude to work. Though the assessments thus obtained do provide some notion of the worker's attitude to his job, they are not interrelated, which is a disadvantage. In order to obtain a fuller picture of the worker's attitude to his job, the main worker types must be distinguished by integrating all the features, since none of them taken separately can provide a general index of attitude to work.

METHODS FOR ARRIVING AT A GENERAL INDEX OF ATTITUDE TO WORK

Two methods were evolved in order to arrive at a general index. Classifications on the basis of quantity and quality were combined and then the results were integrated. The first method involves the treatment of each grade of each index of the worker's attitude to his job in inverse proportion to the frequency with which it occurs. The number of gradations in each index must also be taken into account. The larger the number of gradations, e.g. quota fulfilment has four, where participation in rationalization has only two, the more selective will be the index. The value to be attached to each score by this method may be determined according to the formula

$$S = \frac{N}{kn}$$

where S is the value to be attached to each score (e.g. high quota overfulfilment), n is the number of people in each grade (e.g. the number with a high quota overfulfilment), k is the number of grades for each index (e.g. four for quota fulfilment), and N is the total number of workers interviewed. In the example taken, the value for a high quota overfulfilment will be

$$S = \frac{2415}{4 \times 266} = +2.27$$

The values for each index are as follows:

Quota fulfilment
1. High overfulfilment   +2·27
2. Overfulfilment   +0·53
3. Fulfilment   −0·66
4. Underfulfilment   −5·92

Quality of work done
1. Good   +0·81
2. Average   −0·91
3. Poor   −32·03

Could be given responsible work
1. Yes   +0·70
2. No   −1·74

Took part in movements of advanced workers
1. Yes   +2·49
2. No   −0·63

Took part in rationalization
1. Yes   +4·16
2. No   −0·57

Made proposals to improve organization of labour
1. Yes   +1·96
2. No   −0·67

The plus or minus sign depends on the quality measured and the nature of the distribution in each grade.

The total value of the points the worker scores in each index gives an overall index of the particular worker's attitude to his job.

The advantage of this method is that the total number of workers may be listed in order from best to worst (in the Soviet Union the overall index may range between +12·4 and −40·6). Furthermore, this method can be used to combine an unlimited number of separate qualities. The disadvantage is that it does not provide a clear-cut qualitative classification, with the exception of the extremes, since one and the same index can be obtained by combinations of different qualities.

An additional method was therefore employed to produce worker-type groups. We started by combining the three first and three second qualities separately. In each case the theoretically possible combinations fitted those which actually occurred.

WORK GROUPS AND INITIATIVE GROUPS

As a result we obtained four groups varying in the three first qualities (quota fulfilment, quality of work done, and degree of responsibility) which were conventionally called the 'w' groups.

Group 1. Workers considerably overfulfilling or simply overfulfilling their quotas, doing work of a good quality, and able to undertake responsible work (1,195).

Group 2. Workers fulfilling or slightly overfulfilling their quotas and doing work of a good quality (437).

Group 3. Workers fulfilling and overfulfilling quotas but doing work of average quality (913).

Group 4. Workers underfulfilling quotas but doing work of average, poor, and at times good quality, or fulfilling quotas but doing work of poor quality (118).

Qualities characteristic of initiative were obtained in the following three 'i' groups:

Group 1. Workers with initiative, who are rationalization suggesters, take part in movements of advanced workers, and make proposals to improve labour organization. We included in this group workers displaying at least two of these qualities (376).

Group 2. Workers of average initiative, displaying only one of the three listed qualities (692).

Group 3. Workers with no initiative (1,582).

Our next step was to combine conscientiousness and initiative. The four first groups and three second groups combined produce the following ten groups:

Group 1. Workers who considerably overfulfil or simply overfulfil quotas, do work of a good quality, are trusted with responsible work, and display good initiative (292).

Group 2. Workers of the same first 'w' group but who display average initiative (374).

Group 3. Workers of the same first 'w' group but who show no initiative (526).

H

Groups 4, 5, and 6. These categories of worker fell already in the second 'w' group and displayed varying initiative qualities (respectively 39, 110, and 286).

Group 7. Workers of the third 'w' group and second 'i' group (193).

Group 8. Workers of the third 'w' group and third 'i' group (671).

Group 9. Workers of the fourth 'w' and third 'i' group (116).

Group 10. Workers with mutually exclusive qualities (54).

However, these combinations still do not give us a definitive listing from best to worst. To achieve that, we must express these combinations quantitatively, or in other words revert to our method of defining the value of the main features and compute the range of index fluctuation as regards attitude to work demonstrated by workers in each group.

Provided that the quantitative assessments coincide, we now obtain not ten, but five groups:

Group 1. Front-ranking workers, who are active rationalization suggesters, make proposals to improve the organization of production, overfulfil or considerably overfulfil quotas, do work of a good quality, and are trusted with responsible work. There were 292 of them, or 11·2 per cent of the total. The attitude-to-work index ranged between +12·5 and +5·8.

Group 2. Workers who overfulfil or considerably overfulfil quotas, do work of a good quality, and are trusted with responsible work but who show only average initiative. This group of 413 workers, or 15·9 per cent of the total, included also 39 workers displaying good initiative but fulfilling or only slightly overfulfilling their quotas. The attitude index ranged between +6·4 and 0.

Groups 1 and 2 accounted for nearly one-quarter of the total interviewed.

Group 3. Workers who either fulfil or overfulfil their quotas, do work of a good quality, but display no initiative at all, or display average initiative, but in fulfilling and overfulfilling their quotas, do work of an average quality. There were 829 such workers, or 31·9 per cent of the total.

Group 4. Workers who fulfil the quota, do work of an average quality, and show no initiative. There were 956 such workers, or 36·6 per cent of the total, and the attitude index ranged from −1·5 to +5·1.

Group 5. Workers who either underfulfil quotas and do work of an average quality, or fulfil quotas but do work of a poor quality. There were 107 such workers, or 4·1 per cent of the total, and the attitude index ranged from −6·0 to −41·1.

This classification indicates the attitude to work among the sample of young workers interviewed. Its specific feature is that it provides a measurement of objective factors of work. However, it is limited in that it takes into consideration far from all the objective features characterizing a worker's attitude to his job. It also fails to take into consideration subjective aspects, such as whether the worker is satisfied, or not, with his job or occupation, and whether he understands the social significance of his work. To obtain this information, a special questionnaire was circulated.

Starting with the degree of satisfaction with one's job as the most concrete element in a person's attitude to work, each worker selected was asked whether he was satisfied or not with his current job. As we were interested not in the individual's attitude but in the general picture, each worker was asked to choose one of the following six answers:

1. Quite satisfied.
2. Satisfied rather than dissatisfied.
3. Indifferent.
4. Dissatisfied rather than satisfied.
5. Quite dissatisfied.
6. No comment.

Answers were counterchecked by means of two other questions listed at some distance from the main question. These were 'Would you like to switch to another job?' and 'Suppose you were not working for some reason now, would you like to return to your old job?' An analysis of these questions gave the following categories of degree of satisfaction with the job:

1. Quite satisfied (427).
2. Satisfied (664).
3. Indifferent, vague, or indefinite (1,153).
4. Dissatisfied (297).
5. Totally dissatisfied (124).

In the same way, we obtained a picture of the extent of satisfaction with occupation.

1. Completely satisfied (391).
2. Satisfied (774).
3. Indifferent, vague, or indefinite (1,161).
4. Dissatisfied (216).
5. Totally dissatisfied (123).

Finally, we deduced the worker's understanding of the social significance of his work. The worker was asked to choose one of the four following comments (the number that chose the particular comment is given in brackets):

1. The best kind of job is one in which you feel you are needed and are of the greatest use (617).
2. Though you should not forget pay, the main point of one's job is its social usefulness (830).
3. Pay comes first but neither must you forget the significance of your job (819).
4. Any kind of job is good as long as the pay is good (399).

We thus obtained four classifications, each characterizing one or other aspect of the attitude to work. The extent to which each factor varies indicates its significance.

A GENERAL CLASSIFICATION OF ATTITUDES

However, to get a picture of such variations we must first evolve a general classification index. As before, the groups are ranked from best to worst, and we may designate each group as follows:

Group 1	$+1$
Group 2	$+0.5$
Group 3	0
Group 4	-0.5
Group 5	-1

In each classification we obtain a quantitative average on the basis of the following formula:

$$i = \frac{(+1)a + (+0.5)b + 0(c) + (-0.5)d + (-1)e}{N}$$

$$= \frac{a + \dfrac{b-d}{2} - e}{N},$$

where a, b, c, d, and e are the number of workers respectively in all five groups; and

N is the total number of workers interviewed.

Before analysing the effect of the factors that interest us, we shall present in *Table 2* a general picture of the indices derived according to the above formula.

THE NATURE AND CONTENT OF WORK

Let us now analyse the degree to which the nature and content of work affect the attitude to work. To this end we must compare the picture obtained with that of the attitude to work expressed in different categories of occupations at different levels of skill. We chose six such control groups, which represented about 50 per cent of the total number of workers interviewed.

Table 2. Classification index based on objective and subjective factors characterizing attitude to work

Attitude-to-work factor	Group no. and index					
	1 (+*1*)	*2* (+0·5)	*3* (0)	*4* (−0·5)	*5* (−*1*)	*Average index*
Attitude to work based on objective qualifications	294	413	829	956	107	−0·03
Satisfaction with work	427	664	1,152	297	124	+0·18
Satisfaction with trade	391	774	1,162	216	123	+0·16 +0·21
Appreciation of social significance of labour	617	830	—	819	399	+0·08

Group 1. Unskilled manual labour of a type employing no machinery, and requiring considerable and protracted physical exertion. Included in this group were such occupations as porter, stoker, ash remover, and truck operator. The total was 146.

Group 2. Skilled manual labour requiring special knowledge. This group included fitters of all kinds, electricians, and loom setters. The total was 285.

Group 3. Mechanized labour with no prescribed rhythm of operation. This group included operatives of lathes and of grinding, drilling, and other such machines. The total was 411.

Group 4. Conveyer work with a prescribed rhythm of operation. This group included shoe and garment workers operating machines with a high degree of skill as well as workers on other specialized operations. The total was 307.

Group 5. Panel operators controlling automatic equipment but without training as setters. The total was 54.

Group 6. Operators controlling and setting automatic equipment. The total was 46.

Table 3. Attitude to work in control vocational groups compared with averages for pay, per capita income, and schooling*

Structural and attitude-to-work indices		Totals	Heavy, unskilled, manual labour	Skilled manual labour	Machine-tool operators	Machine operatives, skilled, conveyer labour	Panel operators	Panel operator setters
Number of workers interviewed		2,665	146	285	411	307	54	46
Structural indices	Pay (in roubles)	91	108	96	97	88	90	116
	Per capita income (in roubles)	61	62	61	62	55	58	67
	Years of schooling	7·9	6·8	8·5	8·1	8·0	8·6	9·3
Attitude-to-work indices	Record card data	−0·03	−0·17	+0·11	−0·03	+0·08	+0·07	+0·45
	Nature of work	+0·16	−0·12	+0·68	+0·18	+0·16	+0·26	+0·22
	Satisfaction with occupation	+0·21	−0·14	+0·43	+0·24	+0·15	+0·27	+0·35
	Appreciation of social significance of work	+0·08	−0·31	+0·19	+0·05	+0·15	+0·18	+0·26

* Average pay was calculated on the basis of earnings for the last three months, while the averages for *per capita* income in the worker's family and his schooling are based on the worker's own statements.

Both the choice of groups and the order in which they are listed are deliberate. Each is one rung up the ladder of technical skill. It is now possible to test what influence the nature and content of work under socialism have on the attitude to work.

Table 3 provides two types of indices for the above groups. The first includes *per capita* income in the worker's family and his educational level, which may be called structural indices belonging to those objective factors which, along with the nature and content of work, tend to influence attitude to work. The second type includes indices of attitudes to work, which were obtained from the record cards and questionnaires for these different occupational groups.

An analysis of *Table 3* leads to the conclusion that attitude to work is strongly influenced by type of occupation. The general tendency is for occupations in which the work is more complicated and subject to technical progress to be associated with high indices of attitudes to work, and greater interest in the job. This is a general tendency rather than a uniform series. The tendency is not attributable to subjective factors, such as, for example, a chance high proportion of conscientious workers with a sense of responsibility and initiative in those occupational groups which have been subject to a high degree of technical progress. It arises from the actual opportunities that the job affords for creative work and initiative. These opportunities depend on the content of the particular occupation. The extent to which these opportunities are seized in each occupation depends, in turn, on the degree of the worker's sense of responsibility, initiative, and conscientiousness. These objective factors are decisive, but it would be wrong to discount the role played by such subjective factors as the standard of labour organization, the type of educational work done, and the conscientiousness of the workers before entering employment. The next task is to assess the role each of these factors plays in moulding the new attitude to work.

Table 3 also shows that vocational distinctions do not all have the same effect on the attitude to work. This is because the vocational groups are not equally spaced on a scale of technical complexity. The rungs on the ladder of technical progress are not equally spaced. The differences between occupations are greatest at the extremes. There is a sharp contrast between the group of panel operators and automatic machine setters and the group of occupations requiring heavy manual labour and no vocational training. The distinctions between these two groups are not limited to vocational elements only but acquire a specific social significance. Unskilled manual labour is declining and such occupations as operating and setting automatic machines are typical of new developments in industry and the economy in general. The differences between these occupational groups depend not only on the content of the work done but also on the different nature of the job, expressed as a qualitative difference in the ratio between manual and intellectual work. The least difference in the entire range of averages is found in the group of machine operators. Consequently these are treated as the most 'typical' workers.

STRUCTURAL ELEMENTS OF THE OCCUPATIONAL GROUPS

The structural elements of the occupational groups were next analysed. The deviation below average earnings is relatively small. If the average is 100 per cent, the deviation is no greater than 4·5 per cent. The maximum deviations from average pay in group 1 depend on the extent of heavy physical labour involved and in group 7 on the complexity of the work.

It is important to note that in practically all the occupational groups, with the exception of panel operators and automatic machine setters, the deviation from average earnings and also from average *per capita* income does not correlate directly with the deviations from the attitude-to-work averages, which shows that there is no direct connection between the two. None of these factors operates independently, and the effect they have, the direction in which they take effect, and the strength of their effect depend on vocational differences. Consequently, technical progress under socialism and the related changes in the content of work not only directly influence attitude to work but also affect the various structural components of the different occupational groups through a whole series of intermediate factors.

A survey of the educational standards of young workers in the occupational groups discloses the following. The average standard is fairly high, amounting to nearly eight years of schooling. However, in group 1 it averages only 6·8 years, which is 15 per cent less. Nearly 15 per cent of the workers in this group have only four years of schooling, and this is closely connected with the content of their work. We may further note that the educational standard in a occupational group is higher, the more complex the work done. Education has become a major factor in the attitude to work. In the case of panel operators and automatic machine setters, for example, education is more than simply an advantage; it is a necessity in their work. 'It seems to me', one of the workers in this group said, 'that this job approaches that of an engineer.' The average educational standard in this group is more than 9 years of schooling, and more than half the workers in the group have either 10 years of general schooling or a full secondary specialized education. In this group, the attitude to work improves with the rise in educational level. In group 1, the opposite is to be observed. The higher the educational level, the more the worker is dissatisfied with his job and occupation, and the more eagerly does he look for a more interesting job. In this group there is the greatest labour turnover and the least prospect of increasing skills. This again serves to emphasize the acute nature of the problem of eliminating unskilled manual labour by a comprehensive mechanization of production.

WORK MOTIVATIONS

The dependence between the content of work and the attitude to this work having been established, it is necessary to make a more concrete approach to work motivations. These will be examined not from a general point of view but within the framework of the more characteristic occupational groups. Before attempting this, some initial points must be clarified.

Work motivations are taken to be those inner urges to work, which are more or less stable but which people have in various forms. They could, of course, be divided into motivations of a material and moral character, though both these assume in men's minds a definite ethical tinge, and both are viewed in their ethical and moral aspect by the public at large.

Material motivations do not bear directly on the process of work as such, but rather on what the individual in question derives from work by virtue of the economic laws of distribution operating under socialism.

Moral motivations are associated both with the social significance and with the content of work. These are, in the first place, urges stimulated by the content of the job. A feeling of satisfaction is produced by the application of one's mind and body to creative purposes, or by the realization that one has done one's job well. Second, these are urges associated with the feeling of being a member of a group, with the team spirit, and with mutual assistance. Third, there is an awareness of the social significance of work (including the part work plays in laying the material and technical foundations of communism and in the further promotion of social welfare). There is the related desire to work for the common weal – the feeling of obligation and duty and responsibility to society. Interest in the content of one's work and in public evaluation of it gives rise to a group of motivations such as professional pride, a desire for public recognition within both the framework of one's group and society generally, and the wish to master one's trade more completely and acquire higher skill.

Both moral and material motivations operate together in every kind of work. This arises from the twofold function of work under socialism. On the one hand, it is a means of vital satisfaction, and on the other, a means of asserting and enriching one's personality. It would therefore be wrong to regard material motivations as something 'worse' than moral motivations. However, we can by no means overlook the relation and the tendency for moral motivations to grow in importance relatively. It is also necessary to find out how their relative importance depends on the content of work, and what effect one or other motivation has in different kinds of work.

TABULATION OF MOTIVATIONS IN RANK ORDER

A comparison between evaluations of various aspects of work such as, for example, variety, the possibility of increasing one's skill, and labour organization which we shall call 'job elements', as well as the satisfaction or dissatisfaction with one's work, enabled us to ascertain their relative importance for the workers interviewed. After this, it was possible to tabulate motivations in a definite order, depending on the effect they have in making one feel satisfied or dissatisfied with one's job. We estimated the various job elements according to the formula:

$$V = \frac{(+1)a + (0)b + (-1)c}{n} = \frac{a-c}{n},$$

where a is the number of workers taking a favourable view of the

particular job elements;

b the number of workers taking an indifferent view;

c the number of workers taking an unfavourable view; and

n the total number of workers interviewed.

Table 4 contains two sets of assessments. V_1 is the assessment of various aspects of work by workers satisfied with their job. V_2 is the assessment of these same elements by workers dissatisfied with their job.

Table 4 shows first that all job elements have some motivational significance with respect to satisfaction or dissatisfaction with one's job. In every case, the assessment of job elements by workers dissatisfied with their job is lower than the assessment of these elements by satisfied workers. At the same time, it shows the difference both in the degree to

Table 4. Comparative assessment of job elements by workers satisfied with job and workers dissatisfied with job

Groups of workers	Variety or monotony of job	Requires ingenuity or needs no mental effort	Provides opportunity to raise skill or does not	Causes no fatigue or is physically tiring	Pay: good or bad	Labour organization: good or bad	Uniform or spasmodic flow of work	Attitude of management: concerned or unconcerned	Relations with workmates: good or bad	Interested or not in importance of article produced
						Job elements assessed				
Satisfied with work	+0·33	+0·40	+0·25	+0·13	+0·31	+0·16	+0·01	+0·24	+0·70	+0·42
Dissatisfied with work	−0·15	−0·32	−0·33	−0·19	−0·30	−0·22	−0·20	−0·11	+0·60	+0·07
Difference in assessment	+0·48	+0·72	+0·58	+0·32	+0·61	+0·38	+0·21	+0·35	+0·10	+0·35

which the motivations exert their influence (the difference ranges from 0·72 to 0·10) and in the character of the influence exerted. There are certain job elements, such as attitude to one's workmates and to the importance of the article produced, that are favourably assessed by both categories of worker, and consequently they are not the causes of dissatisfaction with one's job. Conversely, the assessment of the flow of work shows that in the case in question this particular job element is not a cause of satisfaction with one's job. The very low assessment of the work flow by satisfied workers implies that even among this category the number who answered in the affirmative when asked whether the flow of work was uniform or not is only slightly greater than the number who answered in the negative. This shows the importance of ensuring an even flow of work.

The assessment of the other job elements shows that satisfaction or dissatisfaction with them correlates with satisfaction or dissatisfaction with one's work generally. Consequently it is this group of motivations, which, when combined, have the greatest effect in making one feel satisfied or dissatisfied with one's work. Dissatisfaction with precisely these job elements is the decisive reason for dissatisfaction with one's work in general, while satisfaction with them is the reason for satisfaction with one's work in general.

Listing the motivations analysed according to the degree in which they produce satisfaction or dissatisfaction with one's work, we obtain the following order:

1. Content of work (does it require ingenuity or not)   0·72
2. Pay   0·61
3. The possibility of improving skill   0·58
4. Variety in work   0·48
5. Organization of labour   0·38
6. Management's concern for workers   0·35
7. Physical effort   0·32

The content of one's work ranks first among the reasons for satisfaction with one's job. The application, or not, of intellectual effort in the process of work proves to be most important. In comparison, pay comes second, but nevertheless ranks high in the scale. We shall now examine in an analogous fashion the influence and significance of motivations in the vocational control groups, the results of which are set out in *Table 5*.

The control groups are examined in turn, and the data compared with those in *Table 3*.

Table 5. Comparative assessment of job elements by members of control vocational groups satisfied and dissatisfied with work

Control groups Job elements	I			II			III		
	V_1	V_2	V_1-V_2	V_1	V_2	V_1-V_2	V_1	V_2	V_1-V_2
1. Work requires ingenuity or needs no mental effort	0·46	−0·33	+0·79	0·59	0·42	+0·17	0·13	−0·05	+0·18
2. Pay: good or bad	0·0	−0·40	+0·40	0·29	−0·05	+0·34	0·24	−0·40	+0·64
3. Provides opportunity to raise skill or does not	−0·18	−0·69	+0·51	0·44	−0·42	+0·86	0·51	−0·18	+0·69
4. Variety or monotony of job	0·14	−0·27	+0·41	0·53	−0·16	+0·69	0·29	0·10	+0·19
5. Labour organization: good or bad	0·43	−0·44	+0·87	0·05	−0·26	+0·31	0·13	−0·27	+0·40
6. Attitude of management: concerned or unconcerned	0·15	−0·08	+0·23	0·26	−0·11	+0·37	0·29	−0·11	+0·40
7. Causes no fatigue or is physically tiring	−0·64	−0·75	+0·11	0·14	−0·21	+0·35	0·16	−0·02	+0·18
8. Uniform or spasmodic flow of work	0·21	−0·19	+0·40	−0·01	−0·32	+0·31	0·24	−0·22	+0·46
9. Interested or not in importance of article produced	0·43	−0·04	+0·47	0·41	0·42	−0·01	0·05	0·14	−0·09
10. Relations with workmates: good or bad	0·68	0·67	+0·01	0·77	0·47	+0·30	0·83	0·68	+0·15

Table 5 (continued)

Control groups	IV			V			VI		
Job elements	V_1	V_2	V_1-V_2	V_1	V_2	V_1-V_2	V_1	V_2	V_1-V_2
1. Work requires ingenuity or needs no mental effort	0·05	−0·28	+0·33	0·46	0·00	+0·46	0·76	−0·33	+1·09
2. Pay: good or bad	0·37	−0·60	+0·97	0·50	−0·80	+1·30	0·43	−0·50	+0·93
3. Provides opportunity to raise skill or does not	0·07	−0·21	+0·28	0·18	−0·40	+0·58	0·57	−0·33	+0·90
4. Variety or monotony of job	−0·06	−0·52	+0·45	0·16	−1·00	+1·16	−0·10	−0·17	+0·07
5. Labour organization: good or bad	0·22	−0·10	+0·32	0·18	−0·20	+0·38	0·05	−0·17	+0·21
6. Attitude of management: concerned or unconcerned	0·01	−0·45	+0·46	0·16	−0·60	+0·86	0·10	−0·33	+0·43
7. Causes no fatigue or is physically tiring	0·20	0·14	+0·06	0·18	0·00	+0·18	0·19	0·50	−0·31
8. Uniform or spasmodic flow of work	−0·28	−0·43	+0·15	0·37	0·20	+0·17	0·38	0·33	+0·05
9. Interested or not in importance of article produced	0·25	0·07	+0·18	0·46	0·20	+0·26	0·38	0·33	+0·05
10. Relations with workmates: good or bad	0·67	0·55	+0·12	0·50	0·60	−0·10	0·67	0·83	−0·16

Group 1. Unskilled manual labour, *Table 3* showed that this group had the maximum deviation below the averages, despite the relatively high pay. It is also marked by the highest labour turnover and the lowest number of workers satisfied with their job. What motivates this attitude to work? The most disheartening aspects are that the work is heavy and gives very little opportunity for improvement of skill. Outstanding among these negative elements in this group are the different aspects of the content and conditions of work. It is most important to change the working conditions in this group generally and to lessen fatigue. The lack of prospects also derives from the content of work, which in this case requires little knowledge and no special training. Group 1 is the only category in which workers dissatisfied with pay outnumber those who are satisfied. Consequently, pay is a powerful incentive for the entire group generally, and is the only thing that makes the worker stick to this kind of job. Meanwhile the assessment of all the other job elements does not put this group at an advantage over all the others. The diverging assessments point to quite specific factors for the moulding of a communist attitude to work, which could be utilized in this particular group of occupations. Outstanding among motivations is organization of labour, which should provide the worker with a uniform flow of work.

Group 2. Skilled manual labour. This group is at the other end of the scale from group 1 in respect to satisfaction with one's job and also to one's awareness of the social significance of the work being done (see *Table 3*), in spite of the fact that the workers in this category also do manual labour and receive relatively low pay. An analysis of the varying significance of work motivations reveals the following peculiar features in group 2. In the first place, there is a favourable assessment of the element of using one's ingenuity in work, one that ranks quite high both with workers who are satisfied with their job and with those who are not. This job element displays itself as a constant factor within the limits of this group. Also ranking quite high (though negatively) is the assessment of the element of pay by workers who are dissatisfied with their jobs. The assessment of the elements of a uniform flow of work and of labour organization approximates to the average (see *Table 4*). The greatest difference in importance is to be observed in the case of available prospects for improvement of skill. Second and third in diverging assessments are the factors of variety or monotony in work and of the management's attitude.

Group 3. Machine operators. The lower attitude-to-work indices in this group, as compared with group 2 (see *Table 3*), may be explained as follows. This job calls for the application of the worker's mental energies to a lesser extent than in the case of skilled manual labour. It is more automatic. This accounts for the transposition (in group 3 as compared with group 2) of assessments of the job elements of variety or monotony in work and of the need for ingenuity. On the other hand, owing to a more rigid rate-fixing which produces a drop in pay levels, pay exerts a far more differentiated effect on satisfaction or dissatisfaction with one's work. These circumstances tend to make this group of workers possess a relatively less stable composition.

Group 4. Machine-tending, skilled, conveyer labour. Subjectively this group stands nearest to the group of unskilled manual labour. However, in this group we have a lower assessment of interest in the process of work. The work is not attractive, because it is monotonous and does not require ingenuity or intellectual effort. At the same time, the assessment of working conditions is higher. In contrast to groups 2 and 3, the most important element exerting a differentiated influence is pay and not the lack of opportunities for the improvement of skill.

Group 5. Panel operators. A characteristic feature of this group is that none of the job elements assessed received a negative correlating assessment. While no aspect of work is negatively assessed by any of the workers satisfied with this work, several key features, such as a uniform flow of work and the physical effort, which were assessed differently in the previous groups, are assessed positively both by those satisfied with their work and by those dissatisfied with it. Diverging assessments can be tabulated according to their significance in the following order: pay; variety or monotony in work; attitude of management; opportunities for improvement of skill; and organization of labour.

Group 6. Panel operators skilled as automatic machine-setters. In this group assessments largely correlate with the assessments given in group 5. Monotony in work is given a negative correlating assessment. Indeed, once the automatic system is set up and everything works smoothly, all the worker has to do is to keep an eye on the display panel and control production with its aid. The problems arising in this field can apparently be solved by substituting cybernetic control for human control.

In this group the question of physical effort involved no longer counts in making the worker satisfied or not with his work. Also less significance is attached in groups 5 and 6 to relations with workmates. This indicates the great changes which occur in the structural pattern of a factory group following the introduction of automation. The worker develops close links with his group through intermediate channels.

Greater significance is attached to the importance of the article which is being made. This indicates that the worker has a greater sense of responsibility to society generally. This is also borne out by the greater awareness of the social significance of labour to be observed in groups 5 and 6 (see *Table 3*).

An analysis of motivations in these vocational groups supports the conclusion that attitude to work depends on the content and character of work. The pattern of motivations and their relative importance and influence vary from group to group. This analysis also suggests that the division of motivations into material and moral, which is often made in our literature, is too abstract, and does not enable a sufficiently penetrating examination of the nature of work motivations to be made. We therefore consider it to be completely wrong to reduce the problem of material incentives simply to that of pay. The facts show that the worker is interested primarily in better working conditions and opportunities for improving his skill. In other words, he is interested in the opportunities for developing his personality in the course of his work, and for enriching the content of his work. This is a material incentive of a novel kind. The Soviet worker is aware that advance lies not through consumption but through labour. He is most concerned not with pay and distribution but with the business of production. This is a novel attitude to work, which is unthinkable under capitalism. Our survey shows that work in a socialist society is the workers' main interest.

A COMPARISON OF SOVIET AND AMERICAN ATTITUDES TO WORK

A comparison can be made between our results and some evidence obtained by American sociologists and psychologists in an analysis of the work motivations of American workers. Interviews with 6,000 workers employed at 71 different enterprises gave five main factors as key motivations for satisfaction with work. They were, in a descending order of significance:

1. Guaranteed employment (guarantees against possible unemployment).
2. Opportunities for promotion.
3. Pay.
4. Content and nature of work.
5. 'Human relations', chiefly the management's attitude to the worker.[2]

I

Wolfe's interviews showed that male workers rated highly: (1) stability of employment; (2) opportunities for promotion; (3) the type of work; (4) pay; and (5) working conditions. Jurgensen[3] obtained similar data. The interviews showed that American workers attached secondary significance to the job itself.

In the assessment of work, it never enters the head of the Soviet worker to wonder whether work is guaranteed, He is never afraid of being left without employment for his abilities or of being left stranded without a means of livelihood. Consequently he is not concerned merely to get a job, but to get one which conforms to his own interests and inclinations. Material motivations are still important, of course, but they are quite different in kind. The American worker's interpretation of the material incentive in work, is explained by the American researchers S. Strauss and L. Soiles in their observation that, in American society, money was all-important not only to pay for food, clothing, and housing, but also as an indication of 'having made it', of success and social standing. To 'have made it' means to have a high income. A 'good job' means it is well paid. To have opportunities for promotion means chances for making more money.[4] In a socialist society, on the contrary, money has lost its importance as a symbol of wealth and, the main thing, wealth itself is not the basic yardstick of a person's worth.

CONCLUSIONS

The development of a communist attitude to work is most intimately bound up with the effort to lay the material and technical foundations of communism and with the resultant changes in the nature and content of work. However, it is wrong to regard this as merely a direct consequence of technical progress in a socialist society. There are many cases, for example, conveyer operations, in which mechanization and automation do not lead to the enrichment of the content of work, or to the greater use by the worker of his intelligence. On the contrary, they cramp these abilities, and restrict initiative. These are examples in which mounting labour productivity conflicts with the process of transforming work into a prime vital need. This is being overcome by comprehensive, rather than partial, automation of production.

This, however, cannot be done all at once. This must be taken into account in planning the policy of automation for each particular industry. Automation may be effected in a multitude of ways, depending in each particular industry on the nature of the technical progress achieved, the system of equipment which is used, the scientific research in progress, and the degree of importance attached to the industry. The policy can be implemented only when it will lead to a marked rise in labour productivity. When a need for this policy arises, the emphasis should be placed on more flexible patterns of labour organization which will afford the worker the opportunity of following two or three trades in the course of his work.

Our second point relates to opportunities for studying the nature of work subject to technical progress. There is a need for a more concrete approach to the problem of manual labour. The opinion is widely expressed in our literature that manual labour presents a major obstacle against work becoming the basic vital need. A distinction must, however, be made. The manual work done by automatic equipment setters, assembly men, and erection men, which involves the use of tools, does not demand excessive physical exertion. On the other hand, it does call for manual dexterity, a certain amount of ingenuity, and a full understanding of the purpose of the work, which is not at all automatic in character.

The manual work of a porter, or auxiliary labourer naturally presents quite a different picture. It is important to emphasize that the basic objective of mechanization of production is to eliminate precisely this kind of manual labour. This is far more feasible, and necessary, than the elimination of all manual labour generally. It is not accidental that manual work of the former kind gave the greatest measure of satisfaction (63 per cent of the workers in this group said they were satisfied with their job, and 29 per cent said they were very satisfied). This is not surprising, as this kind of work offers the greatest opportunity to use one's intellectual and physical abilities. We shall never solve the problem of making work a prime vital need if this is overlooked.

Heavy physical labour called for in loading and unloading operations is naturally at the other end of the scale, because it offers no prospect of ever becoming an intellectual occupation. The only solution is to eliminate this kind of work. We must not only fix a timetable for this objective to be reached but also state concretely what needs to be done in each industry. The twin tasks of laying the material and technical foundations of communism and of moulding the new man demand that we eliminate this type of labour. Heavy physical labour, which requires no special skill or knowledge, must be eliminated before the building of communism's material and technical base is completed. This must be taken into account in the preparation and implementation of plans for each industry.

The changes which technical progress can be observed to have produced in the content and nature of work exert a twofold influence in making work a basic vital need. First, those which arise directly as a result of changed working conditions and of work itself arousing the worker's interest. Second, those which arise, indirectly, as a result of the changed structural pattern of occupational groups, of improved skill and educational standards and of the broader mental horizons of every worker. In the case of unskilled manual labour, wider mental horizons and rising educational standards serve to impair, rather than to improve, the individual's attitude to this kind of work. They encourage him to seek other occupations. The fact that all labour is socially useful is irrelevant in this case, because other work which is more productive, may be of greater social benefit. It is not surprising that research disclosed that this vocational group had the greatest labour turnover, particularly among young workers.

Our investigations have shown the need for a concrete approach to the problems of communist education in two respects. A concrete approach must take into consideration vocational distinctions. They include the distinction between unskilled labour and skilled labour employing technical equipment. The evidence above shows that, in each of the groups, the factors influencing the attitude to work, and the respective pattern of work motivations, interact in their own particular way. Second, the peculiar features of different groups of young workers, which depend on their attitude to work, must be taken into consideration. One cannot give the same tasks to a worker showing initiative and taking an active part in the organization of production that one gives to a worker who barely manages to fulfil his output quota. One must clearly take into account not merely the attitude to work but also the record of quota fulfilment.

Our research also shows what should be done in the education of young workers. Its aim should be to give greater play to the worker's initiative. This is precisely the factor which places a worker in the front rank and produces the other essential features of the new attitude to work, such as conscientiousness and discipline.

An analysis of what it is that makes the worker feel satisfied with his work will help to define what is required to inculcate in the young worker, taking into account the specific features of the different vocational groups, the idea that he both controls and owns a socialist enterprise. The employment of one's intellectual faculties in the course of work, regardless of vocational distinctions, was shown to be the prime incentive for the young workers interviewed. In addition, a steady flow of work was also seen to be instrumental in moulding a communist attitude to work.

A key objective in fostering a communist attitude to work is to deploy the labour force as far as possible in conformity with the worker's abilities and inclinations. This depends on the standard of education required for each job because, as our analysis has shown, in a whole number of occupational groups a higher standard of education does not necessarily produce an improved attitude to work. The worker with a wider intellectual horizon naturally seeks a more interesting occupation. In each factory a study must be made of the requirements for each kind of work, and of the abilities and inclinations of its workers.

A comparison between the significance of different motivations shows that, during the period of the building of communism, material incentives have changed in content. An examination of material incentives must include not only pay, but also working conditions in the broadest sense of the term, as well as the nature and content of the work. The opportunities available for the improvement of skill are also important especially for the young worker. They depend both on the nature of the work and on how it is organized.

Moral motivations were found to depend least of all on the content of work. The degree of consciousness, as expressed in the assessment of one's attitude to workmates and in one's understanding of the significance of the product, is quite high even in the case of workers dissatisfied with their job. This shows that it is a mistake to adopt a purely verbal approach to fostering a communist attitude to work and that all the problems enumerated above can be solved only by forging a stronger bond between ideological and organizational work.

Some methodological considerations arise from our investigations. It is important to clarify the notions of 'content of work' and 'nature of work'. We have been discussing so far vocational distinctions and their effect on the attitude to work. Occupations clearly differ in the content of the operations performed, or in the content of the work done. These tell us precisely what the worker does during his working time, or the kind of operations he performs. The notion of 'content of work' is closer in meaning to the notions of 'job' and 'occupation'. A stable combination of particular skills in an industry, or a similar content of work, defines an occupation.

The nature of work is slightly different. The differences in the nature of work are more fundamental. They are not merely simple differences between particular skills; they depend also upon certain social factors. The marked distinctions between intellectual and manual labour arise not from specific vocational features, but precisely from their social content. The nature of work is a combination of the qualities of a type of work which has definite social differences. The nature of work fundamentally influences the structural pattern of a vocational group; under socialism the differences in the nature of work are linked with the historical development of the productive forces. These differences have the greatest impact on the psychological features of an occupational group and on the inculcation of a communist attitude to work. We found three groups of workers differing precisely in the nature, rather than in the content, of work.

The first group included occupational group 1, the second, occupational groups 2, 3, 4, and 5, and the third, occupational group 7. Occupational group 6 was, in our view, transitional between groups 2 and 3. The differences between these groups, as we have seen, produce the most marked differences in the structural pattern of the group itself, in the relationship of attitude-to-work motivations and in the objective indications of the attitude to work. The rate at which work is transformed into a prime vital need will largely depend on the future trend of change in the relationships between the occupational groups differing in the nature of work.

One more conclusion arises out of our analysis. The factors influencing the attitude to work which we have examined (content of work, pay, *per capita* income in the worker's family, and educational standards) are by no means of equal strength. This is of fundamental importance from the point of view of methodology. The meaning of the social process cannot be understood if these factors are treated as equivalents.

The structural pattern of the occupational group and the interaction of its different internal elements are not independent. In every case the specific features of this pattern depend on the content and nature of work, which exert both a direct influence on the attitude to work, and an indirect influence through the changes in the structural pattern of the vocational group. This shows the weakness of adopting a structural-functional approach, in which the structural pattern is regarded as something self-contained, forming the foundation for all social changes. If the structural pattern of an occupational group is seen to depend on the content and nature of work, it clearly emerges that the productive forces and relations of production play the decisive and ultimate role in producing these social changes.

NOTES AND REFERENCES

1. The main results of this research were discussed by the authors in an article in *Voprosy Filosofii*, No. 4, 1964, pp. 72-84, under the title of 'Empirical research into the attitude to work'. Some details of the methods employed by the research team are given in this article. A questionnaire was distributed to the sample of young workers up to 30 years of age to assess the extent to which they were satisfied with their jobs and with their occupations, their appreciation of the social significance of work, and also the reasons for their choice of occupation and their satisfaction or dissatisfaction with their jobs. The work record book belonging to each worker was examined to discover the indices of their standard of conscientiousness, discipline, and initiative.

2. R. Bellows, *Psychology of Personnel in Business and Industry*, New York, 1961, p. 134.

3. M. Viteles, *Motivation and Morale*, New York, 1953, p. 303.

4. J. Strauss and L. Soiles, *Personnel, the Human Problem of Management*, 1960, p. 28.

8

Vertical mobility of employees in an enterprise

S. T. GURYANOV

SOCIAL AND OCCUPATIONAL MOBILITY

Sociological investigations at the Moscow electrical engineering plant point to the conclusion that some strata of the Soviet working class display a considerable rate of social and occupational mobility. The subject of the research was a group of 1,000 workers from various workshops. The representative sample accounted for 15·6 per cent of the total number of employees. The principle of random sampling was used: each sixth person in the enterprise's files was included and his work record was traced for ten years (1951-1961). All members of the group under study, with rare exceptions, were found to have begun their careers as semi-skilled operators. During the ten years, 295 persons of this group became engineers or technicians, 680 highly skilled operators, and 25 reached average skills.

A subgroup, consisting of 34 persons in the casting workshop, was found to have started in the workshop as apprentice moulders, tool-sharpeners, cutters, core-makers, mould-pourers, electric welders, etc. During the 10 years, 14 of them became either college-trained engineers and technicians or were promoted to the rank of engineer or technician by virtue of seniority and experience. Their social status changed accordingly.

Thus, K. Dogadina came to work at the enterprise as an unskilled worker, employed in the preparation of parts for assembly, and now she is an economist. E. Kolosova started work as a rate controller, and now she is a rate-fixing specialist. A. Medvedev, once an iron-mould-pourer, became a master finisher of the section. B. Zhuravlev became the senior foreman of the production section, and V. Yevstigneyev a foreman. Twenty employees became highly skilled operators, raised the level of their general educational and technical standards and learnt two or three trades. N. Abramov, who is a lathe operator, can also work as tool sharpener and cutter, I. Dozorov, who is an iron-mould-pourer, as assembly fitter of the 4th rating, and V. Goryachev, who is a cutter, as electric welder.

Along with college-trained engineers and technicians, highly skilled operators are frequently promoted to responsible positions in the workshops and in management. Since 1956, 21 workers (e.g. E. Irinarkhova, E. Bokaryova, and I. Sharov) were transferred to work in the Chief Technologist's Department. Since 1958, 4 workers were transferred to the Chief Metallurgist's Department, 11 to the Chief Designer's Department, 2 to the Labour Department, 6 to the Planning Department, 6 to the Power Department, 5 to the Finance and Delivery Department, 4 to the Technical Information Office, 5 to the Central Laboratory of the enterprise, and 2 to the Laboratory. They are all now ranked as engineers or technicians.

The management consists of former workers, many of whom are continuing their studies. A. Chernikov began his career as an ordinary lathe operator after seven years at school. While still working, he completed his secondary education and graduated from the Steel Institute. He was then appointed chief foreman of the forge workshop. At present he is in charge of production. V. Bogdanovsky joined the enterprise in 1936. Initially he worked as a machine tool operator after seven years at school. He soon became a tool setter, then a foreman, a technologist, a senior technologist, the head of the workshop, and chief engineer of the plant. At present, he is in charge of the Rationalization Office, which deals with improvements in methods of production. During this period he completed his secondary school education, a course at the Moscow Economic Institute, and a Higher Engineering Course. M. Bulykin, formerly a skilled worker, was promoted to the post of foreman, then senior foreman, and is now in charge of shop No. 13. A. Sokolova came to the enterprise in 1939 as a winder. She completed a course at a technical school and is now senior engineer in the Chief Technologist's Department. S. Kurochkin began work in the Chief Mechanic's Department as a mechanic and, in 1959, was promoted to the post of chief engineer of the enterprise.

The fact that an operator learns three or four trades and raises his technical and general cultural standards justifies a change in his social and occupational status. This does not change his social status by itself. Versatility creates conditions for a possible change in the operator's position in the cycle of production.

This point can be illustrated from an example in the tool-making shop.

The department of small- and medium-size dies in the tool-making shop employs 37 persons. Out of the five workers in its planing section, 4 had learnt two or three trades in 1961, and 3 are studying. The lathe operator's groups consist of four men, two of them studying, and three have become highly skilled operators. Thus, B. Magerov could at first machine only simple parts, but could not cut threads. As a result of a course of study he began to apply his theoretical knowledge to his work, soon learned more complex occupations involving tapping, polishing, and other such processes, and became a lathe operator with a wide range of skill. He intends to study at the Polytechnical Institute. More or less the same applies to other employees in the shop. The reboring group consists of five operators. In 1960-1961, three of them began more complex operations, and two are studying: V. Davydov at the Polytechnical Institute and A. Mishin at the Electrical Engineering School. The polishing, milling, and fitting groups include 22 operators. In 1960 and 1961, 13 of them learned two or three trades and became highly skilled specialists. In department No. 11, manufacturing compound dies, there are polishing, fitting, lathe operating, and reboring groups, with a total of 48 employees; 20 out of them are studying and 10 have learnt several trades and have been promoted during the past three years.

THE EFFECT OF TRAINING ON VERTICAL MOBILITY

Training is an important factor making for vertical mobility, and it takes on a number of different forms in this enterprise. Of the 6,000 workers, 262 study at the enterprise's branch of the All-Union Polytechnical Institute by means of correspondence courses, 278 at the branch of the Moscow Electric Engineering School functioning at the enterprise, 498 at the enterprise's evening school, and 138 at courses preparing for college entrance. In addition, many employees have joined in various local study groups; 258 at the University of New Equipment and Advanced Methods of Labour, 195 in economics courses, and 550 in social science study groups.

It is expected that, by 1971, every tenth worker will be an engineer and every ninth a technician. Analysis of the enrolments at secondary and higher educational establishments in the Soviet Union shows that the large-scale attendance of workers at these schools is an important channel leading to a change in their social status. Thus, in the 1960-1961 academic year, the Moscow Power Technical School enrolled 245 students, of whom 25 had been working for two years. In its evening department, the School enrolled 98 persons, of whom 57 had been working for two years. The Moscow Mechanical-Technological School of Light Industry enrolled in 1962-1963 in its evening department 180 persons, of whom 148 had been at work for two years. The Moscow Machine-Building School enrolled in its first year 336 persons in September 1961, and 121 of them had been at work. The evening department admitted 233 persons, 212 of them having a background of industrial work. The number of persons with industrial experience of two years and more constantly increases, as is shown in *Table 1*.

Table 1. Enrolment of workers at Moscow Technical Institutes, showing those with not less than two years' employment (1959-1962)

Institute	Enrolled in 1959-60	2 years' employment	Enrolled in 1960-61	2 years' employment	Enrolled in 1961-62	2 years' employment
Power Institute	1,984	853	1,986	1,056	2,025	1,367
Steel Institute	400	139	613	340	610	462
Mining Institute	230	190	255	226	310	259
Textile Institute	390	200	474	353	496	370
Building Engineering Institute	800	449	803	574	804	630

The general analysis of the total higher school enrolment in the Soviet Union yields a similar pattern.

Table 2. Enrolments at all Soviet higher education institutes

	1957-58	1958-59	1959-60	1960-61
Enrolled at the day-time departments of higher schools, '000	219·7	215·5	227·1	257·9
Including those with work records not less than two years, '000	60·6	97·3	112·5	147·8
Percentage of those enrolled with work records	28·0	45·0	49·0	57·0

CONCLUSIONS

The above data suggest the following conclusions. First, there is a rapid process of vertical mobility in enterprises in the Soviet Union. Second, the two main forms of this mobility are transition of workers into the category of engineers and technicians and the promotion of workers to responsible posts. Third, the number of students who have had previous industrial experience is increasing at a rapid rate.

9

Soviet intellectuals and white-collar workers

V. S. SEMYONOV

COMPOSITION OF SOVIET INTELLIGENTSIA AND EMPLOYEES

The abolition of the distinction between classes and social groups in the period of the building of communism is causing considerable changes among intellectuals and white-collar workers. A new, genuinely people's intelligentsia arose in the Soviet Union during the years of socialist construction. The number of intellectuals and white-collar workers increased from 2,725,000 in 1926 to 20,495,000 in 1959, i.e. nearly 7·5 times. Approximately 80-90 per cent of the socialist intelligentsia, including engineers, technicians, agrotechnicians, teachers, doctors, scientists, artists, cultural workers and so on, are people who came from the working class or the peasantry.

A substratum, which under capitalism was deprived of ownership of the means of production, has become a social stratum that owns the means of production on a par with the working class and the peasantry. From a substratum that under capitalism had no common social interests, the intellectuals and white-collar workers became a stratum with common socialist interests with the working class and peasantry. The vital interests of the intelligentsia are inseparable from the interests of workers and peasants, because both are a part of the socialist labour force and equal owners of the basic means of production.

In the Soviet Union, the intelligentsia began to flourish as a stratum, as a new, socialist intelligentsia, during the building of socialism. The scale and rate of training of intellectuals grew. In the period 1918-1937, a total of 880,000 specialists were trained in institutions of higher learning and 1,112,000 in secondary specialized schools. The number of specialists trained in 1938-1958 was 4·4 times greater, namely 3,220,000 in institutions of higher learning and 5,621,000 in secondary specialized schools. During the five-year period 1959-1963 the numbers trained in these categories were 1,655,000 and 2,404,000 respectively, that is nearly 2·5 times the number trained in the first twenty years (1918-1937).

The qualifications of the socialist intelligentsia, i.e. their cultural and technical level, have changed. In the early years of Soviet rule the acute shortage of specialists, particularly in the technical fields, frequently made it necessary to appoint workers to positions of responsibility in the national economy without giving them any preliminary training. At a later date, these workers studied at evening institutes, and on short-term courses, while continuing their practical work. This form of study, naturally, gave only the fundamentals of knowledge or of technical skill. The training of intellectuals underwent a radical qualitative change in the period when the building of socialism was nearing completion, when numerous educational institutions had been built, a large body of highly qualified professors and teachers had been formed, and all the facilities had been created for skilled instruction.

This sharply raised the general educational standard of the intelligentsia. The proportions per thousand of those with a higher or secondary education are: for cultural workers, 594 in 1939 and 958 in 1959; for agrotechnicians, 622 in 1939 and 936 in 1959; for engineers and technicians, 630 in 1939 and 910 in 1959.

An increase in the number of intellectuals and white-collar workers in one category and a decrease in another is evident during the completion of socialist construction. On the one hand, there is an increase in the number of intellectuals engaged in production, in cultural work, and in science and medicine. On the other hand, a decrease is observed in the number of white-collar workers occupied in economic and state administration, and in the management of co-operative and public organizations, as well as of credit and insurance agencies.

According to the 1959 census returns, the main groups of intellectuals and white-collar workers were as set out in *Table 1*.

The above figures show that engineers and technicians (many of whom are heads of enterprises and subdivisions of these enterprises), together with scientific and cultural workers, form the largest contingents of intellectuals and white-collar workers in the Soviet Union. Then follow office employees, retail trade and catering workers, employees in communal and catering establishments, communications and transport workers, workers in the state, Party, and ideological apparatus, constitute a relatively small contingent (excluding the heads of enterprises).

The stratum of intelligentsia and white-collared workers has a heterogeneous composition. The concepts intelligentsia and white-collar workers have different meanings. Neither is a clearcut social category, because they characterize working people from different points of view. The concept 'intelligentsia' characterizes people from the point of view of the nature of their work, which is intellectual. The concept 'employees',

*Table 1. Numbers of intellectuals and white-collar workers
1959 census*

Type of worker	Number
1. Workers in state administration and public organizations	2,389,000
including:	
(a) heads of state administrative bodies and social organizations and their subdivisions	392,000
(b) heads of enterprises and their subdivisions	955,000
(c) government employees (juridical personnel, inspectors, and so on)	1,042,000
2. Technical-economic intelligentsia	4,991,000
including:	
(a) engineers and technicians (excluding engineers occupying positions as heads of enterprises)	4,206,000
(b) agrotechnicians	477,000
(c) planning engineers and statisticians	308,000
3. Scientific and cultural workers	5,294,000
including:	
(a) teachers, educators, scientific workers	2,836,000
(b) medical workers	1,702,000
(c) cultural administrators	462,000
(d) artistic administrators	190,000
(e) professional writers and journalists	104,000
4. Office employees	2,912,000
including:	
(a) bookkeepers, accountants	1,817,000
(b) cashiers	413,000
(c) clerical personnel	536,000
(d) agents and filing clerks	146,000
5. Transport employees (conductors)	334,000
6. Communications employees (radio-telegraph, telegraph, telephone operators)	476,000
7. Retail trade and catering workers	2,452,000
including:	
(a) shop assistants, kiosk and snack-counter managers, etc.	1,166,000
(b) waiters	184,000
8. Workers in communal and public service establishments	2,307,000
including:	
(a) janitors, watchmen	2,030,000

'white-collar' workers implies that the given category of people are employed by state or public organizations and carry out specific work, functions, and duties for a specific salary.

Under socialism, the vast majority of the intelligentsia are employees. However, not all employees can be classed in the category of intellectual workers. In fact, many categories of employees are not brain workers.

In the conditions obtaining under socialism, the categories engaged in what can be described as genuinely intellectual work include the technical-economic and scientific-cultural intelligentsia, many workers in the state, Party, and ideological apparatus, a considerable number of state employees and of the military intelligentsia, and a part of the militia.[1]

The work of certain categories of office employees, communications employees, retail trade and catering workers (shop assistants and waiters), employees of communal and service establishments (particularly janitors and watchmen), many state employees (of insurance and credit bodies), and a certain section of military personnel and the militia cannot be classed as brain workers.

All these people are not engaged in intellectual work, or in creative activity in its true meaning. Their work combines elements of both physical and mental labour. This work has a specific character of its own and can be called service labour.[2] Most frequently this work amounts to the fulfilment of a certain function, such as that of a filing clerk, watchman, traffic controller, and so on, i.e. a function which itself requires specific labour.

Service work is also required by society, as is physical and intellectual work. It stems from the requirements of social development, particularly the development of the productive forces, the economy, classes and of the state.[3]

The distinction between service labour on the one hand and intellectual and physical labour on the other enables us to use the same index, the nature of the work, for a clearer differentiation between intellectuals and employees, white-collar workers. In this case, if we take the word intelligentsia to mean all intellectual workers, and the concept white-collar workers to cover all the people engaged in service labour, the concepts intelligentsia and white-collar workers will acquire a quite clear social meaning. They characterize two more or less definite parts of the single stratum of intellectuals and white-collar workers.

This differentiation according to the nature of the work is all the more necessary for an understanding of the development of these groups during the building of communism. The crux of the matter is, first, that the development of the intelligentsia and white-collar groups follows quite different trends and, second, that during the building of communism service workers, by virtue of the nature of their labour, are faced with the problem of either changing their activity into intellectual work or the elimination of a number of professions in the service sphere. All these important processes cannot be understood without analysing the intelligentsia and white-collar workers as categories.

CHANGES IN THE COMPOSITION OF THE INTELLIGENTSIA AND WHITE-COLLAR WORKERS UNDER COMMUNISM

The intelligentsia will remain as a stratum in its own right until the highest stage of communist society has been reached. In the Soviet Union the distinction between intellectual and physical work will be finally removed only when communism has been built. During the building of communism, the tremendous development of material and spiritual production will be accompanied by a constant increase in the number of intellectuals and by a growth of their share in the social structure. First and foremost, this includes engineers, technicians, and agrotechnicians in town and country.

The mechanization and automation of production is changing the relation between workers and intellectuals. During the building of communism, the ratio between workers operating an automatic system and the specialists who have designed this system will be very distinctive: it may prove to be 1 to 10, i.e. one worker in a factory department to ten specialists in offices.

Under communism there will be an appreciably larger number of scientific institutions, and of designers and other specialists. In the course of communist construction, an ever-increasing number of factories will be turned into communist-type enterprises. The distinctive features of these enterprises will be the higher cultural and technical standards of the workers, the greater combination in their activity of physical and intellectual labour and the increase in the proportion of engineers and technicians. This process is now gaining momentum. Already today the Soviet Union has factories with 400-500 and more engineers and technicians per 2,000 workers. *Table 2* illustrates the changes in correlation of shares of workers, engineers, technicians, and office employees in Soviet industry.

In the period 1932-1961 the number of engineers and technicians increased 5 times and of workers 3·2 times, whereas the increase in the number of office employees has been very slight.

Table 2. *Correlation of different types of occupation*
(*in percentages*)

	1932	1940	1950	1960	1962	1963
Workers	75	76	80	83	83	83
Engineers, technicians	5	8·5	8·5	9	9·6	10
Office employees	9	7	5	4	4	4

The realization of the spiritual requisites of communism will lead to a growth in the number of and proportion of the scientific-cultural intelligentsia: scientists, teachers, doctors, artists, and writers. In the past 20 years, the size of this category of intellectuals has increased as follows:

Table 3. *Growth of the scientific and cultural intelligentsia*

	Number		1959 as percentage of 1939
	1939	1959	
1. Teachers, educators, scientific workers	1,553,099	2,835,556	183
2. Medical workers	679,550	1,702,487	251
3. Professional writers and journalists	58,033	104,146	179
4. Cultural administrators	285,000	462,272	162
5. Artistic administrators	143,280	190,618	133

During the building of communism these groups of intellectuals will continue to increase absolutely. In view of the rapid development of public health, education, and culture, the number of people engaged in these and other non-productive spheres will show the largest increase, almost threefold in the course of the 20-year period. At the same time, some groups of intellectuals will decrease in number and form a smaller proportion in the social structure. First and foremost, these are employed in state administration and in public organizations. In the period 1939-1959, the number of heads of state administrative bodies and public organizations, and their subdivisions, decreased from 445,244 to 392,131, i.e. by 12 per cent.

The changes in the number and share of employees of state administration bodies, economic managements, co-operatives, and public organizations are shown in *Table 4*:

K

Table 4. Changes in the number and share of public employees

	1940	1950	1955	1960	1962	1963
Number ('000)	1,825	1,831	1,361	1,245	1,316	1,308
As percentage of 1940	100	100	75	68	72	71

Substantial qualitative changes will take place within the intelligentsia during the building of communism. The material and technical basis of communism is being created in conditions marked by scientific and technical progress, the improvement of the productive forces, and new discoveries and inventions. All this is inconceivable without considerable changes in the educational, cultural, and technical standards of the intelligentsia, and an intensified all-round development of intellectual workers. These changes have to take place if the work of scientists, engineers, technicians, teachers, and cultural and medical workers is to be fruitful. At present, far from all brain workers have a secondary or higher education. Higher education will be compulsory for them in the near future. *Table 5* illustrates the rise of the Soviet intelligentsia's level of education.

Table 5. Standard of education of the intelligentsia

Group of intellectuals	Higher or secondary education per 1,000 persons		1959 as percentage of 1939
	1939	1959	
Engineers and technicians	630	910	144·4
Agronomists, livestock experts, veterinary surgeons, and foresters	622	936	150·6
Medical workers	674	969	143·7
Teachers, educators, scientific workers	892	991	112·2
Cultural administrators	594	958	161·2
Artistic administrators	644	894	138·6
Juridical personnel	684	987	144·3

The technical progress that is taking place during the building of communism will lead to changes in the professional composition of the intelligentsia. New groups of technical intelligentsia, which formerly did not exist in the Soviet Union, are rapidly taking shape. These include specialists in atomic power, radioelectronics, and electronic computers. There will be a continuation of the withering away of obsolete professions and of the rise and development of new specialized occupations engendered by the latest achievements of science and technology.

The change in the national composition of the intelligentsia will also continue. Before the Revolution many nations and nationalities of the Soviet Union did not have an intelligentsia of their own. Many of them did not have even a written language and remained ignorant and backward. All the nations and nationalities of the Soviet Union created their own socialist intelligentsia during the years of socialist construction. In the national republics, the intelligentsia grew several times faster than the intelligentsia in the Soviet Union as a whole. For example, in the period 1926-1959, the number of engineers, technicians, and agronomists in the Soviet Union as a whole increased 18 times, whereas in Central Asia and Kazakhstan their number increased 38 times. The number of teachers and cultural workers rose 7 times in the Soviet Union as a whole, and 19 times in Central Asia and Kazakhstan. The number of medical workers increased 8·5 and 21 times respectively.

The territorial distribution of the intelligentsia is changing side by side with the changes in its national composition. Large centres of industry and culture are being built in Siberia, Kazakhstan, Central Asia, and the Far East. The number of intellectuals is increasing substantially in all these regions. The socialist intelligentsia is being distributed more and more uniformly throughout the territory of the Soviet Union, thereby bringing physical and intellectual workers closer together, and helping to erase the distinction between them.

In the process of building communism, the completion of the development of the intelligentsia will be accompanied by the abolition of the distinction between intellectual and physical labour. Under communism labour will, of course, not be devoid of physical effort. It will rationally combine elements of intellectual and physical activity. Automation, too, requires some physical effort. How then will this unification of intellectual and physical work take place? We feel that basically this will happen by combining intellectual work with definite elements of associated physical effort.

In their leisure time, many intellectuals engage in physical work that is not directly connected with their main functions. In industry and institutes engineers, designers, and scientists will expend a certain amount of physical effort in the course of their intellectual work. This is rendered easier by ever closer relations between intellectual work and production, and between science and life. When intellectual work is closely linked with production its quality is improved by associated physical effort. Such a combination of intellectual and physical work yields the greatest economic result and gives the worker concerned the greatest satisfaction.

As in the case of the intelligentsia, essential changes are taking place among many categories of employees in the present period of transition from socialism to communism. With the improvement in the equality of labour, the distinction between service work and intellectual work will be removed for many categories of employees; many present fields of service will cease to exist and the employees now occupied in them will become intellectual workers.

The swift development of technology and automation, the ripening of friendly relations, mutual aid, and comradeship,the fostering of communist consciousness, the surmounting of survivals of the past in people's minds, and the strengthening of communist morals will lead to the elimination of many categories of service occupations.

Very many categories of office employees will become unnecessary. These include cashiers and filing clerks. A movement aimed at paying wages without cashiers has started on a large scale in the Soviet Union. In the course of communist construction, the need for wages clerks will undoubtedly lessen. Their functions will be performed by the working people themselves. With the transition to distribution according to needs, this function will disappear. As the building of communism progresses an even larger share of all clerical work will be done by machines.

In retail trade and public catering, with the ever wider satisfaction of the needs of the population, there will be an increase in many categories of employees. At the same time, the need for other categories of personnel in retail trade and public catering will diminish. Automatic vending machines and self-service shops will lead to a reduction of the number of salesmen. At many factories and offices, the restaurants no longer employ sales staff. Fewer waiters are being employed as a result of self-service. In 1939-1959, despite the huge growth of public catering establishments, the numbers of waiters decreased.

With the numerical reduction in some categories of employees and the disappearance of a large number of occupations many of the employees concerned will be engaged in intellectual work. This applies to some groups of office employees, many communications employees, a section of transport and retail trade employees.

The process of removing distinctions in the nature of labour during the transition from socialism to communism signifies not only the combination of the physical labour of workers and peasants with intellectual work, but also the transformation of the labour of some categories of employees into intellectual work. In other words, the distinction will be removed not only between intellectual and physical work, but also between intellectual work and service work.

The introduction of machines and changes in functions performed by workers form the material basis of this process. The latter factor is of very great importance. Formerly the functions of most employees required service labour and not intellectual work, but now the functions performed by many employees are changing and giving way to intellectual work. Bookkeepers, accountants, and some other categories of office workers, for example, are now making ever greater use of machines, and they are beginning to perform the functions of economic analysis. In future, the work of these categories of employees will merge more and more with the work of planners, inspectors, statisticians, and other specialists.

In railway transport, passenger attendants and conductors are likewise using an increasing number of machines. Automation, radio-television regulation and control, and self-service by passengers will lead to the replacement of conductors and passenger attendants by technicians. The work of communications employees (radio-telegraph, telegraph, and telephone operators) already approximates to the intellectual work of technicians and operators. The further development of radio and telephone engineering and the automation of telephone and telegraph communication will turn the work of communications employees into a form of engineering.

The work of many categories of the militia is also acquiring a different character. Educational tasks are entering into their functions. They do not limit themselves to the maintenance of law and order and to tracking down criminals. They make every effort to prevent violations of the law, and to achieve this object they carry on educational work among the population and keep an eye on the upbringing of young people. This preventive and educational activity is intellectual work in the full meaning of the word.

Thus, step by step, the labour of many categories of employees is turning into intellectual work. The educational, cultural, and technical standards of these categories of employees is approaching the same level as that of intellectuals. The gap between the cultural and education standards of the intelligentsia and service employees was narrowed down considerably during the years of socialist construction, as may be seen in *Table 6*.

Table 6 shows that though most employees (except bookkeepers and clerical personnel) have a lower educational standard than the intelligentsia they are catching up very rapidly. The difference is being removed through a change in the nature of the work and of the functions performed by many employees.

An analysis of the trends of the changes in the various categories of intellectuals and employees in the course of communist construction shows that the basic groups of intellectuals will increase numerically, while some categories of employees will steadily decrease. On the whole, intellectuals and employees will occupy a relatively larger place in the social structure primarily through the rapid increase in the numbers of the technical-

Table 6. Changes in the educational standard of employees compared with that of the intelligentsia

Occupation	Secondary or higher education per 1,000 persons		1959 as percentage of 1939
	1939	*1959*	
Intellectuals and employees	498	884	177·5
Engineers and technicians	630	910	144·4
Office employees:			
bookkeepers, accountants,	535	927	173·4
clerical personnel	624	943	135·1
Transport employees:			
passenger attendants	61	521	854·1
ticket collectors	42	403	959·5
bus, tram, trolleybus conductors	76	626	323·6
Communications employees			
(Post, Telegraph, and Telephone)	368	792	215·2
Retail trade and public catering:			
all employees	182	737	404·9
waiters	49	534	1,087·7
Employees of communal and service			
establishments	197	561	284·7

economic and scientific-cultural intelligentsia. It may be expected that, by 1980, the groups of workers who now come under the heading of intelligentsia and employees will form about 30-35 per cent of the population of the Soviet Union.

In the transition from socialism to communism, the intelligentsia is playing a greater role. It is helping to create the material and technical basis, to raise the standard of education, culture, and technical knowledge among the people, to promote science, technology, the arts, and public health, and to foster communist consciousness and morals.

The increasingly creative character of the labour of workers and peasants and the rise in their educational, cultural, and technical standards are giving them a larger role in science, culture, and the arts. It is becoming and will become quite usual for many workers and peasants to be amateur actors, musicians, schoolteachers, writers, and scientific workers. Material and cultural activity will increasingly merge in the work and life of harmoniously developed individuals in communist society.

NOTES

1. In the Soviet Union the militia is the organization responsible for the maintenance of order and public safety. It supervises the observance of laws, decrees, and decisions of the central and local organs of power which are concerned with the maintenance of public order. Its functions include, in particular, the protection of state and public property, the preservation of personal safety and property, crime prevention and detection, and road traffic regulation.

2. This form of activity must not be confused with the service sphere, a field of the economy in which intellectual and physical workers, and also service workers, are engaged. There are three spheres of socio-economic activity: material production, intellectual production, and services.

3. In our view, the development of the productive forces and the rise of the state brought about three basic forms of labour: physical, intellectual, and service. Just as intellectual work has always differed from physical labour, in the same way service labour has always differed from physical and intellectual work.

10

Social conditions for technical creative activity among workers

B. I. YEREMEYEV

BACKGROUND TO THE INVESTIGATION

A key criterion of growth in technical creative activity is participation in the work of rationalizing production. To solve the problem posed in this paper, the author carried out a series of investigations in 16 work-shops and departments of the Gorky Automobile Works, the Krasnaya Etna Plant, and the Gorky Milling Machine Works, and in the whole Zavolzhsky Engine Works.

Of the 13,474 workers and engineering and technical personnel covered in the inquiry, 1,589, or 11·8 per cent, of them took part in promoting the efficiency of production in 1960. Analysis of comparative data on such activity for a number of years makes it possible to trace the main trends. Some pertinent figures for Gorky region, which show a growing participation in this form of creative work, are set out in *Table 1*.

Table 1. Indices of activity in rationalizing production

Year	Number of participants in rationalizing production	Number of rationalization proposals		Economic effect (in millions of roubles)
		Submitted	Applied	
1957	46,969	98,534	57,996	23·6
1958	55,060	113,882	63,106	29·6
1959	60,877	119,472	68,102	33·4
1960	66,888	130,812	74,755	35·0
1961	68,290	128,635	74,377	41·0
1962	69,434	123,073	69,201	39·7
1963	73,641	113,146	72,545	44·5

From *Table 1* it can be seen that, in six years, the number of partici-pants in rationalizing production in the region increased by more than

26,000, and today it amounts to 11 per cent of the total industrial personnel in the Gorky Economic Area. This means that every ninth person employed there is a promoter of production efficiency, and a direct participant in solving the problems connected with technical progress. Inventions by workers in the Gorky Region have forged far ahead in 40 years, as may be seen from the annual data on rationalization proposals and inventions for the Krasnoye Sormovo Shipyards, one of the oldest enterprises in the country.

Table 2. Increase in rationalization proposals

Year	Number of rationalization proposals and inventions		Total economic effect (in roubles)	Total awards (in roubles)
	Submitted	Applied		
1919	15	9	—	—
1926	62	49	3,760	160
1930	778	302	28,500	1,460
1940	4,613	2,420	520,000	26,700
1950	6,542	3,063	1,550,000	45,000
1959	5,270	2,373	1,700,000	52,600

Comparison of the figures in *Table 2* shows convincingly the tremendous growth that has taken place in the creative activity of industrial workers and engineering and technical personnel. Instead of a mere fifteen persons participating in technical creative work at the Krasnoye Sormovo Shipyards in 1919, there are today over 5,500.

Technical creative work on a mass scale has risen immeasurably not only in quantity but also in quality. One of the first proposals at the Krasnoye Sormovo Shipyards to rationalize production, made back in 1919, was to replace hand saws for wood cutting by electric circular saws. The following is typical of the proposals workers are making today. A. V. Zolin, a distinguished promoter of efficiency in production at the Gorky Automobile Plant, working in collaboration with A. P. Sizov, designed and constructed a multi-station automatic machine for the mechanical treatment of automobile engine bearings. This made it possible to combine three operations in the tooling process, thus considerably lightening labour and releasing about 20 workers. The economic effect of the proposal was an annual saving of 30,000 roubles.

Another inventor at the same plant, a fitter engaged in assembling Volga automobiles, V. D. Ludin, devised and introduced automatic installations for transferring car bodies from one conveyer to another and rotating them through an angle of 90 degrees in the process. Thanks to this, the labour-consuming operation of transferring cars from one shop to another has been fully automated.

The first step in research into the social problems of technical creative work should, in our opinion, be an analysis of the relation between technical creative work and such factors as the content of a worker's labour, his level of education and skill, length of service, and age. In analysing this relation, we confined ourselves to investigating the most important type of technical creative work. This is the effort which is made to rationalize production, or to promote its efficiency. This is also the most widespread mass form of technical creative activity. Study of the movement to promote production efficiency was facilitated by the availability of data on such indices as trade, skill, age, length of service, and education of the rationalizers of production. Without these initial data our analysis would have been made very difficult.

THE NATURE AND CONTENT OF LABOUR

Of the factors directly influencing the creative activity of workers, the nature and content of their labour play the main role. As a basis for studying the influence of the nature of labour on the creative activity of workers a classification of the workers was made by such objective indices as the degree of mechanization of the work and the production functions performed. The classification of the groups is as follows:

    I Automatic machine operators
    II Machine-tool operators
    III Manual workers engaged on machines
    IV Manual workers not engaged on machines
    V Machine-tool setters and maintenance mechanics.

The largest group consists of machine-tool operators (Group II), which include some 36 per cent of all categories of workers in the shops we investigated. Their labour is characterized by the performance of relatively simple, routine operations machining raw materials or semi-manufactured articles. The production functions of such operators include machining, pressing, and certain operations involved in setting, fastening, and removing the work, and routing it on. Creative activity of this group of workers is reflected in *Table 3*, which was drawn up on the basis of a statistical study of 3,493 workers in nine workshops.

With the exception of the last three shops, average percentage participation in promoting production efficiency is no higher than 2·5. This is to be explained above all by the fact that the place occupied by this group in production does not directly prompt them to tackle creative problems. The work of the machine-tool operators in these shops most of the time is limited to a series of simple and monotonous rhythmic movements, mastered to the point where they have become automatic.

Table 3. Participation of machine-tool operators (Group II)
in rationalizing production in 1960 (in percentages)

Shop	Percentage participating
1. Zavolzhsky Engine Works	1·2
2. Engine Shop No. 2, Gorky Automobile Works	< 1·0
3. Cold Forge Shop, Krasnaya Etna Plant	2·5
4. Small Standard Parts Shop, Krasnaya Etna Plant	1·5
5. Bedstead Shop, Krasnaya Etna Plant	2·5
6. Spring Shop, Krasnaya Etna Plant	1·6
7. Measuring Tool Shop, Gorky Automobile Works	10·0
8. Die Shop, Gorky Automobile Works	16·0
9. Shop No. 2, Gorky Milling Machine Works	18·0

The striking thing in *Table 3* is the sharp jump in the percentage of production efficiency promoters in the last three shops. This can be explained by the fact that universal machine operators, who perform a variety of operations, work in the measuring tool and forging die shops of the Gorky Automobile Works. A universal machine operator engaged in short-run production, which is typical for these shops, sets up and adjusts the tools and attachments and, if necessary, sets the equipment. He is a setter-operator. Besides this, universal machine operators are skilled in a number of other trades and have a broader technical range. These factors taken together made possible a four- to five-fold increase in creative activity of this category of workers as compared with the machine-tool operators who are skilled in only one trade.

Table 3 shows that creative activity of the employee is at its highest in Shop No. 2 of the Gorky Milling Machine Works. This is the direct result of a strong element in this shop of one of the main trends in the changing trade structure of the working class, in which a worker combines a number of production functions. The machine-tool operators in that shop have been given the functions of setting, adjustment, and control. Such combination of trades brings the machine-tool operator close to the machine-tool setter and maintenance mechanic in the nature of the functions performed. In role and importance in modern production, the setter-operator comes within the category of industrial personnel with the biggest future.

The main production functions determining the content of his labour are the setting and adjustment of the various parts of the equipment, eliminating faults, and maintaining optimum operating conditions. The setter requires a knowledge not only of modern metal-cutting machine tools and other types of equipment, but of hydraulics, electricity, and of the properties of the materials being worked. Modern production makes no less a demand on the skill of the fitter, who has to deal with highly complicated and multi-purpose equipment. Besides possessing extensive practical skills, and the ability to handle repair jobs of medium complexity on various types of equipment, he must be familiar with the working principles and the mechanism of the various parts of the equipment, the mechanical and chemical properties of the materials being machined, and so on.

A study was made of the percentage participation of workers in this group (Group V) in promoting production efficiency by comparing 10 different shops concerned with quite diverse types of production. The results of the inquiry are shown in *Table 4*.

Table 4. Participation of machine-tool setters and maintenance fitters (Group V) in rationalizing production (in percentages)

Shop	Percentage participating
1. Main Conveyor Shop, Gorky Automobile Works	51
2. Engine Shop No. 2, Gorky Automobile Works	19
3. Die Shop, Gorky Automobile Works	19
4. Cutting Tool Shop, Gorky Automobile Works	54
5. Measuring Tool Shop, Gorky Automobile Works	43
6. Cold Forge Shop, Krasnaya Etna Plant	22
7. Small Standard Parts Shop, Krasnaya Etna Plant	27
8. Bedstead Shop, Krasnaya Etna Plant	39
9. Spring Shop, Krasnaya Etna Plant	29
10. Cold Strip Rolling Shop, Krasnaya Etna Plant	36

The tabulated results of our calculations show that percentage participation in rationalizing production does not drop below 19 per cent. In two of the shops it even exceeds 50 per cent, which means that approximately every third worker in this group contributes to promoting production efficiency. The reason for such a high percentage of creative activity, compared to the other groups, lies in the very nature of the labour of these trades. Constant contact with most widely differing kinds of work, and the daily need to overcome various technical difficulties, compel these workers to be on the constant lookout for the best technical methods and to give creative thought to finding them. In the course of their work workers are continually coming up against various unexpected problems, or 'emergency situations' to use their terminology. In such situations they must make a quick decision independently, and select the best out of dozens of possible variants. All this compels them to keep on thinking and comparing things all the time while working. Every work-day brings new knowledge which becomes integrated with their store of skill and production experience. It is precisely because the workers in this group are able to study the equipment in the course of their work, and are constantly faced with the need to cope with problem situations that they can make significant improvements in the technological process. Maintenance fitters and machine-tool setters are drawn into the creative process in the course of their daily work.

A very low rate of technical creative work is found in the group of workers who perform similar operations involving the manual operation of machines or simple manual labour (Group III). The creative activity of the workers in these groups, as can be seen from *Table 5*, amounts to an average of only 1·2 per cent for the eight shops investigated, and 0·8 per cent at the Zavolzhsky Engine Works.

Table 5. *Participation of unskilled workers* (*Group III*) *in rationalizing production* (*in percentages*)

Shop	Percentage participating
1. Zavolzhsky Engine Works	0·8
2. Engine Shop No. 2, Gorky Automobile Works	0·0
3. Cold Forge Shop, Krasnaya Etna Plant	2·4
4. Bedstead Shop, Krasnaya Etna Plant	2·3
5. Spring Shop, Krasnaya Etna Plant	0·0
6. Cold Strip Rolling Shop, Krasnaya Etna Plant	3·0
7. Shop No. 2, Gorky Milling Machine Works	< 1·0
8. Shop No. 21, Gorky Milling Machine Works	0·0
9. Shop No. 10, Gorky Milling Machine Works	< 1·0

Such a low percentage participation in rationalizing production is to be explained by the fact that the function of the workers in this group is confined to simple operations and to moving raw materials and products. Physical effort only is required of them along with the very simplest of labour skills. Practically no demand is made on their intellectual abilities, and, to a certain extent, repetition of the same work introduces elements of monotony into the character of their labour. Mechanization is at present also beginning to penetrate into these auxiliary types of labour; mechanized conveying appliances of all kinds, and 'mechanical hands' are being devised. This results in the gradual transfer of the functions of loaders and warehousemen to machines, which are then serviced by fitters and maintenance mechanics.

A study of the creative activity of such an expanding group as automatic machine operators (Group I) is specially needed. Mental operations predominate in the work of this category. They consist of complex processes of observation and control of the work of the equipment and require constant attention and mental alertness to make independent decisions. A study was made of 627 automatic machine operators in three workshops of the Krasnaya Etna Plant. The extent of their creative activity, compared with the group of machine operators in the same shops, is shown in *Table 6*.

Table 6. *A comparison of the creative activity of auto-matic machine* (*Group I*) *and machine-tool operators* (*Group II*)

Shop	Trade	
	Automatic machine operators	Machine-tool operators
1. Cold Forge Shop	6·5	2·5
2. Automatic Small Standard Parts Shop	9·0	1·5
3. Spring Shop	10·0	1·6

From *Table 6* it follows that the creative activity of automatic machine operators is 2·5 times higher than that of machine operators in the cold forge shop and 6 times higher than that of machine operators in the small standard parts and spring shops. This is to be explained above all by the character of the work of the automatic machine operators. An automatic machine operator does not take a direct part in the machining; the share of automatic controlled machining rises quite high in his work (58·5 per cent of total working time), whereas manual-controlled machine work predominates for machine-tool operators (59·4 per cent of the total budget of working time).[1] Thus the need for manual labour drops off when working on automatic equipment and production functions boil down to running the machine and controlling its operation, apart from the present unavoidable hoisting and conveying operations. This requires of the workers thorough knowledge of the mechanism of the equipment they are operating and of the principles on which it operates. The higher the degree of automation, the more important become specialized knowledge and its application on the job, This explains the considerably greater activity of automatic machine operators as compared with machine-tool operators.

In order to discover the comparative degree of the promotion of production efficiency in each of the five selected groups of workers, we made a statistical study of three of the shops at the Krasnaya Etna Plant (the small standard parts shop, the cold forge shop, and the spring shop) which included 2,804 workers in all. These shops were chosen because each of them employed all five groups of workers. By comparing the percentage of each group in the shop, on the one hand, with the percentage of promoters of production efficiency in each of these five groups, on the other, we arrived at the conclusions that have been summarized in *Table 7*.

Table 7. Structure of the workers and rationalizers of production representing each of the five groups (in percentages)

	Groups				
	I	II	III	IV	V
Total number of workers	23	38·0	8·8	17·6	14·2
Production efficiency promoters alone	26	11·8	1·6	6·0	56·0

Comparing the figures in each column, we obtained the following ratios: Group I, $23:26 = 1:1$. The proportion of promoters of production efficiency is approximately equal to the proportion of the given group in the total number of workers. Group II, $38: 11·8 = 1:0·32$. The proportion of rationalizers of production in this group among all the production efficiency promoters is less than a third of the proportion of the numbers of workers in the given group among the total number of workers. Group III, $8·8:1·6 = 1:0·16$. Here this variance is down to one-sixth. Group IV, $17·6:6 = 1:0·4$ (or two-fifths). Group V, $14·2:56 = 1:4$. This is the only one of the five groups where the percentage of production efficiency promoters is four times that of the total number of workers in the given group.

The data obtained permit us to assert that it is precisely the trades which have been inevitably swelled in numbers by technical progress (automatic machine operators, machine-tool setters, and maintenance mechanics) which simultaneously yield the largest number of rationalizers of production (82 per cent according to our data).

We also made a study of the creative activity of the workers in each of the groups in the same three shops, using mean data, which are more reliable than the data for one shop. These data are summarized in *Table 8*.

Table 8. The creative activity of the five groups of workers in the small standard parts shop, cold forge shop, and spring shop at the Krasnaya Etna Plant (in percentages)

Groups				
I	II	III	IV	V
8·5	1·8	2	5	24

The data in *Table 8* are convincing evidence that creative activity is, to a considerable extent, determined by the nature of the work being done and varies extensively, rising to a twelvefold increase in the group embracing machine-tool setters and maintenance mechanics as compared with manual workers.

Among the factors affecting the creative activity of workers are vitally important characteristic of the work such as the degree of repetition of production operations, which is determined by the type of production (short-run, serial, and gross), and by the level of the mechanization of labour. In order to study the influence of this aspect of labour on the participation of workers in rationalizing production, we investigated a group of workers engaged in conveyor-line jobs. The inquiry covered 1,122 persons. Shops with different types of production were selected for comparative analysis. These were the main conveyor shop at the Gorky Automobile Works with multiple production; Shop No. 25 at the Gorky Milling Machine Works with medium-scale assembly work, and, finally, Shop No. 6 with small-scale assembly work at the same plant. A choice of shops like these enabled us to find the relation between the scale of lot production and the participation of the workers in technical creative activity. The data for 1960 obtained in this analysis have been summarized in *Table 9*.

As can be seen from *Table 9*, participation of workers in rationalizing production varies with type of production, within the limits of 9 and 24 per cent, and has a clearly defined tendency to increase with the transition from gross and multiple production to short-run and piece production.

Thus, in Shop No. 25, which is concerned with medium-run assemblywork, there are twice as many production efficiency promoters (18 per cent) as in the main conveyer shop (9 per cent). While in Shop No. 6 (where there

Table 9. *Participation of assembly workers in rationalizing production (in percentages)*

Shop	Percentage participating
1. Main conveyor shop, Gorky Automobile Works	9
2. Shop No. 25, Gorky Milling Machine Works	18
3. Shop No. 6, Gorky Milling Machine Works	24

is short-run production), the degree of creative activity is the highest of all three, 24 per cent, which exceeds the participation in rationalizing production in Shop No. 25 (where there is medium-run production) by 25 per cent.

This is to be explained by the fact that work on the conveyer line (split up as it is into small separate operations), especially in conditions of multiple production, becomes monotonous and tedious owing to the constant repetition of one and the same simple operation, which is not conducive to the employment of the workers' abilities.

On the other hand, a worker engaged in short-run production, and the more so in piece production, where the range of goods handled is quite extensive, has to deal with constantly changing materials, and hence has to carry out a diversity of operations, which greatly stimulates creative thought. Lessening the variety in production work has an adverse effect on the creative activity of the worker. The fact that this is not an accidental conclusion is also confirmed by the results of a study of the creative activity of another category of workers, namely machine-tool operators. For the comparison, we chose a group of machine shops with diverse types of production at the Gorky Milling Machine Works (*Tables 10* and *11*).

Upon comparing the data on participation in rationalizing production for these two shops, we arrive at conclusions analogous to those we came to after a study of conveyer-line production. Indeed, the percentage of workers taking part in Shop No. 2 (where there is short-run production), namely 14 per cent, is nearly three times the corresponding figure for Shop No. 3 (4·8 per cent), where there is serial production and, hence, the nature of the work is more monotonous.

It would be erroneous, however, to draw the conclusion that the degree

L

of creative activity will drop as production goes over from piece production to large-scale and wholesale manufacturing (which is, in fact, the main trend in the development of technology). With the transition to the more progressive quantity type of production, based on improved techniques, it becomes possible to decrease the number and percentage of workers

Table 10. Participation of workers and technical and engineering personnel in Shop No. 3 in rationalizing production (serial production)

Category of employees	Number of employees	Employees participating in rationalizing production	
		No.	%
Workers	717	37	4·8
Engineering and technical personnel	55	32	59·0
Total	772	66	9·0

Table 11. Participation of workers and technical and engineering personnel in Shop No. 2 in rationalizing production (short-run production)

Category of employees	Number of employees	Employees participating in rationalizing production	
		No.	%
Workers	302	42	14·0
Engineering and technical personnel	37	24	78·0
Total	339	66	20·5

involved in operations on materials and, accordingly, the group of persons engaged in maintenance, adjustment, and setting work is increased. Economists have calculated that setters and fitters make up 12 per cent of the total number of workers in piece production, 18 per cent of their total in serial production, and 24 per cent in mass production. Increase in this group of industrial production personnel will inevitably be accompanied by growth in technical creative activity among them, as we indicated above.

The widespread introduction of new technology and the mechanization and automation of production processes will radically change the nature and content of the workers' labour. The modern automatic production line, for example, combines in itself a complement of different types of machine tools and equipment, interlinked by conveyors and a single system of control and operation. It carries out a considerable number of technologically dissimilar functions as regards both manufacturing the goods produced (various kinds of mechanical and heat treatment, and quality control) and technical services (self-adjusting, lubrication, and readjustment). Such a line unites in a single technical system heterogeneous technological processes: for example, casting, machining, induction hardening, etc. The resultant simultaneous rise in level of mechanization makes it possible to increase sharply the share of manually operated machine time and automatically operated machine time, thus reducing manual labour to a minimum. All these processes, which take place in the technical basis of modern production, permit the combination of a number of functions in the trade of a single worker.

As automatic systems are introduced, the old form of division of labour begins to be replaced by a new form which has, as its main features, the introduction of trades involving a broad field of skill, and the functional mobility of the worker, who is capable of carrying out the most diverse operations. All this provides the necessary basis for the transformation of technical creative work into a necessary element of the production activity of the worker.

CREATIVE ACTIVITY AND LEVEL OF SKILL

In order to study the correlation between the creative activity of workers and their level of skill, we conducted an inquiry in two of the machine shops of the Gorky Milling Machine Works: Shop No. 2 with short-run production, where we investigated 227 workers (over 90 per cent of whom are machine-tool operators), and Shop No. 3 with multiple production, where the survey covered 537 machine-tool operators. Two groups of statistical data were obtained: (i) all the workers in the shop grouped according to grades of pay and (ii) those among them participating in rationalizing production, also grouped according to grades of pay. It was possible to establish a definite relation between them.

Shop No. 2 had a mean per cent participation in rationalizing production in 1960 equal to 18.

A comparison of *Tables 12, 13,* and *14* enables us to draw a number of conclusions:

1. Workers in the first and second grades, who account for 45 per cent of the shop's total (see *Table 12*), contributed only 14·7 per cent of all its production efficiency promoters (see *Table 13*). At the same time, 38·3 per cent of all the rationalizers of production in the shop come from the group of workers in the fourth grade, who account for 19 per cent of the

Table 12. Distribution of all the workers in the shop according to grades of pay

Grades	I	II	III	IV
Percentage distribution	10	35	36	19

Table 13. Distribution of the shop's production efficiency promoters according to grades of pay

Grades	I	II	III	IV
Percentage distribution	0	14·7	47	38·3

Table 14. Participation in rationalizing production among workers of each grade (a measure of the creative activity of workers in relation to their skill)

Grades	I	II	III	IV
Percentage participation	0	6·5	20	32·5

shop's total. Thus, the creative activity of workers in the first two grades is less than one-third of the percentage of these two groups in the shop's total, whereas the creative activity of the workers in the fourth grade, on the contrary, is twice as great as their percentage in the shop's total.

2. The investigation also revealed appreciable fluctuations in extent of participation in technical creative activity among the workers in the different grades (see *Table 14*):

(*a*) there are no rationalizers of production at all in Grade I;
(*b*) in Grade III (degree of creative activity = 20 per cent) there are more than three times as many production efficiency promoters as in Grade II;
(*c*) nearly every third person in Grade IV (degree of creative activity = 32·5 per cent) engages in technical creative work.

In other words, a rise in skill of a worker equivalent to just one grade increases his creative contribution two- to three-fold.

Shop No. 3 had a mean percentage participation in rationalizing production in 1960 equal to 4.

Table 15. Distribution of workers in the shop according to grades of pay

Grades	I	II	III	IV
Percentage distribution	18	61·5	16·5	4

Table 16. Distribution of the shop's production efficiency promoters according to grades of pay

Grades	I	II	III	IV
Percentage distribution	0	33·3	47·6	19·1

Table 17. Percentage participation in rationalizing production among workers of each grade in the shop

Grades	I	II	III	IV
Percentage participation	0	2	10·6	17·3

Roughly similar conclusions follow from an analysis of *Tables 15, 16,* and *17* to those arrived at after considering the results of the survey of the previous shop. Only one-third of the production efficiency promoters figure among the workers in Grades I and II, who make up nearly three-quarters of the total number of workers in the shop, whereas Grades III and IV, which together account for 20·5 per cent of the shop's total number of workers, yielded 66·7 per cent of the production efficiency promoters. Hence, at the present technical level of these shops, it is attainment of the Grade III rating (under a five-grade pay-scale) that makes it possible to draw workers into technical creative activity on a mass scale.

Increase in creative activity with rise in skill can also be observed by comparing the creative activity of workers with that of engineering and technical personnel, along with a comparison of their respective percentages in industrial production personnel as a whole.

Table 18. Percentage of engineering and technical personnel in total staff

Shops of Gorky Milling Machine Works				Shops of Gorky Automobile Works			Shops of Kras- naya Etna Plant		
No. 25	No. 6	No. 3	No. 2	Main con- veyor	Measur- ing tool	Cutting tool	Small standard parts	Cold forge	Cold strip rolling
9·5	9·4	7·1	10·8	3·4	13	8	6·3	7·5	8

Table 19. Engineering and technical personnel participating in rationalizing production as a percentage of the total number of production efficiency promoters

Shops of Gorky Milling Machine Works				Shops of Gorky Automobile Works			Shops of Kras- naya Etna Plant		
No. 25	No. 6	No. 3	No. 2	Main con- veyor	Measur- ing tool	Cutting tool	Small standard parts	Cold forge	Cold strip rolling
36	26	42·2	40	26	29	34	24	29	27

From a comparison of *Tables 18* and *19* it follows that the engineering and technical personnel, though constituting a relatively small proportion of the total staff employed, contribute three to four times the percentage of production efficiency promoters that can be observed in each of these ten shops.

If we take mean data, we get the following figures: of the total number of workers and engineering and technical personnel surveyed at the four industrial establishments which were investigated in Gorky Region, 36 per cent of all those participating in rationalizing production, in 1960, fell into the category of engineering and technical personnel, and 64 per cent into the category of workers, although the percentage of these two categories of industrial production staff was equal to 9·2 and 90·8 per cent, respectively. Thus, although they amounted to only 9·2 per cent of the total staff employed, the engineering and technical personnel supplied 36 per cent of the production efficiency promoters, or four times that percentage. Technical progress is undoubtedly the material basis for a steady increase in the proportion of skilled personnel. In conditions of socialism, technical progress makes much higher demands in terms of the skill and of the specialized and general educational standards of all the working people.

The process of a sharp growth in the proportion and number of skilled personnel, and of a reduction in unskilled and heavy physical labour, can be observed at a number of the plants in Gorky. *Table 20* presents data for the Krasnaya Etna Plant:

Table 20. Increase in number and change in grading of skilled workers (in percentages)

Year	Grade						
	II	III	IV	V	VI	VII	VIII
1945	4·3	28·4	19.0	20·3	15·8	9·3	2·7
1959	0·2	14·0	27·9	22·1	17·4	12·4	5·8

Table 20a shows the same data for the Gorky Milling Machine Works.

Table 20a

Year	Grade							
	I	II	III	IV	V	VI	VII	VIII
1943	4·1	35·6	21·4	13·1	14·5	8·5	2·2	0·4
1959	0	1·9	21·5	28·7	24·0	14·0	7·3	2·0

From *Tables 20* and *20a* it may be seen that during 14 years at the Krasnaya Etna Plant and 16 years in the Milling Machine Works the category of skilled workers with Grades I to III was reduced 2·3 and 2·6 times respectively. At the same time, the total number of highly skilled workers (Grades VI to VIII) increased at the Krasnaya Etna Plant 1·3 times and in the Milling Machine Works 2 times. A similar picture of the increase in the proportion of the highly skilled groups in the total labour force may be seen in the remaining examples.

EDUCATIONAL STANDARDS

To ascertain the relation between the technical creative activity of workers and their educational standard, we made a study of three shops at the Krasnaya Etna Plant.

As can be seen from *Table 21*, creative activity increases parallel with a rise in educational standards. There is an especially abrupt jump in activity between 10th grade and higher education. This is to be explained by the fact that ability for creative work, which is built up in a person on the basis of individual experience throughout his lifetime, develops in particular under the influence of any type of instruction which trains the human mind to solve diverse problems involving logical thinking. Education widens the horizon of a worker, and enables him to approach his job more creatively.

Table 21. Creative activity (participation in rationalizing production) of workers with different levels of education (in percentages)

Shop	Education							
	Less than 4 grades	*4 grades*	*5-6 grades*	*7 grades*	*8-9 grades*	*10 grades*	*Technical secondary*	*Higher*
Small standard parts	0	2	7·0	12·0	4	10·0	54	80
Cold forge shop	1	4	6·4	9·6	11	—	47	86
Spring shop	0	4	7·2	6·2	—	9·3	34	87

LENGTH OF SERVICE

The creative ability of an individual is complex and dependent upon many different factors, among which length of service is important. This is understandable, because a longer period of contact with complex equipment leads to the accumulation of a large amount of production experience and learning, which forms the foundation for creative activity.

In this study of production efficiency promoters according to length of service, there is striking evidence of the influence of the length of service upon the person's occupation. *Tables 22* and *23* illustrate this dependence.

From the data given in *Tables 22* and *23*, it can be seen that the possibility of participating in rationalizing production arises much earlier in occupations which involve less complex work. Thus, 16·6 per cent of all automatic machine operators and 33·3 per cent of all workers on conveyor lines, who participate in rationalizing production, have a service record of less than 10 years, whereas the corresponding figure for setters and fitters is only 5·6 per cent, or from 3 to 6 times less. This can be attributed to the greater complexity of the occupation of setter or fitter, which takes much more time to learn thoroughly. That is why in the setter and fitter group there are to be found the largest number of production efficiency promoters among workers with a service record of 16 to 25 years. As the tables show, length of service can influence creative ability in two ways. If the objective need to create is always there in the labour of the worker, which demands of him constant creative efforts, or 'steady thinking', as

Table 22. Composition of production efficiency promoters according to length of service at the cold forge shop, Krasnaya Etna Plant (in percentages)

Trade	Length of service					
	6-10 years	*11-15 years*	*16-20 years*	*21-25 years*	*26-30 years*	*31-35 years*
Setters and fitters	5·6	1·1	27·7	22·2	19·4	13·9
Automatic machine operators	16·6	25·0	16·6	25·0	16·6	—

Table 23. Composition of production efficiency promoters according to length of service at Shop No. 6, Gorky Milling Machine Works (in percentages)

Trade	Length of service			
	up to 5 years	*6-10 years*	*11-20 years*	*21-30 years*
Workers on conveyor lines	12·5	20·8	20·8	46·7

Pavlov called it, then the longer the service, the more developed will be the ability for technical creative work. On the other hand, when the work is of a monotonous nature, or does not in itself require a creative approach, there is a curbing influence on the ability to create.

Age of the worker, irrespective of length of service, does not directly influence creative activity. Nevertheless, certain interrelationships are to be found here too. At the start of a career in production, following a definite period (2-5 years) for the person to learn his trade, an upsurge of creative activity is observed, which subsequently remains for many years at the same level. Then, after a certain age, such activity is found to drop. *Table 24* presents the results of an inquiry into the age composition of 65 promoters of production efficiency in the main conveyor shop at the Gorky Automobile Works.

In order to discover how the influence of age on creative activities vary with occupation, we made a study of two groups of workers (fitters and automatic machine operators) employed in the cold forge shop at the Krasnaya Etna Plant (*Tables 26* and *27*).

Table 24. *Age composition of workers participating in rationalizing production in the main conveyor shop at the Gorky Automobile Works*

Age group	21-30 years	31-40 years	41-50 years	Over 50 years
Percentage participation in creative work	24·6	44·6	27·7	3

Table 25 gives similar data for 97 participants in rationalizing production at the Zavolzhsky Engine Works:

Table 25. *Age composition of workers participating in rationalizing production at the Zavolzhsky Engine Works*

Age group	21-30 years	31-40 years	41-50 years
Percentage participation in creative work	56·6	30	10·4

Table 26. *Age composition of workers participating in rationalizing production at the Krasnaya Etna Plant (in percentages)*

Trade	Age group				
	26-30 years	31-35 years	36-40 years	41-45 years	46-50 years
Fitters	11·1	22·2	27·7	16·6	22·2
Automatic machine operators	33·3	16·6	25·0	8·4	16·6

Table 27. *Age composition of fitters participating in rationalizing production in Shop 6, Gorky Milling Machine Works*

Age group	Under 20 years	21-30 years	31-40 years	41-50 years	Over 50 years
Percentage participation in creative work	4	20·8	29·1	43·3	4

The data cited suggest that there is no one definite age-range, either for maximum upsurge of creative activity of workers, or for a drop in it. The beginning, increase, or decrease of creative activity depends mainly upon the nature and content of the labour performed by the given group of workers in the course of their lifetime, and also upon their cultural and technical standards.

CONCLUSIONS

The development of science and engineering, and the introduction into production of up-to-date equipment, make it possible continuously to transfer new types of technological processes to machines. This process, accompanied by a steady rise in skill of the workers, extends the limits of application of creative labour. The need to solve complex technical problems, when operating modern equipment, requires of the worker extensive theoretical knowledge and the ability to make independent decisions when technological conditions have been upset. The worker puts ever more thought into the production process, and overcoming technical difficulties encountered on the job provides more favourable conditions for the development of creative thought. Engineering and technology continually make new and greater demands on the worker. Formerly, the main question posed in most forms of manufacturing was 'how is it to be done?' Now there have been introduced into a large number of occupations operations which cannot be performed merely on the basis of experience but require an extensive, specialized, scientific knowledge, founded on answers to the question 'why?' As the nature and content of labour changes, the role of intellectual work in labour increases. Technical progress in the conditions of socialist society rids man of many exhausting types of work, and opens up unprecedented scope for applying his creative abilities.

NOTE

1. The data on the measurement of labour functions were taken from Voronin, *The Division and Content of Labour of the Machine Tool Operator and the Machine Tool Setter*, Moscow, 1960.

11

Improvement of the cultural and technical standards of workers

M. T. YOVCHUK

TECHNICAL PROGRESS AND THE TRAINING OF WORKERS

The rise in the cultural and technical standards of workers in a number of industrial enterprises in Sverdlovsk Region was studied in 1957-1959 by research institutes headed by the Institute of Philosophy of the Academy of Sciences of the Soviet Union. A survey of some factories in Sverdlovsk Region, by A. I. Katsenelinboigen of the Institute of Economics of the Academy of Sciences of the Soviet Union, showed that mechanized labour is playing a steadily growing role. In 1958, from 50-54 per cent (Nizhniy Tagil Iron and Steel Works) to 67 per cent (Urals Heavy Engineering Plant) of the workers were engaged in mechanized operations.

The inadequate mechanization of some operations (particularly in transport), still leaves a high percentage of workers engaged in manual labour. At the Nizhniy Tagil Iron and Steel Works, for example, from 29 per cent (open-hearth furnace department) to 40 per cent (blast-furnace department) of the auxiliary workers are engaged in manual labour. The data obtained by a survey of factories, made by A. I. Katsenelinboigen and other investigators, indicate that the division of labour among individual workers engaged in a standardized simple task is being replaced by the combining of trades, by the combining of functions of varying complexity, and by the learning of several trades. This frees workers from having to perform one and the same standardized task all their lives.

Through the overall mechanization and automation of production, the existing division of functions between a machine operator and a more highly skilled worker, such as a setter, is giving way to the combination of the functions of an operator and a setter in one worker with higher standards of skill, general education, and special training (e.g. at Sverdlovsk Bearing Works and other factories).

Workers acquire a knowledge of more intricate equipment while operating several semi-automatic machines. Overall mechanization (at the Pervouralsk Pipe Works, for example) has sharply reduced the number of unskilled workers, and increased the number of skilled workers such as setters and electricians. Formerly the '220' mill was operated by workers with 3 to 5 years of secondary education, but after the mill was automated, all the workers employed had 7 to 10 years of secondary education, while many of the workers in the principal trades (e.g. rollers) have a secondary technical education, or are studying at technical institutes.

A worker requires extensive knowledge in order to be able to operate the modern machines made at the Urals factories. For example, the crews of the mobile excavators ESH 75/15, which are made at the Urals Heavy Engineering Plant, usually consist of workers with a specialized secondary education. The operators of automatic steel-smelting furnaces spend more than three-quarters of their time on computations and on regulating the work of their machines.

Particularly highly trained operators are required for the modern machinery now being installed in factories. For example, after a computer had been installed on the up-setting machine of the new '306' mill at the Nizhniy Tagil Iron and Steel Works, many of the operators, who had 7 or 8 years of education, had to be replaced by skilled workers who had a full secondary, technical education. Many of them were also studying at technical institutes. Automation is leading to a rise in the skill of the workers operating automatic machines and production lines. For example, on the automatic production line installed in a factory in Sverdlovsk Region, the same worker adjusts milling, boring, and drilling machines. Formerly, workers looked after only those machines that they had been trained to operate.

Overall mechanization and automation make it necessary for workers, particularly skilled tradesmen like setters and fitters to have an increasingly high standard of skill and general education. At the Sverdlovsk factories surveyed by A. I. Katsenelinboigen, G. V. Mokronosov, and others, the discrepancy between technical progress and the cultural and technical standards of the workers is being successfully surmounted. With this aim in view, new workers are given additional training in order to enable them to handle new machinery. Many factories have organized classrooms and production training courses.

D. H. Liberman and V. V. Petrov, who studied the forms and methods used by factories in Sverdlovsk Region to give workers production and technical training, found that far from narrowing down and shortening the training term, technical progress is broadening out and lengthening the technical training programme, with emphasis on all-round knowledge.

The broadening-out of elements of engineering and technical knowledge in the production training programme, as envisaged by the decisions of the Plenary Meeting of the Central Committee of the Communist Party of the Soviet Union, held in June 1959, is all the more important in view of the fact that nearly three-quarters of the new workers, for the most part secondary school leavers, are being trained within factories, and only about a quarter come from vocational schools and colleges.

The programmes of many of the production-technical courses, foremen's schools, and other forms of technical training at factories in Sverdlovsk Region provide for the study of the appropriate branches of physics, chemistry, mathematics, design, production economy and planning, rate-setting, and so forth. In the training course of, say, the driver of a mine electric locomotive, these subjects occupy 48 per cent of the study programme, of a sintering plant operator 42·7 per cent, and so on.

One-sided training, which is usual under the apprenticeship system in which little attention is paid to elements of theoretical training, is being eliminated. At the Urals Pipe Construction Trust of Sverdlovsk, young workers are formed into teams headed by skilled instructors. In their training, they pass from simple to difficult operations and, at each stage of their production training, they study a specific section of the theoretical programme based on the technology and the organization of production. At the Urals Carriage-Building Works, new workers are given a systematic production training in study workshops and, at the same time, take a theoretical course in their trade. After passing the examinations in theory and a rating test, they are assigned to work-benches in the appropriate department.

Factories have set up numerous refresher courses, re-training courses, and also schools of advanced experience, in order to help workers to learn how to use new machinery. In 1959, the Urals Heavy Engineering Plant had 484 schools of advanced experience located in its departments. These schools were attended by 4,000 workers, who studied under a special programme in which the most rational methods of work were taught scientifically. Inter-factory schools with courses of training in the most advanced methods of work have become widespread in Sverdlovsk Region. For example, more than 30 of these schools were organized at non-ferrous metals enterprises in 1959.

Training in allied trades has also become widespread. At the Pervouralsk and Sinarsk pipe factories many workers are studying the trades of fitter, electrician, and oxy-acetylene welder. At the Nizhniy Tagil Iron and Steel Works more than half of the workers have two or more trades. Many machine-tool operators have learnt the trade of fitter, and this has enabled the works to reduce the number of auxiliary personnel and considerably increase labour productivity. A questionnaire conducted among the workers of five factories representing different industries showed that from 31 to 44 per cent of the workers have two trades, and from 12 to 23 per cent three or more trades.

Special training courses were organized when automatic production lines and other new machinery began to be installed. Nearly 40,000 workers attended these courses in Sverdlovsk Region in 1959. At the production automation courses, workers study electronic automation, photocells, photorelays, and so forth. The setting up of technical classrooms in factory departments is helping the workers to learn to handle new machinery.

It must be noted, however, that these advanced experience schools and courses are unable to close the gap between general education and technical training. The courses in general subjects are very short (if taught at all) and the workers are not given a thorough grounding in physics, chemistry, electronic engineering, and other subjects. Yet the interests of socialist society require that workers be given all-round production training and general education. The reorganization of the public education system, as required by the decisions of the Communist Party and the Soviet Government, will go a long way towards eliminating this shortcoming.

In the Sverdlovsk Region, it is proposed to set up study departments (or production training departments) at industrial enterprises. These will be attended by young men and women who have completed 8 years of secondary education. In the course of three years, these young workers will receive a production rating, take part in actual production and, at the same time, receive a full secondary education. At the end of this course they will be given a qualification rating and a school-leaving certificate. The first of these departments has been set up at the Communal Engineering Plant in Sverdlovsk. It has been given modern equipment and is staffed by skilled engineering and technical personnel.

In Sverdlovsk Region, the training system at 150 secondary schools for young workers is being reorganized in order to close the gap between general education and production training. These schools will train skilled workers able to operate many types of machines. In addition to a general education, the pupils of these schools study technical drawing, the principles of metallurgical science, the latest developments in science and technology in their particular field, labour organization, and production economy.

Leading industrial enterprises in Sverdlovsk Region, like the initiator of this movement (the Kupavna Fine Cloth Mills), are drawing up and carrying out long-term plans to raise the cultural and technical level of their workers. In the current seven-year period, the Nizhniy Tagil Iron and Steel Works was the first Urals enterprise to draw up such a plan. The management has set a compulsory educational minimum for 250 trades. Under the works' present requirements, a rolling-mill control-panel operator, rolling-mill, heating-furnace, and press operator, and also a rolling-mill fitter and other workers must have completed an education of at least 10 years, while blast-furnace operators, slab-cutters, picklers, and other workers must have an education of at least 7-8 years.

After the training standard of the works' personnel had been carefully studied, and the workers themselves consulted, the management worked out a rational system for raising the general educational and technical level of the entire personnel. The aim is to give all workers (with the exception of older workers) an education, equivalent to 7 to 8 years' secondary education, within the next seven years, and to increase considerably the number of workers with a full secondary or higher education. Workers under 35 years of age are encouraged to attend a secondary school for young workers, where they are given a basic technical education. Experienced technicians, team leaders, and workers in basic trades, who because of their age or other reasons cannot study at schools for young workers, attend the school for foremen set up in the works.

The Nizhniy Tagil Works began its seven-year plan of technical training in the autumn of 1959. More than 4,000 workers went to schools for young workers (1,700 in 1959), over 840 enrolled in a correspondence institute or a technical school, and more than 940 studied at the school for foremen, which has become a four-year secondary special school, offering not only vocational training but also a full secondary education. The Nizhniy Tagil works is not an exception in Sverdlovsk Region. For example, the Pervouralsk Pipe Works has a study network that is gradually turning it into a higher technical school. This network has a branch of a technical institute, a technical school, a school for foremen, schools for young workers, and numerous refresher and retraining courses.

The experience gained by Sverdlovsk Region's industrial enterprises in raising the cultural and technical standards of their workers shows that, on the basis of the technical progress achieved during the full-scale building of communism there is not only a growth in the need for greater engineering and technical knowledge on the part of the workers, but also a development of new techniques for achieving it. In addition to the methods we have already described, mention must be made of the public discussions of the technical development of young workers. These debates, which have become popular in Sverdlovsk Region, publicize advanced work methods and give young people a taste for technology. In addition, there are scientific and technical education universities and also composite teams consisting of engineers, technicians, and workers in various trades.

THE RISE IN THE STANDARDS OF GENERAL EDUCATION AND TRAINING OF YOUNG WORKERS

Parallel with the different methods for improving working skill and for technical training inside factories, the cultural and technical standards of the workers are being substantially raised by the facilities which enable them systematically to improve their general education. The study conducted at factories in Sverdlovsk Region, by P. O. Kosyakov, F. R. Filippov, G. P. Zatevakhina, and others, confirms that among industrial workers the number of people receiving a 7-year, or a full, secondary education is steadily growing from year to year.

For example, of the large number of workers questioned in various departments (where different trades are needed), at the Urals Heavy Engineering Plant in 1958, from 20 to 37 per cent had a primary education, from 40 to 50 per cent from 5 to 7 years of education, and from 13 to 30 per cent a 7-year, or a full, secondary education. The dynamics of the growth of the general educational level of the workers at this plant shows (according to G. V. Mokronosov) that in the ten-year period 1950-1959 the numbers of workers with a 7-year education increased from 18·8 to 27·7 per cent, and with a full secondary, a secondary technical, or a higher education from 2·5 to 13·9 per cent. Consequently, the number of workers with a 7-year, incomplete secondary, full secondary, or secondary special education has increased from 25·5 to 53·6 per cent, i.e. it has about doubled in nine years.

Interesting data have been obtained by G. V. Mokronosov on the raising of the general education standard of new workers at the same plant (excluding new workers coming from industrial trade and

M

technical schools) in the period from 1950 to 1959 inclusively. The number with less than a 7-year education dropped from 71·5 to 34·2 per cent, with an education of 7 to 9 years increased from 26·5 to 43·7 per cent, and with a full secondary education rose from 2 to 22·1 per cent (more than 10 times). Thus, already in 1959, nearly two-thirds of the new workers had 7 to 9 years', or a full secondary education. The Urals Heavy Engineering Plant itself, called 'the father of factories' by Maxim Gorky, has become a personnel training centre, and a centre of education and culture. It has seven evening secondary schools for workers, evening and correspondence engineering technical schools, and an evening and a correspondence department of the Urals Polytechnical Institute. Each department has branches of industrial trades schools which offer a 7-year education. In the 1955-56 school year, 1,100 workers of the plant's personnel attended institutes or secondary special schools. Today, their number has risen to 1,800. In 1955-56, the plant's secondary schools for young workers had 200 students; today, they have more than 2,900. A total of 600 workers are taking courses preparing them for enrolment in an institute. As a result, nearly 70 per cent of the young people under 25 years of age already have at least a 7-year education. An engineering research institute was set up in 1959.

There are many factories like the Urals Heavy Engineering Plant. Similar educational activity is undertaken at other factories in Nizhniy Tagil and Pervouralsk. For example, at the Nizhniy Tagil Iron and Steel Works, which compared with the Urals Heavy Engineering Plant has many more unskilled transport and other auxiliary workers, the number of workers with an education of up to 6 years dropped, in the period 1952-1959, from 46·5 to 31·4 per cent, while the number of workers with a 7-9 years' education increased from 22·2 to 41·8 per cent, and the number with a full secondary education from 1·1 to 18·4 per cent.

A characteristic feature is that after attending a school for young workers (or a vocational school) and then a technical school, and even an institute, many of the workers continue to work in the factory departments, combining their engineering knowledge with extensive practical experience, and become worker-intellectuals. For example, in one of the communist work-teams at the large unit machine department of the Urals Heavy Engineering Plant, A. Khramtsov, leader of a team of gear-cutters, attended a technical school, and Y. Gondev, a Polytechnical Institute. Both continue to work as machine operators. Khramtsov is a deputy of the Supreme Soviet of the Soviet Union. A steelworker, named V. N. Lukyanov, who attended a school for young workers, continued his studies at the evening department of a technical school and, in 1956, was decorated with the title of Best Steelworker of the Soviet Union. He also is a deputy of the Supreme Soviet of the Soviet Union. G. K. Ogorodnikov, another steelworker, attended a vocational school, then went on to a school for young workers and the evening department of a Polytechnical Institute. He is now foreman of an open-hearth furnace department.

The rapid rise in the general educational standard of young workers is being accompanied, not very evenly it is true, by an influx of young people with a 7-year or a full secondary education.

Before its reorganization in 1959, a major shortcoming of the public education system was its partial isolation from practical work. The one-sided training given to young people in schools did not conform with the requirements of society in a period of rapid technical progress. Many older pupils left school before completing their education, took jobs in factories, and continued their education at evening schools.

A steadily growing number of secondary-school leavers are, on their own initiative and with the approval of their parents, taking jobs in factories. In Sverdlovsk Region, their number reached 8,000 in 1957, to over 12,000 in 1958, and to more than 11,000 in 1959. In Nizhniy Tagil, according to data obtained by F. R. Filippov, a little over 24 per cent of secondary-school leavers took jobs in industrial enterprises and studied at technical schools run by factories. In 1957, their number rose to over 57 per cent. Prior to the reorganization of the public education system, some of the town's leading secondary schools (Nos. 5, 9, and others) gained some experience in training their pupils for work in industry. They fitted out excellently equipped workshops, and their pupils had production training at the Iron and Steel Works and other factories. As a result, in Nizhniy Tagil, an increasing percentage of secondary-school leavers are taking jobs as skilled workers. Unfortunately, the pattern is not the same everywhere. The law on strengthening the link between the school and life (1958) opened up tremendous perspectives for raising the educational level of the rising generation and preparing it for productive labour.

A considerably larger number of young people are enrolling in schools for young workers. In Sverdlovsk Region, the enrolment in these schools was over four times bigger in the 1959-60 than in the 1955-56 school year. However, judging by the data for some factories, the wide opportunities for receiving a secondary education without discontinuing work are still being insufficiently utilized.

The encouragement given to young people to enrol in schools for young workers is uneven. At the Urals Heavy Engineering Plant, for example, in some departments most of the workers are studying, while in other departments a fairly large number are doing nothing to raise their level of education. In the large assembly department, of the 300 workers up to the age of 22, most have full secondary education or its equivalent at an evening school, and at present 131 are studying: 51 in institutes and technical schools, and 80 in schools for young workers. In the neighbouring forge and press department, the level of education of more than 80 per cent of the workers is below the 7-year standard, and until the autumn of 1959, most of them did not go to schools for young workers. One of the reasons for this was that these schools did not directly improve the workers' skill and did not have any effect on their wages. They did not attract the attention of young people as much as the schools for foremen, courses offering training in allied trades, and other forms of production-technical training.

The positive experience of combining general education with technical training at some schools for young workers in Sverdlovsk Region, which concentrate on specific trades and give their pupils a higher qualification side by side with a general education, ensures (as the data obtained by F. R. Filippov confirm) enrolment stability and efficiency in this form of training. Hardly any of the young people enrolling in these schools leave before completing the study programme. Their pupils acquire technical knowledge quickly, and considerably increase the labour productivity at factories.

Unfortunately, judging by the literature of recent years, hardly any estimates have been made in our country of the economic efficacy of the higher standard of education among workers, such as were made by Academician S. G. Strumilin. As long ago as 1924, he made a statistical analysis showing that the profit obtained from an increase in labour productivity exceeded the state's expenditures on school education 27·6 times, and that the investment made by the state is paid back within the first eighteen months. For approximately the next 35 years the state gets a clear profit from the increase of labour productivity of workers who had received a primary education, while the expenses on secondary education are repaid within seven years, after which a profit is received for approximately 30 years. In 1931, S. G. Strumilin showed that each rouble spent on tuition in a 7-year school raises the national income by a minimum of 6 roubles a year.[1]

A new, and now widespread, form of scientific and cultural education in people's universities of culture came into being in recent years. In Sverdlovsk Region, 72 of these universities, which attracted thousands of the most able workers, were opened in 1958-1959. At first they concentrated on literature and various aspects of the arts, and then established departments which have come to be known as people's universities of science and technology. In Sverdlovsk Region, in these departments, which run two-year courses, the students study science and technology, and the prospects for further scientific and technical development in connection with the practice of building communism.

Vocational-technical training at secondary schools and Labour Reserve schools (or trade schools) is playing an important role in training young workers. Already in 1959, according to data obtained by G. P. Zatevakhina, among the pupils of technical schools and factory trade schools in Sverdlovsk Regions 78·7 per cent had an education of 7 and more years, and 22·4 per cent a full secondary education. Within the next few years, in connection with the reorganization of the Labour Reserve system, most of the people going to vocational schools will have completed 8 years at a secondary school.

Vocational schools have begun training workers in new trades, such as automatic production line and machine setters, computer operators, workers with a wide range of skills, and workers skilled in several trades. This has made it necessary to lengthen the courses of study. The curricula of these schools now provide more hours for general subjects, and embrace new technology and advanced methods of work.

The thorough general educational and polytechnical training given at the 8-year school is to be augmented by sound vocational training, in which engineering and technical knowledge will occupy a steadily growing place. This will be a further step towards erasing the distinction between mental and physical work and will help to train a new type of worker, a worker-intellectual, for industrial enterprises.

PASSING ON THE EXPERIENCE OF OUTSTANDING WORKERS

The survey made at industrial enterprises of Sverdlovsk Region by D. T. Posdnyakov, L. N. Kogan, O. N. Zhemanov, and others shows that these enterprises are successful in teaching new technical developments. This is a very important aspect of raising the cultural and technical standard of workers. The nation-wide socialist emulation movement, aimed at speeding up mining, which was started in Sverdlovsk Region by N. Minzarilov and I. Pronichkin in 1947, made it possible gradually to increase mining speed in horizontal workings from 181 to 364 linear metres in the same working-time (1958). To a large extent this is due to the higher qualifications of miners, who have followed the lead given in the North Urals. They are successfully working at two or three trades, combining drilling with the removal of the ore, the laying of tracks, and so on.

At the Nizhniy Tagil Iron and Steel Works, the latest work methods have helped the teams led by Morozov, Sofronov, and Zashlyapin, of Open-Hearth Furnace Department No. 1, to obtain a stable yield of 10·7 tons of steel per square metre of furnace hearth. The spread of these and other methods of steel-making enabled the Sverdlovsk Region as a whole to produce 8·5 tons of steel per square metre of furnace hearth. Overall automation of open-hearth furnaces at the plant will make it possible to produce 15, and more, tons of steel per square metre of hearth.

Valuable initiative has been shown by the workers of the Urals Carriage-Building Plant. They recast many of the indices in the bonus system and made them dependent on the fulfilment, and overfulfilment, of the plan for reducing costs, provided that the plan of output in the prescribed range of items and the targets in labour productivity are achieved. The plant put its departments on a self-supporting basis, and drastically reduced the consumption of metal and other materials per unit of output. This experience has been adopted by other industrial enterprises.

The dissemination of advanced work methods is not the affair solely of economic bodies, engineers, and technicians. They become effective, and a powerful stimulant to technical progress and cultural and technical growth, when they are spread by the workers themselves. According to a questionnaire conducted at several enterprises in Sverdlovsk Region in 1958, 11 per cent of the workers questioned at the Nizhniy Tagil Iron and Steel Works, 31 per cent at the Urals Heavy Engineering Plant, and 77 per cent at the Sverdlovsk Instrument-Making Factory pass their experience on to other workers through individual or group arrangements, or through training schools that have been set up at the Urals Heavy Engineering Plant and other factories in the region. At these schools (departmental, factory, inter-factory, inter-district), workers demonstrate their improved work methods at the workbench (sometimes after introductory theoretical instruction by specialists). Formerly these were, as a rule, short-term schools, but now permanently functioning schools are becoming widespread (for example, the school for forge-operators at the Urals Heavy Engineering Plant, which studies advanced methods used in the Soviet Union and abroad). Patronage, a form of individual tuition of young workers by skilled workers, engineers, and technicians, as practised in Sverdlovsk Region, is likewise gaining popularity. This form of instruction was initiated in the spring of 1958 by V. D. Gagarin, a grinding-machine operator at the Sverdlovsk Instrument-Making Plant.

THE EMULATION MOVEMENT

Under present conditions, the emulation movement of communist work teams and shock workers is a new and higher stage of socialist emulation. It induces not only these, but also all other workers, continuously to raise their trade, educational, cultural, and technical standards, and teaches them to work, acquire knowledge, and live in a communist way. This movement has swept through all the industrial enterprises in Sverdlovsk Region. By 1960, more than 312,000 people joined the movement, aspiring to earn the title of communist work team or communist shock worker. The workers at 59 industrial enterprises entered into competition for the title of communist work enterprise. On the initiative of communist work teams, Sverdlovsk Region started a movement aimed at achieving the Seven-Year Plan output target in six years.

In the movement of communist work teams and communist shock workers, the raising of the cultural and technical standard of the workers has become a compulsory and important element. For example, in a team of boiler-assemblymen, led by A. Markin at the Urals Heavy Engineering Plant, six of the workers will complete their higher education by 1965, and four will complete their technical and full secondary education. At the same plant, in a communist work team of five workers headed by N. Tulenev, two are completing an engineering technical course and one is studying at an evening secondary school. The team has permanent contact with scientists of the Urals Polytechnical Institute, attends their lectures, uses their blue-prints to modernize equipment, and makes wide use of the scientific and technical knowledge they receive.

INVENTIONS AND IMPROVED METHODS OF WORK

Technical creative work by workers is a clear indication of the close link between a communist attitude to work and cultural and technical growth. In the nine-year period, 1950-1959, the number of production rationalizers and inventors in the Soviet Union more than trebled (from 555,000 to 2,000,000), and the number of applications for patents for inventions and improvements increased from 1,241,000 to 3,300,000. At the Pervouralsk Pipe Works, for example, the number of production rationalizers was one to every fifteen workers in 1950-1953, and one to every three workers in 1959.

A questionnaire conducted by D. T. Posdnyakov and L. N. Kogan at several industrial enterprises in Sverdlovsk Region shows that from 12 per cent (Verkhisetsk Works) to 27·7 per cent (Nizhniy Tagil Iron and Steel Works) of the workers had taken part in production improvements, and that most of them have made at least five or six improvement suggestions. The largest percentage of rationalization improvements come from skilled workers who have had a good general education and technical training.

One of the features of the movement of production rationalizers and inventors, which shows the development of comradely mutual assistance, is the fact that, in the majority of cases, production rationalizers and inventors come forward not alone, but as teams, resolving intricate problems of invention and production rationalization. At the Pervouralsk Pipe Works, for example, only 17 per cent of the inventors and rationalizers worked by themselves, while 83 per cent combined into teams. In 1959, major technical developments were started by 45 composite teams of rationalizers, consisting of workers, engineers, and technicians of various specialities. One of these developments was the introduction in the pipe construction industry of the '160', '200', and '140' automatically controlled pipe-rolling mills.

Young rationalizers' clubs and circles, set up on the initiative of the Young Communist League are playing an important role in promoting the movement for production improvements. In Sverdlovsk there is a regional young rationalizers' club, which regularly holds contests. In the second half of 1958, these contests drew more than 6,000 young workers, who made more than 9,000 rationalization suggestions that lead to a saving of 35 million roubles in a year.

At the Urals Carriage-Building Works and other industrial enterprises in Sverdlovsk Region almost all the large departments have voluntary designing groups and bureaux consisting of production innovators (workers, engineers, and technicians) who develop and introduce new technology. Many of the production innovators in Sverdlovsk Region have made important contributions to science. One of these is an electronic design for remote control for mining conveyors developed in 1958 by an electrician-fitter, A. I. Shapovalov. This work required a detailed study of the latest scientific and technical literature.

The co-operation between scientists and practical workers is inducing many workers to study. For example, the long-standing contact between the Department of the Metallurgy of Steel at the Urals Polytechnical Institute and the workers in the open-hearth furnace department of the Serov Iron and Steel Plant has given the leading workers of the plant an incentive to acquire knowledge. Zlobin, Popov, Nosov, Uralsky, Golovanov, Sokolov, and other workers of the open-hearth furnace department have, in the course of these years, taken a course at the correspondence department of the Polytechnical Institute.

Many leading workers in industrial enterprises in Sverdlovsk have written books, pamphlets, and articles on scientific and technical subjects. Among them is a handbook on gear-cutting by technologist V. T. Ponomarev, a former gear-cutting machine operator of the Urals Heavy Engineering Plant, and a book on the operation of turning lathes by L. N. Mekhontsev, a worker.

Scientists and industrial workers of Sverdlovsk Region are jointly resolving scientific and technical problems. With the co-operation of scientists from research institutes, production innovators of the Nizhniy Tagil Iron and Steel Works have developed a new design for the overall automation of the thermal régime of open-hearth furnaces. This design makes it possible to maintain the furnace's optimal thermal capacity during smelting, thus considerably stepping up its productivity. Scientists, engineers, and leading workers have jointly developed a new method of smelting steel in revolving furnaces, and experimental smelts at the Nizhniy Tagil Iron and Steel Works showed that such a furnace can be used for the production of a semi-finished product as well as finished steel.

A composite team, consisting of scientists from the Urals Polytechnical Institute and engineers and workers from the Verkhnepyshminsk Copper Electrolytic Works have worked out, and helped to introduce, a new method of producing and stabilizing powdered copper. This was a new development in chemistry and the heads of the team were awarded the Mendeleyev Prize, First Class. Co-operation between scientists and leading workers in production has also manifested itself in the setting up of communist work schools for communist work teams and shock workers. At these schools, organized at the Urals Heavy Engineering Plant and other factories, prominent scientists conduct courses of lectures on the latest developments in science and technology.

In Sverdlovsk Region scientists co-operate in preparing for Innovator's Day, on which leading workers explain and demonstrate new methods of work. Scientists of the Urals Polytechnical Institute have helped S. Y. Barin, a worker-innovator at the Urals Carriage-Building Plant, to work out the scientific development of his new method of lining and charging electric furnaces. This method made it possible to achieve an unprecedented exploitation of furnaces (10,000 instead of the usual 60-80 smeltings without repairs). These and numerous other examples of the development of scientific elements in the creative efforts of workers show clearly the growing community of interests between them and scientists, and the forms of co-operation between them that are leading to the abolition of the distinction between mental and physical work.

THE DEVELOPMENT OF COMMUNIST CONSCIOUSNESS AND ITS INFLUENCE ON THE CULTURAL AND TECHNICAL STANDARDS OF WORKERS

The facts accumulated by L. M. Arkhangelsky, V. A. Shandra, and other researchers, with the participation of B. S. Kruzhkov, a corresponding member of the Academy of Sciences of the Soviet Union, show that the rise in the cultural and technical standard of workers is organically linked up with the moulding and development of communist consciousness and morals, and with the struggle against survivals of the past.

The production activity of advanced workers and entire factory staffs is inseparable from their social and political activity. A striking example of this combination is given by the workers of Machine Department No. 29, at the Urals Heavy Engineering Plant, which has become a centre for the training of skilled workers for this, and for other, industrial enterprises. The plant has trained many fine workmen, who are active in public affairs. Veteran workers like A. M. Chugunov, who has time and again been elected a member of the Plant Party Committee, a member of the City Committee of the Communist Party, and a member of the Supreme Court of the Russian Federation, and who was a student at an evening university of Marxism-Leninism, have trained many of the plant's foremost workers, who are active in plant affairs. Every second worker in this department is studying, every third worker is a production innovator, and more than half of the machine operators have been given the highest qualification rating. Most of the workers in this department are active in the Party, the Young Communist League, the trade union, and other organizations at the works.

At the sheet-rolling department of the Verkhisetsk Factory, despite the fact that most of the equipment in the department is old, the shift headed by foreman S. S. Borikhin has made considerable progress in the past ten years, learned how to make many new grades of steel and produce many thousands of metres of rolled stock over and above plan. Following the example of other workers, the personnel of this shift realized the benefits of education and the number attending evening or correspondence schools more than trebled in ten years. The production successes of this shift are closely linked up with the workers' social and political activity. They helped to build a Young Pioneer summer camp and modernize the factory and settlement, are members of voluntary detachments which help in the maintenance of law and order, and engage in other voluntary public activity.

The force of public opinion and its influence on the cultural and technical standard of workers is growing at industrial enterprises. Criticism is levelled at workers who do nothing to improve their knowledge, who do not keep in step with technical progress and make no effort to raise their cultural and technical standards, thereby hindering advance. At the Serov Iron and Steel Plant, a blast-furnace gas watchman and State Prize winner, E. Fukalov, and other leading workers sharply criticized people who had formerly been outstanding but had failed to keep themselves abreast of progress in the smelting of pig-iron.

The experience of Party and public organizations at the Urals factories, surveyed by A. G. Davydov and L. D. Mitrofanov, shows that the cultural and technical standard of the workers and, consequently, the level of their labour productivity depend directly on a systematic acquisition of political and economic knowledge. In recent years, the study of economics has become widespread at industrial enterprises in Sverdlovsk Region. The technical-economics seminars, economics groups, and other forms of economics education in the departments of the Nizhniy Tagil Iron and Steel Works have given many hundreds of workers a grounding in economic science. Theoretical conferences on economic problems have been held at the plant. One took as its theme 'Production costs and ways of reducing them', preceded by a thorough study of the economic indices of the plant's work. Various organizational and technical improvements were recommended that have helped to reduce the number of rejects and have saved the plant 11,000,000 old roubles over and above plan.[2]

The passing on of the old traditions of the working class is playing a substantial role in the economic training of young workers. This is done, for example, through meetings with veteran workers. Veteran workers' councils are organized in factories (in Sverdlovsk Region they have more than 350,000 members). These pay particular attention to the individual needs of the young workers under their patronage, help them with lessons, arrange outings and other forms of recreation, and so on. Veteran workers, communists, and members of the Young Communist League concern themselves with the well-being of young workers and their behaviour at work and in the community.

Children's establishments, such as boarding-schools, play a big part in the upbringing of the rising generation. Every working man's family feels the concern of the Soviet Government for the upbringing of children, and for creating conditions suitable for the new generation of workers. L. M. Arkhangelsky and V. A. Shandra quote the example of a working couple, T. M. and D. D. Svechkin, who are leading workers at the Rubber Technical Goods Factory in Sverdlovsk. They have three small children and, thanks to assistance from the state, have achieved considerable success in raising their qualifications and cultural standard. D. D. Svechkin studied in the evening department of a technical school and has become a foreman. His wife is studying at a technical school. The state has given them a separate apartment and pays the major portion of the expenses for the care of their children, first of all in a boarding nursery and then in a kindergarten. The Svechkins together earn on average 210 roubles a month and pay 12 roubles a month for the upkeep of each child. This is not a burden on their budget. They have a television set and a radio in their home and give much attention to their children. After the working day had been shortened to seven hours, they were able to spend more time in study and reading.

This is only one of the many thousands of families in Sverdlovsk Region whose life shows that in the Land of Socialism the workers combine education with diverse cultural interests and personal happiness.

Workers actively oppose all manifestations of the old life and ideology that distract their fellows from the socialist way of life, from advanced methods of work, from education and culture. At their meetings and in the press, they criticize backward people who make no attempt to improve their qualifications, fail to study, or show idleness and laziness.

REFERENCE

1. S. G. Strumilin, *Problems of Labour Economy*, Moscow, 1957, pp. 163, 598.
2. See p. 36, note 22.

12

Trends towards the combination of intellectual and manual labour

A. N. MASLIN and G. V. OSIPOV

HISTORICAL BACKGROUND

The problem of combining brainwork and manual labour[1] exercised some of the finest minds of mankind as long ago as the eighteenth century. Saint-Simon, Fourier, Owen, Chernyshevsky, Pisarev, and many other thinkers tried to resolve it. They scathingly criticized the division of labour under capitalism and made remarkable predictions about the fusion of brainwork and manual labour in the future. Capitalist industry, as they rightly observed, is based on the separation of brainwork and manual labour. 'Factory industry', D. I. Pisarev wrote, 'rests on physics, chemistry, and mechanics, but the factory worker knows as little about these sciences and is able as little to apply their results as the steam-engine valve which the worker has to open and close. . . constantly. The worker turns out to be . . . a tool in the hands of the manufacturer who possesses material and intellectual capital. . . .'[2]

Although these progressive thinkers were unable to offer a scientifically substantiated programme for the abolition of the gap between brainwork and manual labour, they believed that this gap would inevitably be closed in the course of mankind's progress. 'Combine knowledge and labour, give knowledge to the people who will necessarily derive from it all the practical value it contains and you will see that the wealth of a country and its people will begin to multiply at an incredible speed.'[3] This was the conclusion drawn by Pisarev.

The problem of abolishing the separation of intellectual and manual labour and of effacing the distinctions between them has been scientifically elaborated in Marxism, based on a scientific materialistic analysis of specific phenomena of social life, the nature of, and tendencies in, the development of large-scale machine production.

'Modern industry', Marx wrote in *Capital*, 'never looks upon and treats the existing forms of a process as final. The technical basis of that industry is therefore revolutionary. . . . It is continually causing changes in the technical basis of production.'[4] Revolutionary changes in the technical basis lead to changes in production processes and in the functions of the workers, and thus inevitably bring about the technical prerequisites for changes in the division of labour. In other words, these changes prepared the technical conditions for the obliteration of the distinctions between intellectual and manual labour. The necessity arises, as Marx put it, 'to replace the detail-worker . . . the mere fragment of a man, by the fully developed individual'.[5] But standing in the way of this tendency, engendered by large-scale capitalist production, are the economic relations of capitalism with their inherent social and technical division of labour into intellectual and manual, and the conversion of the worker into 'a fragment of a man', or an appendage to the machine.

In addition to material and technical prerequisites, there are social conditions necessary for the accomplishment of this task. The revolutionary transformation of capitalism into socialism alone makes possible the overcoming of the separation of manual and intellectual labour. The record of history has shown that this task can be accomplished only in the course of development of the communist form of social organization, based on a socialist pattern of industrial relations and the highest level of science and technology, where labour is freed from all forms of exploitation. Even under communism, the accomplishment of this task is a long and intricate process which will pass through several consecutive stages.

THE TWO FORMS OF WORK UNDER DIFFERENT SOCIAL SYSTEMS

The separation of intellectual and manual labour was determined by the social development of labour and the rise of antagonistic classes. This separation in the slave system and in conditions where private property was dominant, gave rise to a class which was released from direct productive work. It assumed charge of such affairs of society as the management of production, the administration of the state, and of justice, science, and the arts.

As human society developed and passed from one antagonistic formation to another, this abyss between the two forms of labour was widened and deepened, reaching its most pronounced form under capitalism. Under conditions of capitalist production, the working class is denied full access to knowledge. It is unable to rise to the level of engineering and technical personnel and is engaged chiefly in manual labour.

The separation of the two forms of labour and the monopolization of intellectual work by the ruling classes has inflicted tremendous harm on the intellectual development of mankind and has tended to warp the individual personality. This division of labour into intellectual and manual is also expressed in the marked social inequality between manual and 'brain' workers.

The process of eliminating the separation of intellectual and manual labour was begun by the Great October Socialist Revolution. This separation was completely and finally eliminated only by the victory of socialism in the Soviet Union, when the abolition of the exploiting classes changed the structure of Soviet society, and relations of hostility between manual and brain workers disappeared. The working class and the peasantry became entirely new classes, previously unknown in history. A new, people's intelligentsia arose and developed. In the Soviet Union the interests of workers and peasants engaged in manual labour and the interests of intellectuals are not antithetical; on the contrary, they are closely identified. Equal opportunities for participating in all spheres of economic, political, and cultural life are provided for all members of society under socialism.

The social composition of intellectual workers is radically changing in a socialist society. Statistics show that, in socialist countries, people engaged in intellectual labour come chiefly from the ranks of the workers and peasants.[6] The differences in earnings of manual and brain workers have been considerably reduced. Before the revolution the difference in earnings in Russia was approximately 550-570 roubles a month (the monthly wage of a worker was 30 roubles and of a technical specialist 600 roubles); today the difference is 200 roubles on the average (100 and 300 roubles respectively). Even this disparity will disappear in the course of building communism.

Lastly, the most important consequence of combining manual and intellectual labour is the change in the nature and content of both. This can be illustrated by the nature and content of the work in a long-established industry such as steel smelting and in a comparatively new occupation such as that of a setter. Striking changes have occurred in the work of a steel smelter. In the past, many operations were done by hand and in smelting steel the worker relied on his intuitive knowledge of the process and on his keen vision. Now, as a result of mechanization and automation, functions associated with mental effort predominate in his work. According to data from the Ukrainian Metallurgical Research Institute, the working time of the steel smelter is divided as follows: analytical calculations, 3 per cent; preparatory operations, 7 per cent; control of the production process, 50 per cent; carrying on the technological process, 20 per cent; direct performance of labour operations, 15 per cent; keeping the production record, 5 per cent. All this shows that the steel worker must have today considerable scientific and technical knowledge.

As for the new occupations, for example that of setter, they offer at the present stage an example of the harmonious combination of intellectual and manual labour in the process of productive activity. The work of a setter, which is a leading trade in modern automated industrial production, is made up of the following components:

Table 1. Breakdown of the setter's work

Subdivisions of working time	Expenditure of working time as percentage of total time in shift
Setting up and readjustment of equipment	34·9
Grinding of tools	0·9
Size inspection	6·5
Repairing defects	4·7
Performance of processing operations	21·0
Inspection of operation of equipment	12·2
Instruction of machine-tool operators	1·1
Fetching jobs to be done and delivery of those completed	3·2
Obtaining tools from tool-store	4·4
Taking over and handing over of the shift	1·8
Unaccounted time	9·3

These figures indicate that 80·2 per cent of the working time of the setter now relates to control of the equipment, that is to the sphere of mental labour.

THE TWO FORMS OF WORK IN A COMMUNIST SOCIETY

Once the separation of intellectual and manual labour has been done away with, an advanced socialist society proceeds to the next stage, which is the effacing of essential distinctions between them. The solution of this problem is bound up with building the material and technical basis of communism, the development of a communist economy. It has profound social meaning, in that it signifies the final abolition of the old division of labour, in which the worker was tied to one, narrow, specialized trade. The emergence of the new division of labour presupposes people of versatile education who organically combine intellectual and manual labour.

Essential distinctions between intellectual and manual labour under socialism are social, cultural, and technical, as well as professional and functional. Of course, all these distinctions in the last analysis are social distinctions. Thus, we speak here separately of social distinctions as class distinctions. Social distinctions exist at the socialist stage of development of the communist socio-economic formation, because the level of development of the productive forces and the nature of the division of labour are such that classes are preserved. In these conditions distinct classes or groups of people hold a definite place and play a definite role in the system of production. There are, in the main, two groups of people in the system of social production: the group engaged in manual labour (workers and peasants) and the group engaged in intellectual labour (technical intelligentsia). In other spheres of social life (state administration, science, art, etc.) intellectual labour (labour of the intelligentsia) is characteristic; manual labour holds an insignificant place in these fields (chiefly service personnel, concerned with the cleaning of premises, transport, etc.). The different positions and roles in social life under socialism are marked by certain differences in earnings. Earnings of brain workers, especially those engaged in state administration, are to a certain extent higher than those of manual workers.

In an advanced communist society, social differences between individuals engaged in intellectual and manual labour will gradually disappear. This will come about through the development of production, a high level of technical progress, abundance of material and cultural necessities and comforts of life, and the transition from state administration to communist public self-government. There will no longer be separate groups of people engaged exclusively either in manual or in intellectual labour. Man's creative work will combine elements of intellectual and manual labour in rich and varied form.

Simultaneously with the abolition of social distinctions, differences will gradually disappear in the cultural and technical standards, which exist under socialism, both between the majority of the workers and the engineers and technicians, and between the collective farmers and the agronomists and livestock specialists. These differences are determined by the level of development of the productive forces. Technical progress

N

will require that the workers have ever greater engineering and technical knowledge. At the same time there will remain in use equipment which manual workers can operate without special knowledge.

In the course of building the material and technical basis of communism and the spread of overall mechanization and automation, jobs that involve manual work and do not require special engineering and technical knowledge will be greatly eliminated. At the same time, the importance of occupations associated with automated production will rise steadily. In the initial stages the number of workers tending automatic machines will also increase, along with an increase in the number of setters, maintenance men, and control-board operators. The extension of automation will, in future, make the work of the setter, maintenance man, and control-board operator more and more widespread. As technical progress advances, workers in these jobs will require greater engineering and technical knowledge. The worker in automated production in an advanced communist society will have become a new type of man, who will organically combine in his work intellectual and manual activity. Thus, the building-up of the material and technical basis of communism demands a continuous cultural and technical advance of the workers and, at the same time, creates the conditions necessary for this advance. Hence the unparalleled scale of training and retraining of personnel with a higher or specialized secondary education.

In 1959, there were in the Soviet Union, according to the population census, 3,778,000 people with a higher education (1·8 per cent of the population), 1,734,000 people with a partial higher education (0·81 per cent), and 7,830,000 people with a specialized secondary education. Altogether 6·4 per cent of the country's population had a higher, a partial higher, or a specialized secondary education (13,400,000). The proportions of these specialists in relation to the entire personnel in various branches of the economy were as follows: industry, 7·2 per cent; building, 5·2 per cent; transport and communications, 4·2 per cent; trade, 5·2 per cent; agriculture, 3·5 per cent.

The essential distinctions between intellectual and manual labour are also manifested in occupational differences, that is, differences in the content and nature of the work done. At the stage of socialism these distinctions are of an essential nature, inasmuch as different kinds of work are essentially dissimilar in both nature and content. Alongside the highly skilled work of the setter, for example, there is the hard monotonous work on the conveyor; the extent of manual labour is still great, particularly in agriculture. Moreover, a survey has shown that parallel with the main tendency towards a rise in the skill of workers, in some sections (for example, where assembly lines are introduced) the demand for skilled labour is lowered.

The elimination of occupational differences will proceed on the basis of the further extension of the automation of production, especially comprehensive automation, in the course of the steady building-up of the material and technical basis of communism. This will be evident, in particular, in the combination of the trades of setter and machine-tool operator, which was mentioned above. The harmonious combination of intellectual and manual activity in the job of the new type of worker, and, consequently, the abolition of the old division of labour with its characteristic narrow specialization will not imply, as stated earlier, that a variety of skills and types of work will no longer exist. The elimination of occupational differences must not be understood to mean that the worker of the future communist society will be able to specialize simultaneously in chemical production, in nuclear physics, electronics, engineering, and so on. He will be a man with a wide range of knowledge in allied sciences; a worker with a great technical and general knowledge, which enables him, when necessary, to change his job with minimum difficulty. In addition to his productive activity he will be able to join in artistic activities and take part in social affairs. The removal of the essential distinctions between intellectual and manual labour will thus signify the disappearance of one of the biggest sources of social inequality – a source, moreover, that cannot be abolished at once merely by the conversion of the means of production into public property, or by the expropriation of the capitalists.

FACTORS NECESSARY FOR THE COMBINATION OF THE TWO FORMS OF WORK

The effacing of essential distinctions between mental and manual labour has several interconnected aspects. First, it is necessary radically to alter the nature and content of both mental and manual labour. This, above all, necessitates the abolition of both arduous physical work (manual labour, on assembly lines) and monotonous mental work (the work of an accountant, bookkeeper, stenographer, etc.). Second, it is necessary to raise the cultural and technical level of the workers to that of engineers and technicians. Third, it is necessary to ensure such a sufficient growth of the productive forces to make it possible 'to distribute work among all members of society without exception, and thereby to limit the working day of each individual member to such an extent that all have enough free time left to take part in the general affairs of society, both theoretical and practical.'[7]

The transformation of industry and agriculture on the basis of extensive mechanization and automation is the material basis for solving these problems. Automation of production is an unprecedented means of increasing labour productivity. It has now become the objective basis for changing the character and content of labour, and for raising the cultural and technical level of all the working people to that of engineers and technicians. It has already been pointed out that as a result of the automation of steel-making, intellectual activity has begun to predominate in the work of the steel smelter.

A graphic example of the change in the content and nature of labour in the course of technical progress is also afforded by the extension in the functions of an automatic machine operator, during the period 1946-1959. In 1946, the functions of an operator of an automatic machine included: (*a*) knowledge of the methods of operating the automatic machine and of its design; (*b*) knowledge of machine-tool technology; (*c*) knowledge of the methods of sharpening ordinary cutting tools. By 1959, the scope of the operator of automatic machines had widened considerably. He had to have good knowledge of (*a*) the design of the automatic machines he operated and the principles for using the appliances for setting them up; (*b*) the designation and principles for using the main cutting tools and control and measuring instruments and also the principles for the sharpening of cutters and drills; (*c*) basic data on tolerances, accuracy of machining, etc.

These and similar examples show the rise in the level of knowledge of the workers in the course of building the material and technical basis of communism. It should be stressed that the acceleration of technical progress, the change-over to new kinds of goods, and the development of production are inseparably associated with the process of combining mental and manual labour in modern production. The introduction of new equipment and learning the techniques for the production of new goods introduce elements of creative endeavour in the work of the operator, bringing it closer to the work of the engineer or designer. For example, in order to machine the new shaft for the GAZ-150 motor vehicle, it was necessary to study the blueprints, to overcome faults in the course of practical trials, to set up the necessary machine-tools, to make a prototype, to work out the most rational sequence of operations in machining the shaft, etc. Consequently, in the first stage of learning the technology of production of this component, the work mainly involves the expenditure of mental energy; in the second stage, after learning the technology of production, the elements of mental activity are to a certain extent replaced by manual activity.

The above analysis is very important for understanding the basic tendencies in changing the nature and content of labour as society advances to communism. With each improvement in the material and technical basis of communism, part of the mass production of goods by established methods will be automated. The labour of the worker will be converted into the labour of an experimenter in research centres, laboratories, and experimental workshops. Production, while serving as an experimental basis for science, will become the material embodiment of science itself. Science is becoming a direct productive force in full measure.

EDUCATION AND TRAINING

The development of modern technology, and the elimination of occupational distinctions, as pointed out above, are inseparably bound up with the cultural and technical advance of all the working people. Trades, formerly based on little knowledge, will be replaced by specialisms requiring much knowledge and long technical training. In this steady growth of knowledge of all working people and the effacing of the essential distinctions between intellectual and manual labour, a big part is played by the polytechnization of the school in which the process of education is closely linked with productive labour. '. . . An ideal future society cannot be conceived without the combination of education and the productive labour of the younger generation: neither training and education without productive labour, nor productive labour without parallel training and education could be raised to the degree required by the present level of technology and the state of scientific knowledge. This thought was already expressed by the great utopians of the past. . . .'[8]

Much work has already been done, in the Soviet Union, to combine the education of the younger generation with productive labour. The Soviet educational system has set out, as its main task, the raising of a cultured, technically trained generation of members of communist society, capable of working competently in conditions of developing technology, and also of managing production and administering all the affairs of society.

It is important, in this respect, to overcome the disconnection between the general education and the vocational training both of the working population of young people. These aims will be achieved in the wide network of school and inter-school workshops, where pupils will gain technical knowledge and working skill, will learn about the management of production, and will take part in controlling the distribution and consumption of the social product they themselves produce. At the same time, in order to eliminate the differences in the technical and cultural level of a number of categories of the working people, and to raise sharply the cultural and technical level of all the working people, it is necessary considerably to extend the number of educational establishments, particularly evening institutes. The education of the working people in the fundamentals of social sciences, the humanities, and the arts must be ensured by the wide development of a network of correspondence and evening institutes, providing an education in economics, history, philosophy, and the arts.

THE INFLUENCE OF WORK ON THE WORKER'S PERSONALITY

The combination of intellectual and manual labour in the productive activity of man is most intimately connected with the all-round development of the personality. This is an intricate and complicated process, which begins with changes in social relations and in the nature of work itself. Work is the determining element and source of man's all-round development. If social production, the creation of material wealth and, consequently, the work of people form the basis of society's life, it follows that the all-round development and perfection of man in the process of work will bring the greatest benefit to society and to the individual. Work that is free from the fetters of exploitation is the prime and decisive condition for the spiritual enrichment of the personality. But it must be intelligent and creative, based on scientific and technical knowledge and on the principles of a high social consciousness.

What is needed for the development of the personality is such a change in the nature and content of work, which will combine harmoniously elements of manual work and of creative technical engineering and scientific labour in the work of man. The labour of the machine-setter is characteristic in this respect. The manual of skill ratings points out that a setter who operates gear-cutting and thread-milling machines must perform many calculations in setting up the machines (technical engineering and scientific labour); select and install gear changes (technical engineering and manual labour); determine the sequence of operations in machining the parts and select the cutting speeds and feeds (technical engineering labour); mount the parts which require combined clamping (manual labour), etc. All these elements of work, constituting an indissoluble whole, are woven into the system of labour of the machine setter.

One-sided and specialized employment, in which the worker, as Marx put it, was a fragment of a man, is converted into the labour of a man with a broad intellectual horizon who applies scientific and technical knowledge. The worker already acts as the vehicle of intellectual and manual labour in their unity. It is this that constitutes the basis, the corner-stone of the all-round development of the personality.

This, however, does not cover fully the concept of the all-round development of man. This concept also includes such aspects of man's life as the performance of the duties of a citizen, active participation in the affairs of society, and his moral, aesthetic, and physical development. Active participation in social life and high moral traits are major features of the fully developed man. Moral education during the period of the building of communist society is a primary, historically necessary element in the all-round development of man. Without moral wealth there can be no man of all-round development. The moral wealth of man is expressed above all in his conscious and practical devotion to the ideals of communism.

Society cannot advance to communism successfully without preparing morally all the people, every individual, for a life based on the principles of communism. A man of all-round development, a highly qualified worker, a politically conscious and active member of society who constantly advances culturally, technically, and artistically, must at the same time be brought up in the spirit of communism. Such a personality is moulded by our society's entire way of life. The school, as pointed out earlier, is of prime importance in educating the fully developed man. The role of the school in aesthetic education is growing considerably. In this respect a big part is to be played by amateur theatres, organized at a school or group of schools. Participation in their activities will be an important element in the upbringing of each pupil from an early age.

The Soviet intelligentsia and public organizations are doing much to help in the education and cultural and technical development of all working people. They make increasing use of the premises placed at their disposal by the state, of libraries, the cinema, radio and television to organize universities of culture, art, science and technology, and correspondence courses. Students of these universities will be able to undergo practical training in the laboratories of universities and institutes and also in special factory laboratories. Special examination commissions will be set up for them. In future, those who graduate from correspondence courses will receive diplomas.

The publication of textbooks and other literature will be of great help in self-tuition. Special television channels and radio programmes are assigned for lectures and advice for those who study at home for diplomas in secondary or higher education. All this will facilitate the accomplishment of a primary task connected with completing the construction of communist society, namely, to make all members of society cultured people with a wide education, and to raise their cultural and technical level.

The all-round development of man signifies the full realization of his abilities and gifts. In the era of building communism, man's abilities and gifts have every opportunity for development. The people are taking an increasing part in the improvement of production, in the management of the economy and the administration of state affairs, and in scientific and artistic endeavours. These are not matters of the remote future, but of the present. Many thousands of factory workers now organically combine in their work intellectual and manual activity, and are, in addition to their main occupation, active as musicians, poets, writers, painters, political leaders, etc. The life of V. A. Krupenin, a mechanic in Assembly Shop No. 4 of the Likhachov Automobile Plant, is a good example. After demobilization from the army in 1958, he came to work in the shop, where he soon began to fulfil the monthly plan by 170-180 per cent. At the same time, he continued his activities in the literary association which he had joined in 1948. Krupenin writes poetry and has already published some fifty poems. One of them, entitled 'We Coevals', won first prize in a competition arranged by the journal *Rossia* in 1960.

Creative work and diverse intellectual activities are becoming a natural requirement of the Soviet citizen. Here is what S. A. Antonov, a worker of the Likhachov Plant, says: 'I cannot work automatically, I always feel like improving the part or the method of machining it. Improvements originate in different ways; you ponder over some of them for a long time. It is difficult to get a designer to make a change. There was a case when my proposal was rejected time and again until I, on my own responsibility, worked it out. Only after prolonged testing did the designer agree to accept my idea. When you do something new, you are gripped by it and time passes unnoticed. You are still more elated when your idea succeeds, when a part is ready and you can show it. I could work more successfully on improving production if I had more knowledge. It would be good to organize groups consisting of workers and engineers who would concentrate on the same problem.'

More free time is a major prerequisite for the all-round development of the personality. The experience of socialist and communist construction in the Soviet Union and the People's Democracies shows how the reduction of the working day and the increase in the amount of free time facilitate the task of the all-round cultural development of the personality. More leisure provides the time for engaging, as Marx put it, in ennobling activities. Science, art, participation in artistic societies, advanced professional training, and active political work are all forms of man's activity in his leisure time, which play a big role, both in removing the specialized occupational limitation of the worker, and in promoting the all-round development of the member of the new communist society.

NOTES AND REFERENCES

1. The Russian words 'fizicheskii' (physical, manual) and 'umstvennyi' (intellectual, mental) when applied to work or labour are roughly equivalent to the manual and non-manual categories usually employed in Western sociology. The rather awkward expressions 'brainwork', 'mental labour' and 'intellectual labour' have been retained from the prepared translation into English partly in order to avoid the constant repetition of the word 'non-manual' and partly to ensure that the sense of the Russian original is retained.
2. D. I. Pisarev, *Works* Vol. II, Gospolitizdat, Moscow, 1955, p. 312.
3. ibid., p. 311.
4. Marx and Engels, *Collected Works*, 2nd edition, Vol. 23, pp. 497-8.
5. ibid., p. 499.
6. *From Socialism to Communism, a Handbook*, Moscow, 1962, p. 256.
7. Engels, *Anti-Dühring*, p. 272.
8. Lenin, *Collected Works*, Vol. 2, p. 472.

13

The elimination of vocational limitations in conditions of scientific and technical progress

L. N. KOGAN

INTRODUCTION

In the course of scientific and technical progress in the Soviet Union not only does the productivity of social labour rise and its character change, but also a new type of worker is formed. The old division of labour is ended, vocational limitations which hampered the wider development of the individual are removed, and full scope is given to the abilities and talents of the Soviet people. The elimination of the worker's vocational limitations, which were inherited from capitalism, proceeds in two closely connected ways. First, intellectual and physical labour is combined owing to changes in production, new wide-range occupations appear, and new skills are learned. Second, there has been a combination of productive occupations with public activities which people choose to undertake in their leisure time.

THE SOURCE OF VOCATIONAL LIMITATIONS

Vocational limitations were inherited from capitalism. One of the antagonistic contradictions of a society based on exploitation is the contradiction between the development of the material and of the animate elements of the productive forces. This contradiction inevitably leads to the perpetuation and further growth of vocational limitations. These limitations arise from the following main causes.

First, scientific and technical progress under capitalism inevitably widens the gap between intellectual and physical labour. In capitalist societies, of course, the development of science and technology may raise the skill of some workers who are involved in new techniques of production. It is possible for these workers to combine physical and intellectual work. At the same time, mechanization and automation in capitalist societies are bound to increase considerably the mass of unskilled workers, who are transformed into performers of partial, strictly limited operations at machines, acting as 'appendages' to machines or automatic installations. For instance, in West Germany the proportion of skilled workers in the total labour force dropped from 50·3 per cent in 1935 to 44·8 per cent in 1958.[1] In the United States, the proportion of skilled workers in the gainfully employed population as a whole has remained practically unchanged in the last 50 years (11·7 per cent in 1910 and 12·9 per cent in 1959).[2] According to the American sociologists E. Mann and L. Hoffman, wages up to 85 dollars a week were received on average by 29 per cent of the workers in non-automated power enterprises, as against 44 per cent in automated power enterprises.[3] The American sociologist G. B. Baldwin has admitted that a considerable reduction of skilled and semi-skilled trades is one of the chief consequences of automation.[4]

Second, in capitalist societies the ruling classes maintain a monopoly of education. The overwhelming majority of the working people have little hope of receiving a full secondary education, let alone higher education.

Third, under capitalism, workers in general have no opportunity of combining productive labour with participation in the management of state affairs. Management is preserved as a 'holy of holies', and working people are unable to take an active part in changing it.

Fourth, improvement of a worker's skill is, under capitalism, his personal affair, and there is no general state system for the improvement of the productive skill of the workers.

The capitalist relations of production hamper the tendency for occupations to change. On the one hand, 'the old system of the division of labour is thrown overboard by machinery', but, on the other hand, under capitalist relations of production, 'machinery is put to a wrong use, with the object of transforming the workman, from his very childhood, into a part of a detail-machine', as Karl Marx writes in *Capital*.[5]

THE ELIMINATION OF VOCATIONAL LIMITATIONS IN A SOCIALIST SOCIETY

Some bourgeois sociologists argue that the lowering of the skill of considerable groups of workers is an inevitable consequence of automation. These assertions are convincingly refuted by the experience of the socialist countries. Socialism alone is capable of ensuring a wide development of the productive forces, both animate and material. Technical progress is an indispensable condition for the development of the worker's personality. Social progress under communism ensures 'the all-round development of the abilities of all members of society through the removal of the old division of labour, through vocational education and changes of occupation . . .'.[6]

The elimination of the vestiges of the worker's vocational limitations arises mainly from (a) changes in the occupational composition of the labour force, (b) scientific and technical creative work, (c) the integration of occupations, and (d) a gradual realization of the free choice of occupation. Let us examine each of these in turn.

CHANGES IN THE OCCUPATIONAL COMPOSITION

Scientific and technical progress leads to changes in the occupational division of labour, which reflects both specialization of workers through a subdivision of different types of work, and the specialization of production itself. There is a differentiation of occupations from the point of view of the methods, skills, experience, and knowledge used in work. Vocational division of labour will exist under communism as well. The transition to communism is accompanied, not by the abolition of vocational division of labour, as some Soviet writers have suggested[7] but by changes in the content of the occupations and in the entire vocational structure. Two opposite trends now operate in society: on the one hand, technical progress gives rise to new occupations, and on the other, some of them die out or merge with others. It would be incorrect and narrow-minded to concentrate on either one of these tendencies.

V. I. Lenin wrote that '. . . specialization by its very nature is as infinite as technical developments'.[8] Science, technology, and the arts have developed to such an extent that a lifetime is insufficient for a man to become a perfect master of his trade. Their development at an unprecedented pace naturally leads to the narrowing down of special branches of knowledge. It is no longer possible to be a doctor or physicist 'in general'. People have to specialize in individual branches of medicine or physics. Before the Revolution, mining colleges trained engineers for only two professions. Today, the Sverdlovsk Mining Institute alone turns out specialists in almost forty fields.

Scientific and technical progress gives rise to new occupations.

Thirty years ago the mining industry did not have coal-combine operators, setters, electricians, scraper operators, etc. In the engineering industry, delivery truck drivers, electric crane operators, pyrometrists, specialists in automatic welding, automatic lathe operators, automatic lathe setters and so on, have recently appeared. The application of hydromechanization, a new method of coal-mining, has created such occupations as operators of hydromonitors, crushers, and coal pumps. Many new trades have appeared at atomic power stations or new chemical plants.

The number of workers learning these new trades is growing rapidly. According to the 1959 census, between 1939 and 1959, the total number of miners increased by 202 per cent, while that of drillers by 610 per cent. With a 213 per cent increase in employment in the metal industries, the biggest growth was among electric and gas welders (405 per cent) and electricians (294 per cent). In the building trades (total growth: 206 per cent), the number of excavator operators went up 14 times and of operators of road-building and building machines, 70 times.[9]

At the same time, some trades are gradually dying out. This was foreseen by the founders of Marxism-Leninism. 'A fine sort of socialism that would be, perpetuating the occupation of porters!' Engels wrote.[10] The planning of socialist production makes it possible to foresee the disappearance of some of the present widespread occupations. For instance, in the next five years the number of timbermen in the mines of the Middle Urals Economic Area will go down by 30 per cent and that of top cagers and signalmen by 50 per cent. At the same time, the number of fitters will increase by 35 per cent and that of crane operators and electricians by 30 per cent. In the Soviet Union as a whole, the trade of coal-cutting machine operators will disappear towards 1975 and that of pneumatic pick operators by 1970.[11]

Considerable groups of workers will soon have to change occupations. In a capitalist society, the dying-out of old trades increases unemployment and worsens the condition of most workers. The official report of the U.S. Congressional Subcommittee on Automation and Energy Resources mentions that, in 1958 alone, more than 3 million American workers were compelled to change their place of work 11·5 million times. As a result, two-thirds of these workers transferred to lower-paid and less skilled jobs. The authors of the report declare cynically that the dismissal of workers as a result of automation is an inevitable result of technical progress. They compare redundancy arising from automation with the 'liberation' of millions of horses as a result of the invention of the tractor.[12]

The situation in the socialist countries is entirely different. The Communist Party Programme sets, as one of the most important tasks of the transition from socialism to communism, the planned training and rational utilization of those workers who have been released from some sectors of production as a result of mechanization and automation, for work in other sectors. Usually these workers take up jobs involving greater skill, at the same enterprise. This transfer is beneficial to the workers because they no longer have to perform relatively unskilled heavy work. This is illustrated in *Table 1*, drawn up on the basis of data for the engineering plants of Sverdlovsk Region.[13]

Table 1. Occupational composition (in percentages)
(Engineering industry, Sverdlovsk Region)

	Automatic equipment	Semi-automatic equipment	Non-automatic equipment
Lathe operators	55·0	66·4	80·6
Setters	29·6	16·4	3·4
Fitters	13·8	9·3	7·4
Auxiliary workers	1·6	7·9	8·6
Total	100	100	100

The table shows that automation is accompanied by a considerable increase in the number of setters and fitters and a reduction in the number of operators and auxiliary workers. As automation develops the setters and fitters become the main figures in production. Their work is, as a rule, more skilled, interesting, and varied than the work of the operator. Whereas the latter has to overcome certain inadequacies in the design of the lathes and, above all, maintain direct control over the production process, the setter of automatic equipment has to be the real commander and master of a complex machine. As distinct from the operator, he must have a thorough knowledge of the design of the machine and of its operations. He has constantly to solve complicated technical problems demanding ingenuity and intellectual effort. A 6th-grade automatic lathe setter will not be able to perform his work efficiently if he does not know the fundamentals of mechanics, electrical engineering, electronics, applied and physical optics, telemechanics, and radio engineering.[14] This shows the breadth of the setter's occupational span, and the complexity of his duties. The researches conducted by V. F. Dolbyshev at the Likhachov Motor Works show that the introduction of automatic lathes increases the proportion of working time spent on processes which demand the combination of intellectual and physical labour by 11 to 64·2 per cent.[15] According to similar research done at the Pervouralsk Pipe Plant, such processes constitute up to 75 per cent of the working time of the operator of a semi-automatic rolling mill.

SCIENTIFIC AND TECHNICAL CREATIVE EFFORTS

The new occupations arising from scientific and technical progress not only demand more profound knowledge from the worker, but also stimulate scientific and technical creative efforts. There are workers operating machines who are ignorant of their design and of how to repair and set them. The new occupations arising in industry and agriculture demand, as a rule, that workers have a thorough knowledge of the mechanisms entrusted to them. Such a worker does not limit himself to operative functions alone; he no longer tries to overcome the deficiencies of the machine by his own effort, but becomes a director and organizer of production. Most new industrial and agricultural occupations demand that scientific knowledge be applied, which is one of the ways of turning science into a direct productive force. The February Plenary Meeting of the CPSU Central Committee (1964) set before the workers in agriculture the task of learning how to use chemical fertilizers and herbicides.

In practice, it is precisely those workers who are involved in the most modern techniques of production who constitite the majority of rationalizers, and their suggestions bring the most tangible economic benefits. An analysis of the composition of rationalizers working in shops No. 4 and No. 5 of the Pervouralsk Pipe Plant has revealed that rationalization suggestions are made by 50·5 per cent of the setters working there, 42·5 per cent of the electricians, and only 23·2 per cent of the operators. The average economic benefit resulting from one suggestion made by an electrician is 510 roubles, while that by an operator only 190 roubles. Similar results have been produced by the study of the composition of rationalizers in the section mill shop of the Nizhniy Tagil Iron and Steel Plant. Rationalization suggestions were submitted there by 23·8 per cent of the electricians and by only 1·5 per cent of the operators. More than 70 per cent of the 53,000 workers of Sverdlovsk Region who are members of the Soviet Society of Rationalizers are workers in highly skilled occupations.

Rationalization and invention are important means for the elimination of the vestiges of vocational limitation. In his creative endeavours a worker-rationalizer can extend the limits of his own occupation, broaden his technical outlook, and begin to tackle the problems of the organization of production.

The first occupations which die out in socialist enterprises are the ones which involve heavy physical labour, excessive nervous strain, or monotonous operations. The workers do not regret their departure, although, of course, the need to change one's occupation involves some difficulties: older workers may have to attend study courses.

Research at a number of enterprises in Sverdlovsk Region shows that the overwhelming majority of workers who have acquired new occupations connected with a high degree of mechanization are satisfied with them and have no intention of changing them for others. On the contrary, those whose occupations do not allow them to combine physical and intellectual labour feel dissatisfied and want to train themselves for new occupations.

Research carried out at enterprises in Sverdlovsk Region in 1962-63 shows that, as a rule, the higher the degree of mechanization of labour, the greater the number of workers who derive satisfaction from their work. At the Pervouralsk Pipe Plant 175 workers from 'A' shift of 'T-4' shop were questioned. Of these, 112 (64·1 per cent) were satisfied with their occupation, 19 (10·7 per cent) were not fully satisfied, and 44 (25·2 per cent) disliked their occupations. Of the latter, 9 were technical quality inspectors, and 17 were, for the most part, unskilled workers engaged in fairly heavy physical work.

At the Sverdlovsk Pharmaceutical Factory, only 60 (15·4 per cent) of the 389 workers in the basic shops did not like their occupations. Characteristically, in the central laboratory and the electrical department not a single worker wished to change his occupation. Forty fitters and setters were questioned, and only four, all of them young workers who had come to the factory recently, felt dissatisfied; while in the less mechanized refrigerator-compressor shop seven workers out of 32 would have liked to get new jobs. There were nine workers in the factory yard, and all of them disliked their occupation.

In January 1964, M. A. Sokolovsky, a post-graduate student of the Urals University, studied the occupational attitudes of the whole team of workers in the 2nd '140' rolling mill in the 1st shop of the Pervouralsk Pipe Plant. There were 153 people in the team. One-hundred and nine were operators, and 25 of them, i.e. almost one in four, felt dissatisfied. None of the 24 setters wanted a change. Eighteen out of the 19 electricians declared firmly that they liked their occupations, and only one man gave an evasive reply ('Yes and no'), explaining this by the over-growing complexity of his work.

It is indicative that the greater complexity of work with new equip-ment was mentioned by all the other electricians and mechanics, but they took a positive view of this, and regarded the more complicated work as more interesting. Characteristically, the majority of the workers who wished to change their occupations stressed that they liked work and realized its social necessity and usefulness. For instance, out of the 44 'A' shift workers of the 'T-4' shop who did not like their occupations, only one explained this by his dislike for physical work.

Only two of the 196 women workers in the sewing department of the Uralobuv Shoe Factory replied in the affirmative to the question: 'Would you like to live without working if you were fully maintained?' One of them was a 17-year-old girl who wanted to be a doctor; she would agree to live without working in order to study in a medical college. The other was a 23-year-old mother of a young child.

Those workers who wish to change their occupations express their hope in scientific and technical progress, in the social conditions of socialism, and for the gradual elimination of unskilled heavy work. It is interesting that nine out of the 14 workers of the fermentation depart-ment of the pharmaceutical factory who disliked their work wanted to study in technical schools and colleges in the same branch of science with which their present work was connected (chemistry), and seven of them were already studying.

Satisfaction with occupation reduces labour turnover. Research into the causes of the movement of 5,524 workers from one factory to another (18·7 per cent of the monthly labour turnover at the enterprises of the Middle Urals Economic Area in 1960), conducted by L. F. Pysin and Y. P. Rybakov, research workers in the economics faculty of the Urals University, showed that 13·4 per cent of them changed employment because of dissatisfaction with their occupations. A repeat investigation, conducted in 1962, showed that the number of workers changing jobs for this reason had dropped to 10·4 per cent.[16] In the most highly mechanized and automated enterprises the percentage was still smaller. For instance, at the Nizhniy Tagil Iron and Steel Combine the per-centage of those who left because they were dissatisfied with their occupation went down from 14·6 in 1960 to 7·4 in 1962; at the Urals Heavy Machinery Plant, from 19·6 to 12; at the Urals Electrical Apparatus Plant, from 10 to 4·2; at the Middle Urals Copper Refinery in Revda, from 12·9 to 2·7.[17] At the same time, at the Urals Shoe Factory,

o

which is slow to mechanize, the percentage grew from 3 in 1960 to 16·4 in 1962.

These data show how scientific and technical progress influences the workers' attitude to occupations and leads to an increase in the number of people who derive satisfaction from their work. Changes in the occupational composition of the labour force resulting from scientific and technical progress under socialism are connected with a broadening of occupations and with the growth of the interest of the workers in their occupations.

INTEGRATION OF OCCUPATIONS

The combination of occupations, which is widely practised in socialist enterprises, is one of the ways which will lead to the complete elimination of workers' vocational limitations and to the free choice of occupations most suitable to their inclinations and desires. It considerably lightens work; a combination of operations which differ in character involves different groups of muscles, makes work more varied, and is therefore less tiring than the constant repetition of the same operations. It demands more knowledge and new skills, and thus raises the cultural and technical standards of the workers. In addition, the learning of a new occupation with a wider range gives the worker a better idea of the production process as a whole. It gives him a more intelligent approach towards rationalization, and towards the fuller use of productive resources. The broadening of his occupational span makes it easier for him to learn new techniques, and to understand his part in the complex system of production. Not every combination of trades and not every change of occupation is of benefit to the worker. The combination of several unskilled operations is of little advantage.

FORMS OF INTEGRATION OF OCCUPATION

Integration of occupations in socialist enterprises takes several forms:

(a) The combination of a number of closely related trades into one broad occupation. This arises from scientific and technical progress. For example, the introduction of new, multi-position metal-working machine-tools performing several operations (drilling, boring, milling) makes it necessary for the operator to combine the functions of a driller, a borer, and a miller. Several allied trades are also combined by an automatic equipment setter, who has to work as a fitter, an electrician, and a specialist in electronics and telemechanics. The number of such broad occupations is growing constantly in our country.

(*b*) Integration of several occupations by a member of a composite team. This form has arisen from a better organization of labour. In a composite team every worker can perform several trades and can replace a team-mate. The establishment of such teams has eliminated time wastage and makes labour more collective. For example, at the Bulanash 2-5 mine of the Yegorshin Coal Administration composite teams have existed since 1957. Ten old trades have been combined into one, called a 'face worker', who can act as a cutter, getter, timber-hauler, driller, prop-remover, and roof-setter. The team leader allots to members of the team different jobs in the course of the working day. Composite teams are widespread in the building industry. The team of Hero of Socialist Labour Y. A. Popov (the Urals Aluminium Refinery Building Administration in Kamensk-Uralsky) has six sections. Every member of the team works in one of the six sections but is able to perform two or three trades and can, when necessary, work in some other section.

(*c*) The acquisition of several related skills. For example, following the initiative of three workers at the Pervouralsk Pipe Plant, L. A. Koshkarov, M. V. Nikitin, and N. V. Khlebnikov, thousands of rolling mill operators of the Urals iron and steel industry are also learning to be fitters. When something in the mill goes wrong they do not wait for the fitter on duty but do all the necessary repairs themselves. All these forms of integration of occupations are closely connected with each other. At present only closely related trades are combined, as a rule, but the limits of integration are broadening.

Instruction in related skills is one of the most important factors of the entire system of vocational training at socialist enterprises. Figures for the industries of the Middle Urals Economic Area[18] are set out in *Table 2*.

Table 2. Retraining of workers in the Middle Urals Economic Area

Year	Total number of workers who raised their skill	Number of workers who have learnt allied skills
1957	112,915	9,624
1958	126,524	14,018
1959	147,004	18,219
1960	193,643	24,020
1961	218,147	29,521
1962	226,204	39,165
1963	267,977	39,103

In 1957, workers who had learnt a second and allied skill constituted only 8·5 per cent of the number of workers who were given production training, but in 1963, they had risen to 14·2 per cent. The number of workers learning allied skills is growing in every enterprise. In 1957, the number of workers who were taught a second skill at the Nizhniy Tagil Iron and Steel Combine was 943, and in 1963, 1,789. In enterprises with a high level of mechanization, the majority of workers have already mastered some allied skills. For example, they include 61 per cent of the total number of workers in the section rolling mill of the Nizhniy Tagil Iron and Steel Combine, and three-quarters of all workers at the Sverdlovsk Pharmaceutical Factory, which is a communist labour enterprise.

Integration of trades not only enriches the knowledge and raises the skill of the workers, but also makes the work more attractive. Teams, in which very worker can perform a team-mate's job and can replace him, offer greater possibilities for the exchange of experience, and for the organization of mutual assistance and instruction. Such teams are, as a rule, more closely knit, and are able to put into practice the principle of the moral code of communism: 'each for all, and all for each'. Integration of occupations thus becomes the most important form of turning work into a prime need for everyone.

FREEDOM OF CHOICE OF OCCUPATION

The changes in the vocational composition of the working class in the Soviet Union show that the time is not far off when every man will have a free choice of occupation. Already the choice of occupation in our country is free from national, religious, and racial qualifications, and property, status, and other obstacles to entry, such as exist in a capitalist society. Racial discrimination exists, for example, in the United States. According to United States official statistics, Negroes make up 10 per cent of the labour force, but only 3·9 per cent of the number of persons engaged in intellectual labour; they form 4·1 per cent of the number of works' superintendents and foremen, but 69·8 per cent of domestic servants; 11·5 per cent of skilled workers, but 25·9 per cent of unskilled labourers.[19] All such obstacles have been removed in the socialist countries, where a person may follow any occupation of his choice provided he is trained for it. This means that there is still a certain limiting influence on the choice of occupation by people who have an inadequate general or special training. At the Nizhniy Tagil Iron and

Steel Combine 212 jobs were provided for workers having at least an incomplete secondary education and 43 for those who have finished secondary or specialized secondary schools. Only a man who has a good general and special education is really free in the choice of occupation. It should be noted that people whose inadequate education prevents them from entering certain jobs have unlimited opportunities to raise their educational and vocational standards.

Free choice of occupation is also hampered in our country by the high degree of specialization of vocational training in some branches of production and by the comparatively narrow range of knowledge and skill needed for a particular occupation. Standardization of machinery and installations will in the near future eliminate this limitation as well. Industry, and especially agriculture, still retain quite a few processes involving heavy non-mechanized labour or work which may be injurious to health. The worker's physical condition may, in such cases, limit his choice of trade: women and physically weak men cannot be employed on certain jobs. These limitations will disappear with the elimination of such heavy work and with the introduction of remote control of processes which are detrimental to health.

Finally, choice of occupation greatly depends on the vocational training of secondary school pupils. The introduction of polytechnical education has certainly played a positive role. Some schools, however, substitute for polytechnical education a narrow vocational training without due regard for the abilities and inclinations of the pupils. M. Solodov from Bashkiria wanted to be a radio technician. He built his own wireless sets, and studied technical literature. In his school, however, all pupils were taught to drive tractors. 'And what about those who want to become lorry drivers, radio technicians, combine-harvester operators?' the boy asked in a letter to *Komsomolskaya Pravda*.[20]

All these factors which limit the free choice of occupation will disappear under communism, when the choice will be determined by a man's personal inclinations, with due regard for the interests of society. Under socialism, the social need for the development of a particular trade is met primarily by the provision of personal material incentives. Occupations which are in demand or which involve heavy labour are more highly paid; some categories of worker have a shorter working day (6 hours), or receive special meals. The social interest is also secured by the high degree of social consciousness of Soviet people. For example, patriotic young people respond to the appeal by the Young Communist League to take up occupations as farm machinery operators, cattle-breeders, or builders. Under communism, the material incentives to the choice of occupation will die out, and the social interest will be secured by the high degree of social consciousness of every citizen, and also by public control over the appraisal made by an individual of his own abilities (as we know, not everyone imagining himself to be an actor or writer really has the necessary talent). In the choice of occupation, public and personal interests will coincide and maximum account will be taken of personal inclinations and endowments. Every occupation will become creative and everyone will be able to find satisfaction in his work.

THE COMBINATION OF AN OCCUPATION WITH VOLUNTARY PUBLIC WORK

Elimination of vocational limitations in socialist enterprises is being effected not only through the integration of occupations, but also by means of combining a productive occupation with voluntary public work. This combination is a new phenomenon which has not yet been adequately dealt with in our literature.

Public forms of workers' participation in managing production have become widespread in recent times. At the end of 1963, Sverdlovsk Region alone had 1,463 voluntary design offices (14,263 people), 1,427 economic analysis bureaux and groups (12,355 people), 494 technical information bureaux (3,343 people), 348 voluntary rate-setting and organization of labour bureaux (6,820 people), 248 institutes and research groups (5,537 people). Workers make up from 50 to 73 per cent of the members of these public organizations. A lathe operator may be at the same time a designer or an economist. There is also a vast contingent of workers acting as propagandists and lecturers, heads of amateur art and sports clubs, members of voluntary comrades' courts, and so on. More and more people are performing public activities, which indicates not only the growth of the moral incentives to labour, but also the broadening of the occupational range of the Soviet worker. Some of the duties arising from public activities are performed in working hours, but most public work is done in leisure time. Every year, more and more workers take part in educational activities. They conduct classes for training workers in improved techniques and methods of production, and train apprentices assigned to them. Last but not least, service in elective public office plays an important role in broadening the occupational interests of workers. Participation in the work of Soviets and of Party, Komsomol, and trade union bodies develops in the worker a statesmanlike approach to the solution of production problems and broadens his political outlook.

In addition to performing a public office, a conscientious Soviet worker devotes part of his leisure to some useful hobby. Many of our workers are at the same time amateur actors, artists, poets, philologists, historians, journalists, and radio operators. Thus, elimination of vocational limitations takes place both in work and in leisure. The main role is played, naturally, by the changing character of work due to scientific and technical progress. Elimination of vocational limitations in the course of man's productive activities is the main prerequisite for his harmonious development. This is an objective condition which makes possible the elimination of vocational limitations. A subjective factor, primarily the education of the worker, makes this possibility a reality. Communist education not only pursues the aim of urging the worker to study, and to learn allied skills. It also considerably broadens his outlook, and is an important and necessary factor for the thorough development of the individual. The necessary conditions for the elimination of the vestiges of the old division of labour are created by the working people of our country themselves under the guidance of the Communist Party. Workers in socialist enterprises, by the promotion of technical progress, and by the perfection of techniques and processes of production, accelerate the elimination of vocational limitations and bring nearer the time when every worker will have an absolutely free choice of occupation.

NOTES AND REFERENCES

1. *The Structure of the Working Class of the Capitalist Countries*, Peace and Socialism Publishing House, Prague, 1962, p. 88.
2. *Ekonomicheskaya Gazeta*, No. 12, p. 28.
3. E. Mann and L. Hoffman, *Automation and the Worker*, New York, 1960, p. 28.
4. G. B. Baldwin, *Automation and the Skills of the Labour Force in Improving the Work Skills of the Nation*, 1955, p. 93.
5. K. Marx and F. Engels, *Collected Works*, Vol. 23, p. 433.
6. K. Marx and F. Engels, *Collected Works*, Vol. 4, p. 336.
7. See the discussion on this question in the journal, *Voprosy Filosofii* in 1962-1963.
8. V. I. Lenin, *Collected Works*, 4th edition, Vol. 1, p. 84.
9. *U.S.S.R. National Economy in* 1960, Gosstatizdat, 1961, pp. 29-30.
10. K. Marx and F. Engels, *Collected Works*, Vol. 20, p. 206.
11. *Ekonomicheskaya Gazeta*, 27 November 1961, No. 17, p. 9.
12. *New Views on Automation*, Papers submitted to the Subcommittee on Atuomation and Energy Resources, Joint Economic Committee, Congress of the United States, 86th Congress, 2nd Session, Washington, 1960, pp. 20 and 54.

13. V. V. Breyev and M. D. Nelyubin, *Automation of Processes and Workers' Skills under Socialism*, Sverdlovsk, 1961, p. 23.

14. *Unified Manual of Tariffs and Qualification Standards, Related Trades*, Moscow, Gostoptekhizdat, 1959.

15. V. F. Dolbyshev, Technical Progress and Working Time, in *Technical Progress and Problems of Labour during the Transition to Communism*, Moscow, 1962, p. 110.

16. *Works of the Economic Research Laboratory*, 1st issue, Sverdlovsk, 1963, p. 20.

17. ibid., p. 22.

18. See p. 244, note 1.

19. Calculated on the basis of figures contained in the magazine *Amerika*, No. 29, p. 27.

20. *Komsomolskaya Pravda*, 21 February 1964.

14

Main problems of raising workers' skills under conditions of intensive technical progress

A. I. KATSENELINBOIGEN

OCCUPATIONAL STRUCTURE

There are still some old technical equipment and processes remaining in modern Soviet industry, and this has resulted in the existence of a great variety of occupations and degrees of skill. Nevertheless, two major groups may be distinguished: workers who are engaged in mechanized processes and operating machines and equipment, and those in manual work.

Table 1 was drawn up on the basis of data furnished by some enterprises from different industries in the Urals,[1] and it shows that workers engaged in mechanized labour are in a majority.[2] This is quite natural for advanced enterprises, and reflects the high degree of the mechanization of processes which has been achieved in our country.[3] At the same time, the proportion of workers engaged in manual work is still quite large.

In many branches of production, the problem of the all-round mechanization of jobs has not been solved yet. This applies chiefly to auxiliary jobs, in which about half the workers are engaged; in building construction, about 60 per cent of the workers are still engaged in manual work.[4] One may see from *Table 1* that from a third to a half of the workers at the enterprises of key industries of the Urals perform manual work.

In an analysis of large-scale machine industry, Marx stressed that, at a certain stage of its development, large-scale industry got into a technical contradiction (*Wiederstreit*) to its handicraft and manufacturing basis.[5] The later historical development resulted in the manufacture of machines being carried out chiefly by machines. However, this contradiction between the product of labour and the means of manufacture of this product has not been fully overcome. It finds its expression in the fact that there still are some remnants of manufacturing labour in modern industry.

Table 1. Level of mechanization in some enterprises in Sverdlovsk Region
(in percentages)

Type of work	Enterprises						
	Ural Machine building Plant	Ural Turbine and Motor Plant	Krasno-gorsk Central Power and Heating Plant	Middle Ural Thermal Power Plant	Nizhniy Tagil Steel Plant	Ural Alu-minium Plant	Polev-skoy Cryolite Plant
I. Workers engaged in manual labour including:	33·0	36·0	46·0	42·0	46·0	35·0	44·0
(a) assembly work	3·6	2·0	—	—	—	—	—
(b) transport and handling of materials	8·1	7·0	17·0	12·2	18·9	10·4	21·0
(c) equipment repair and overhaul	8·0	9·0	23·0	24·0	19·0	15·0	13·0
II. Workers engaged in mechanized labour	67·0	64·0	54·0	58·0	54·0	65·0	56·0

Let us examine the work of those workers who are engaged directly in changing the shape or substance of the object of labour on which they are working. The basic thing, which was decisive during the transition to the manufacturing division of labour, is the changes in technology. This means the choice of a new principle on which to carry out the technological process, since the other technical elements underwent relatively small changes. The implements of labour became more specialized in conformity with the requirements of the new technology. The principle of the differentiation of operations and job specialization replaced the principle of concentration of all operations on one work bench.[6] The changes in technical resources that attended these processes created the prerequisites for a new qualitative advance in the development of production mechanization.

The specialization of jobs increased the productivity and, at the same time, reduced the need for skilled labour. In the pre-war years, and particularly during the war and first post-war years, as the scale of output of homogeneous products increased, a number of industries went over to mass production on conveyor lines. Operations were broken down to correspond to the given flow of production, and a lower level of skill was required. Industry developed at a very rapid rate and some of the operations could not be mechanized. The breaking down of operations, along with improved productivity of labour, provided an opportunity to bring in new workers whose training took relatively little time. This was quite important, since at that time there was a shortage of workers with a high level of general education and training. Since the steady growth of industry in the Soviet Union was attended by an increase in the number of workers, it was the new workers who were employed mostly on the jobs that involved work broken down into manual operations. The skilled workers were employed on other jobs where they were badly needed.

It should be borne in mind that the subdivision of the technological process should not be in all cases identified with the division of labour among the workers. The subdivision of operations and the performance by one worker of a particular operation in the course of one shift leads in many cases to greater fatigue and lower output. The experience of the Moscow Electric Lamp Factory shows that, if a worker has mastered several trades, his or her cultural and technical level becomes higher and at the same time the work is less fatiguing and output increases.[7]

When the worker combines the performance of various operations, his functions may be of varying complexity. Although such combination involves an incomplete utilization of the worker's high skill in one of these operations, it has, nevertheless, proved to be beneficial and useful. If such combination of functions brings about a general rise of labour productivity, then we may consider the combination of jobs of varying difficulty to be a rational practice.

Thus, for instance, at the Nizhniy Tagil Steel Plant, in Sverdlovsk Region, there is a worker named Yedovin who does outstanding work at the rail and girder finishing shop. When the rolled rail, girder, and channel bars arrive at the shop, Yedovin does the job of assistant rolling-mill operator; when square or round stock is handled, he works as a flame cutter or press-cutter operator. At the 'Ekspluatatsionnaya' Pit of the Vysokovsk Mines, advanced workers obtain good results when working at the coal face because they have mastered the trades of both coal-cutting operators and timbermen.

The combination of trades brings positive results, of course, if it is based on rational organization of labour. When workers are shifted from one operation to another because of bad organization or are untrained for the new job, their performance of different kinds of jobs will not yield the desired results in higher productivity or in improvement of skill. A study of conveyor lines with a relatively low level of automation at a number of Ural enterprises, including the Chelyabinsk Tractor Plant and the Ural Automobile Plant, has shown that such useless shifting of workers from operation to operation is one of the most serious causes of lower output.

Improved management on the conveyor lines and the allotting of each operation to specific workers have resulted in a considerable increase in output mainly as a result of the productivity of labour. Thus, in the piston ring section of the Ural Automobile Plant, output increased by 68 per cent as a result of a 40 per cent increase in labour productivity.[8]

The extent to which it is possible to subdivide manual operations depends on the volume of mass production. In a number of manufacturing industries where the output cannot be mass-produced in uniform products, the technical processes are much less subdivided. The more complicated the product, the more knowledge and skill the worker needs to have. For example, much more knowledge and skill is required of a radio-set assembly worker than of the worker who assembles ball-bearings, since the two products differ in complexity of design. Technical progress, which also includes the improvement of the quality of the product, with the technological processes and means of labour basically unchanged and the product (or a part of it) more complex, gives rise to an improvement in the workers' skill.

The job of the worker who deals with complicated manual processes is of a contradictory nature. On the one hand, such a worker must have considerable experience, skill, and knowledge while, on the other, his work still involves both considerable physical effort and a number of operations of rather low productivity.

In future, with the steady development of a general mechanization and automation of production on the basis of improved designs, materials, and technology, this contradiction in the nature of manual work in the production of complicated products will be resolved. The constant growth of production, which arises from the very essence of a socialist economic system, increases the need for more workers and greater skill. In the Soviet Union, the change in the nature of the labour of workers who perform partial operations is ensured, in particular, by the fact that they are able to perform them intelligently and are not forced to perform such partial operations for the rest of their lives.

MECHANIZATION AND AUTOMATION: EFFECTS
ON WORKERS' SKILL

In conditions of planned development, all the opportunities exist for the complex mechanization and automation of all jobs, within a relatively short period of time. Complex mechanization and automation will serve to wipe out the contradiction between the development of large-scale machine industry and the remnants of unmechanized labour with little automation. It will also serve as a foundation for a steady rise in the cultural and technical levels of all the workers.

Thus, in the erection of the '650' rolling mill at the Nizhniy Tagil Steel Plant all loading and unloading jobs, usually done by simple manual labour, have been almost fully mechanized. The project was serviced daily by as many as 100 lorry drivers and 100 crane operators. It was at this plant that steel smelting was started in the first rotary furnace in our country. The thermal cycle in the coking batteries and air heaters in the blast-furnace shop are regulated by automatic controls, and there is a complex automation of the controls of two open-hearth furnaces.

Mechanization and automation are steadily raising the technical level of production. It is interesting to note that, in the last ten years, the number of blacksmiths and strikers engaged in manual work has come down by 28·6 per cent, that of navvies digging earth and clay by 72·6 per cent, and of lumbermen working at manual labour by 82 per cent.[9] It should not be forgotten however, that in our industry, in August 1959, some 47 per cent of the workers were engaged in manual work (according to Central Statistical Board data). The current seven-year-plan period will see the solution of the problem of mechanizing comprehensively all labour-consuming production processes. Thus, in the coal industry all-round mechanization and automation of mining will relieve 130,000 workers engaged in manual labour. In building construction, the transition to industrial methods and to all-round mechanization and automation will relieve, for example, over 133,000 navvies and over 100,000 loaders, making a total of about a million workers who are now engaged in manual work.[10] In the Sverdlovsk Region, in the course of a year, the work of over 165,000 workers has been lightened and about 20,000 men have been relieved of hard, labour-consuming operations.

The rise in labour productivity, accompanied by a considerable easing of the work, provides the opportunity both for increasing the output of goods and for fixing shorter working hours.

What are the changes that mechanization introduces in the level of the workers' skill? As compared with manual labour, with the introduction of machines less skill is required, since the machine itself provides the precision, ease, and rate of performance which could not be attained by the most skilled workers. At the same time, the machine still calls for considerable experience in manual work necessary to perform successfully the remaining manual operations.

The machine makes new demands on the workers: the worker must know its construction in order to be able to adjust it and to do the essential repairs and maintenance. In order to work on a machine in conformity with a fixed technology, it is essential to carry out the feed, stopping, discharge, control, adjustment, and maintenance operations. Raising the productivity of labour depends very much on whether the operator is able to perform all these operations and to repair the machine in case of breakdown without outside aid.

At present, however, in most cases these functions are distributed among the operators who do the feeding operations, supervise the work of the machine, etc., the workers who adjust the machine (the setters), and repair workers. At a certain stage of production development there is a definite sense in this distribution of functions, which follows from the very essence of specialization: by specializing in a specific type of work the worker can master it quicker and better. It should, however, be borne in mind that these jobs vary in complexity and call for the employment of workers of various levels of training. In other words, the very nature of breaking down the processes is objectively conditioned by the workers' skill.

The knowledge and skills required of an operator are fairly elementary and simple, whereas a machine-setter must be higher qualified to be able to restore malfunctioning equipment to good working order. The cultural and technical level of setters and repair workers is incomparably higher than that of the workers who perform the individual technological operations, since these workers must have, apart from a certain skill, a fundamental knowledge of the design of the whole machine.

In the conditions where operations are subdivided between the above three groups of workers, most of them are machine operators. The more complicated the machine used for performing the given jobs, the higher is the skill of the operator who does them. Thus, the mechanization of transport workers' jobs, involving quite complicated equipment, makes the machine operators raise the level of their skill.

The shortage of skilled personnel, due to a lack of training time and facilities, made the breaking up of operations between operators, machine-setters, and repair workers a necessity. When the number of workers on the permanent staff is stabilized and their cultural and technical level has risen, opportunity occurs to revise this subdivision of jobs in many respects, even if the kind of mechanization remains the same. The practice among skilled workers has shown that the worker who combines the functions of operator and machine-setter has a higher productivity of labour, even if only for the simple reason that, in case of a breakdown, time is not wasted waiting for a machine-setter.

An investigation conducted by the author at the roller shop of the Sverdlovsk Bearing Factory has shown that the machine-tools were operated mostly by workers who were both operators and setters. Out of 43 operators, the proportion of those who fulfilled their work quota, in the course of each of the months April to June 1958, by as much as 250 per cent, was 97·6, 92·9, and 95·5 per cent, respectively. Those operators who had also taken upon themselves the functions of machine-setter showed a constant high output. Thus, V. Nesterov performed his output quota for these months, which was identical with that of the other operators, by 272, 284, and 334 per cent. and N. Yelokhin did the same by 320, 283, and 297 per cent. If we bear in mind that the quota for an operator working with a setter and that for an operator who also performs the functions of setter are identical, it becomes quite evident that those workers who combined both functions obtained much better output results and made much better use of the equipment at less labour expenditure.

The experience gained at the Yaroslavl Motor Works, Volgograd Tractor Plant, Rostov Farm Machinery Plant, State Ball Bearing Plant No. 2, 'Krasnyi Oktyabr' Confectionery Factory, and numerous other enterprises, also shows the desirability of one worker combining the jobs of operator and machine-setter. The cultural and technical level of workers who are able to perform independently the functions of operator and setter is and will be higher, of course, than that of workers who work as operators only. It is only natural that the workers' cultural and technical level will rise, chiefly because they are relieved of all kinds of manual operations by automation.

However, in the cases when there are no possibilities of introducing such mechanization and automation, a good way to raise the cultural and technical level of the workers is to combine various functions in their work.

Automation brings about steady progressive changes in the process of labour. To give an accurate answer to the question of how automation affects the workers' skill, it is necessary first to choose an adequate basis for comparison. Comparison should first be drawn on the assumption that the other elements of production (design of the products, materials, technology, design of machines) remain unchanged, with the same volume of work in conformity with a particular type of production (mass, serial, or individual). The comparison should cover all the workers (strictly speaking, all personnel who are engaged in the enterprise, including the engineering and technical staff).

With automatic equipment the worker is relieved of the need to perform the standardized, simple manual functions of operating the machine, since the movements of the tools and products during machining is fully automated. The more complicated nature of the machines that arises from automation makes new and increased demands on his knowledge. The setting and repair of such complicated equipment calls for particularly extensive knowledge. The worker's job becomes more interesting.

A distinction should be made between the absolute and relative changes in the worker's skills for separate occupations and as a whole, in comparison with the level of these skills prior to automation. This may be illustrated by the work of semi-automatic machines which are extensively used at the Sverdlovsk Bearing Plant, Chelyabinsk Tractor Plant, and other enterprises. The equipment of this kind has not yet been fully automated. These semi-automatic machines still have to be periodically fed, the machining operations have to be supervised and checked, and so on. The number of manual operations involved for each machine is insufficient to occupy the operator for the whole of the shift, and the usual practice is to have one worker to operate several of these machines at a time. It is possible for some workers to carry out the less skilled operations of feeding the machines and controlling them, while others perform the more complicated tasks as setters. Such a subdivision of operations is practised when the production process involves many semi-automatic machines and it has proved to be fully justified.

The more complicated equipment with automation calls for considerable knowledge and experience on the part of the setter. The level of skill of operators who perform the simplest operations seems at first sight to differ but little from that of the workers who operate non-automated equipment. This is not quite true. In operating semi-automatic machines, a little less experience is needed, but the complicated nature of the equipment places higher demands on the knowledge of the worker: an operator must have some knowledge of the design of semi-automatic machines, and must be able to operate several of them at a time. Thus, the worker acquires the elements of controlling the production process.

The skill of an operator who works on several semi-automatic machines does not, on the whole, differ markedly from that of the machine operator who works on non-automated equipment, but the former has the important advantage of having a knowledge of more complicated equipment and of being able to operate several machines at a time.

Meanwhile, practice shows that these changes in the functions of the workers who are transferred to operate automated equipment do not always occur. In some enterprises it is wrongly assumed that an operator needs to be trained in only a narrow range of operations. The additional requirements that such an operator has to meet are often ignored. When new workers have to be rapidly drawn into production and there is no pre-trained personnel, the functions of an operator may be performed by a worker who has been doing the simple job of feeding the machines, checking the part against a standardized instrument, etc. But such a worker, having inadequate knowledge of the equipment and experience in operating several machines, works with a great deal of waste, reduces the output of the equipment, and is quite helpless if the machine breaks down or some other emergency arises.

With the introduction of automatic machines, which differ from semi-automatic ones in that the feed and discharge operations are performed with the aid of special devices, the division of labour between workers changes, because there is less reason for the operator's and setter's jobs to be done by different people, since the amount of operation work has been considerably reduced.

Thus, with the existing level of automation, in which a certain number of ordinary workers are still employed, there remains a division of labour between the operators and the machine-setters. Moreover, as production becomes automated, the role played by machine-setters becomes increasingly important. According to the author's calculations, the ratio of the number of machine-setters to that of operators (in conditions of long-run production) is as follows. When the equipment is not automated it is from 1:12 to 1:15; when the equipment is partly automated, 1:8, when working on semi-automatic machines, 1:2 to 1:3; and with automatic equipment, 1:2 to 1:1. With fully automatic flow lines, where the operator's functions are performed to a still greater extent by automatic devices, this ratio becomes 1:6 to 16:1. There are already some automatic lines which, owing to the extremely small amount of operator's work, are fully operated by setters alone.

P

We have confined ourselves to examining two groups of workers, machine operators and machine-setters. Though this simplifies to a certain degree the analysis of the problem under examination, it is quite feasible in practice, since the introduction of some automatic machines makes very little change in the workers' cultural and technical level. With complete automation and its introduction on a large scale, an ever larger group of workers is involved. In this case, for a full comparison, it is essential to include in the analysis all the groups of workers connected with the production process.

Practice has shown that with all-round automation the tasks which are eliminated first are the comparatively simple manual operations (those involved in handling the articles during the manufacturing process, distributing and checking the products, etc.), which call for relatively low skill on the part of the workers. When the performance of all these jobs passes over to automatic machines, other conditions being equal, a relatively larger number of skilled repair personnel is required for their operation.

Thus, the all-round automation of the '160' and '220' rolling mills at the Pervouralsk New Pipe Plant brought about a sharp reduction in the number of semi-skilled workers and, at the same time, an increase in the number of maintenance personnel (fitters, electricians, etc.). In many cases, the latter were enlisted from among the workers engaged in the basic operations. This called for a considerable improvement of their skill. As a rule, the '220' rolling mill used to be operated in the post-war years mainly by workers with 3 to 5 years of general education, whereas now, after it has been automated, the workers operating it have had 7 to 10 years of secondary education. At the same time, many of the workers in the more skilled occupations have already acquired a secondary technical education and are now studying at institutes. For example, technicians Alexandrov and Danilov work as senior rolling-mill operators. Operators Sychov, Shititsin, and Malezhin are correspondence students at the Urals Polytechnical Institute.[11]

When automation merely involves the installation of automatic devices on the equipment and does not result in a marked increase of equipment efficiency, the gross number of skilled workers engaged in setting and repairing the equipment increases, and the gross number of less skilled workers (operators, etc.) becomes smaller. The skill of machine-setters and repair workers is raised because the equipment has become more complicated. When, however, automation is attended by considerable fundamental changes in all or some elements of the equipment, it may happen in some cases that the machine-setters and repair workers do not have to be so very highly skilled, since the technique has become so simple that the addition of automatic devices does not affect the simplification of the technology as a whole.

The absolute number of workers required for the same volume of work to be carried out always diminishes under the progressive development of automation because the output capacities of equipment increase sharply (for example, the introduction of engineer L. N. Koshkin's automatic rotary lines). When the introduction of automation leads to an absolute reduction of the number of workers required for carrying out an equal amount of work, i.e. there is a growth of labour productivity, it becomes possible continuously and rapidly to increase production and shorten working hours. In a society where there is a constant increase in production and decrease in working hours, the changes that take place in the skill of the workers associated with automation are necessarily connected with a continuously increasing demand for skilled personnel.

With extensive automation, a machine-setter must be capable of dealing with various automatic devices. Increased demands are made on his skill and objective prerequisites exist for a considerable rise in his cultural and technical levels. On one of the automatic lines installed at a plant in Sverdlovsk Region, the same worker does the job of setting the milling, boring, and drilling machines, whereas formerly each of these machines was operated by a separate worker in the particular trade.

The extension of all-round automation leads to the entire process of manufacture of a given product gradually becoming fully automatic. The setter who deals with fully automatic equipment must be a master of various operations, such as cutting, milling, grinding, heat treatment, etc. Thus, in many branches of industry the divided technological processes are being replaced by all-round automation, based on a concentration of operations, accompanied by a rise in the level of workers' skill and by the elimination of their narrow trade limitations.

THE COMBINATION OF PHYSICAL AND MENTAL WORK

With the present level of the development of automation, the workers will be performing, to an increasing degree, the functions of controlling the production process and repairing the automatic equipment. When we speak of someone as an 'experienced steel smelter', or 'skilled electric locomotive driver', we usually imply by the word 'experienced' that the given person possesses extensive knowledge and skill which permit him to take the most adequate decision when working conditions suddenly change. Now, with electronic computers, it is possible to reach a stage at which the entire production process is controlled automatically in the best possible way. This means that there will be a steadily increasing demand for specialists who are able to control the precise operation of an automatic machine.

An electronic computer has been installed at the rail and girder shop of the Nizhniy Tagil Steel Plant for an '800' rolling mill. The computer controls one of the most labour-consuming processes, that of regulating the space between the rollers in the process of shingling. The introduction of this automatic device has fundamentally changed the required cultural and technical standards of the workers involved. An investigation has shown that, in the past, the operational jobs in the mill were done mostly by workers with 7 to 8 years of education. Now the electronic computer is operated by I. Merkulov, who has a secondary technical education, and S. Bogdanov, who is a correspondence student. The four electricians who are connected with operating the computer also have a secondary technical education, and some of them are continuing their studies.

The current seven-year plan will see a 4·5 to 4·7-fold increase in the output of computing machines, and this will make possible the continuous all-round automation of production processes. At the same time, it will lead to a further rise in the workers' cultural and technical standards. Taking into consideration the actual prospects of technical progress, we may say confidently that in the 10-15 years to come, as mechanization and automation of production continue to expand, the need for skilled machine-setting and repair personnel will steadily increase. They will have to possess extensive knowledge to understand production techniques; at the same time, these workers will have acquired the experience essential for manual setting and repair jobs involved.

This type of worker, who organically combines mental and physical work, will become more and more characteristic of our industry. It has been stressed repeatedly in Soviet literature that, with the development of automation, there will be constantly rising demands for higher standards in workers' knowledge. This, naturally, is important. At the same time it is often forgotten that, with the development of automation, the worker's physical labour will still remain as an important factor which is essential for performing a wide range of jobs involved in the setting and repair of machinery. The very nature of this physical labour will change. A disregard of the role of physical labour in the course of the development of automation may lead to wrong conclusions, to an underestimation of physical work and of the role of the workers' skill and experience.

In the development of modern production there emerges a contradiction between the degree of the mechanization and automation of technological processes and the manual repair of machinery and equipment. With automation, when the equipment becomes more complex, the volume of repair work increases. This increase sometimes becomes so great that it may 'eat up' the entire savings obtained by automation (for example many hydro-electric power stations controlled by automation). The worker who carries out the repair work must be highly qualified, sometimes as highly as an engineer. On the other hand, repair work is chiefly done by hand with the simplest kind of tools. A rise in the stability of the performance of machines which are fitted with automatic devices presents a basis for resolving the contradiction. This will provide for a rise in the productivity of labour and at the same time for change in the nature of the labour of workers, who will no longer have to perform the labour-consuming manual work involved in the setting and repair of machines. In this connection, the creation of synthetic materials, with much longer service life, is of paramount importance. On the other hand, since a certain amount of repair work will have to be performed anyway, it is essential that this work should be reduced, as far as possible, to a rapid replacement of worn units by those which have been prepared in advance, and that the repair personnel's job should be made easier by means of mechanical aids.

Developments in engineering pose the objective demand that the very character of the work performed should be changed, and with this that the worker's trade should be altered. General polytechnical knowledge makes it possible for the worker to move rapidly from one field of activity to another. Workers are transferred from one production branch to another in a planned way. In planning technical progress and personnel training, a socialist society is able to move workers from one sphere to another without great effort and expense. The improvement of technology presents an objective material foundation, which requires of the workers extensive polytechnical training, which in turn, makes possible the rapid acquisition of special knowledge and skill essential for movement to another job.

TRAINING OF PERSONNEL

The introduction of new equipment, by means of mechanization and automation, calls forth a certain conflict between the more complicated machines, which call for higher-skilled workers, and the level of training of the available personnel. It is a contradiction arising from growth, which reflects the ongoing, progressive development of a socialist society. An analysis of the conflict helps to resolve it. The steady improvement of the system of training skilled workers is an important task in this direction. The conflict between the new, complex machines and their rapid development and the lag in the cultural and technical level of large groups of workers can be resolved by improved training. The disparity is, to a certain degree, aggravated by the incorrect employment of workers with a high cultural and technical level, which may be observed in some cases.

Workers who have a full secondary education, as well as those who are continuing their studies at young workers' secondary schools, part-time and correspondence technical schools often possess more knowledge than is essential for manual work or the operation of the simplest kind of equipment. An investigation of a large number of enterprises, conducted by the Sverdlovsk Economic Council in 1958, has shown that the workers who had a full secondary education were mostly employed in skilled work. At the Serov Steel Plant, the Pervouralsk New Pipe Plant, and other plants and factories, the school-leavers, after being given the relevant course of training, were employed as electricians, electric-crane operators, etc.

A high general-educational training permits those who have received it to do the most skilled jobs. Meanwhile, there are some enterprises that employ the workers with the higher educational level on lower-skilled jobs and, vice versa, men with a low level of culture and knowledge, who are thus incapable of showing initiative and creative abilities in their work, on the more responsible jobs.

The recruitment of workers into the various fields of training, the very increasing employment of young people with secondary education, and the constant replacement of highly skilled workers create the very important task of the mass promotion to more complicated jobs of those workers who have raised their general educational, industrial, and technical standards.

CONCLUSIONS

Technical progress leads to a situation in which, in the near future, every employed person will be able to combine physical labour with mental work, and to work on highly efficient equipment which calls for constantly greater skill. Extensive introduction of highly efficient machines, with mechanization and automation, is the chief solution for this problem. The automation of machines and equipment makes the man who does the job of setting and repairing the machines the predominant type of worker in the shop. He must have a high level of knowledge and skill in order to ensure the maximum operation of his machine. The operation of different types of equipment puts still higher demands upon the cultural and technical standards of the workers. They attain the standard of the engineering and technical staff in the extent of their knowledge. The introduction of automatic machine systems will be accompanied by the elimination of manual operations and by the ever-increasing importance of mental work.

The all-round improvement of equipment, the use of effective kinds of products and synthetic materials made by chemical and biochemical methods will make possible the realization of highly efficient and stable processes. Today, there exist some highly automated enterprises that cover the entire production cycle of a particular product. In the same way, in future, there will be an automatic system of machines that will integrate the entire process of producing all the goods that man needs. Unified automatic systems already exist in embryonic form. For example, thanks to the high level of automation of each production process, remote-control, and electronic computers, the mining, transporting, and refining of oil, and the manufacture of the resulting products, have been gradually united into an integral system.

The setting-up of integrated automatic machine systems based on the intensive development of all aspects of technology will raise the cultural and technical level of the workers and do away with inefficient manual labour in setting and repairing the equipment. This will open up before every employed person still wider horizons of creative endeavour.

NOTES AND REFERENCES

1. These data have been calculated by the author from the records of the Sverdlovsk Statistical Board.

2. The data for the census of the occupational structure refer to 5 May 1954. Since then there has been a further growth in the proportion of workers engaged in mechanized labour. The data in the table are approximate, though sufficiently accurate for the analysis.

3. The proportion of workers engaged in mechanized labour for industry as a whole, according to calculations made by Ya. B. Kvash, is 37.9 per cent, i.e. much lower than that at the Ural plants. See Ya. B. Kvash, *Statistical Studies of Labour Mechanization*, Moscow, 1959, p. 123. This may be explained by the fact that the data refer to the more advanced and better mechanized enterprises among the Ural plants.

4. The Nizhniy Tagil Coke-Chemistry plant has not been included.

5. K. Marx, *Capital*, Vol. 1, p. 389, 1955.

6. This question has been considered at length in relation to manual work because similar processes are also involved in the initial forms of mechanized labour, though with particular features. Without repeating at this point later discussion, it should be noted that with the introduction of differentiation of operation in place of concentrated, mechanized, technological processes there was a reduction in the need for a high level of skill and knowledge on the part of the worker.

7. See D. Kaidalov, The building up of communism and the problem of man's all-round development in labour, *Kommunist*, No. 10, 1958, pp. 13-14.

8. *Vestnik Mashinostroenia* (Bulletin of Mechanical Engineering) No. 7, 1955, p. 83.

9. *Pravda*, 8 August 1960.

10. ibid.

11. Reported by Rakhnovsky at a theoretical conference at the Pervouralsk New Pipe Plant, December 1958.

15

An analysis of systems of vocational training in industry[1]

M. KH. LIBERMAN and V. V. PETROV

GENERAL FEATURES OF VOCATIONAL TRAINING: TRAINING OF NEW WORKERS

In the Soviet Union the vocational training of workers has the following main features. First, there is close co-operation and mutual assistance between engineers, technicians, scientists, and workers. Second, the equipping of the workers with professional knowledge and skill is directed by engineers, technicians, and veteran workers, organized on a national scale and planned by state bodies. All the expenses of providing vocational training are borne by the state. Third, it includes the training of people to become fully conscious, harmoniously developed, and educated workers in a communist society. Fourth, there are unlimited possibilities for workers to move from the lowest stage of study to the highest, from vocational training in a narrow field to a broad one, and to the mastery of the elements of engineering and technical knowledge. Fifth, vocational training is intended to raise the general educational level of the worker, to stimulate his efforts to continue his education and to add to his knowledge.

New workers are trained through individual and team study at factories, and also at vocational and general, secondary, polytechnical schools. At present, about 75 per cent of new workers are trained within the factory itself and approximately 25 per cent at vocational schools (see *Table 1*).

A total of 8,800,000 people improved their skills and received a vocational training at factories, in 1959. In 1958, in the Sverdlovsk Economic Area, more than 47,000 skilled workers were trained on the job and 18,000 at Labour Reserve schools; the following year saw 49,460 new workers trained in production (see *Tables 2* and *3*).

The number of workers trained at the enterprises now controlled by

Table 1. Training and refresher courses for manual and white-collar workers at factories and offices ('000)

Training or course	1940	Annual average for five-year period			1957	1958	1959
		1941-1945	1946-1950	1951-1955			
Training of new personnel							
Total (manual and white-collar)	1,950	2,672	2,673	2,790	2,618	2,761·0	2,860·4
Manual workers alone	1,606	2,261	2,261	2,480	2,457	2,604·5	2,702·8
Refresher courses:							
Total (manual and white-collar)	1,655	2,556	4,459	4,907	5,203	5,596·3	5,966·4
Manual workers alone	1,472	1,851	3,228	3446	4,074	4,438·8	4,643·5

Source: *U.S.S.R. in Figures. Statistical Returns*, Gospolitizdat, Moscow, 1958 p. 333, and *National Economy of the U.S.S.R. in 1959*, Moscow, 1960, p. 626.

Table 2. Workers trained in the Sverdlovsk Region

	1957	1958	1959
	Total		
Total number trained	45,965	47,769	49,460
1. By individual training	27,922	30,046	32,454
2. By team training	10,732	9,868	10,668
3. At schools and courses			
(a) full-time study	2,993	3,541 ⎫	6,338
(b) after working hours	4,318	4,314 ⎭	

These figures are taken from 'Statistical Reports for Branch Administrations' prepared for the Sverdlovsk Region as a whole by K. A. Vishnyakova, an economist in the Labour and Wages Department.

Table 3. Training of new workers in the Sverdlovsk Region

	1950	1955	1957	1958	1959
	1950=100 per cent				
Total number of new workers trained	100	110	105·6	108·8	112·8

the Sverdlovsk Region rose from 41,804 in 1950 to 49,460 in 1959. There has been a particularly marked growth in the number of workers trained for building enterprises: from 5,040 in 1950 to 8,354 in 1959. At factories, training is combined with actual production, thus saving society a tremendous amount of labour and means required for full-time study. The system of team and individual apprenticeship in production accelerates the training of large numbers of skilled workers. Instruction is given by highly qualified workers and foremen who pass on their experience and knowledge to a great number of new workers. In the Sverdlovsk Economic Area alone more than 14,000 people act annually as industrial training instructors.

In the system of individual and team training, there is a tendency towards individual apprenticeship, in which a new worker is apprenticed to a skilled worker. This is becoming one of the basic forms of training new skilled workers. At the largest enterprises in the Sverdlovsk Economic Area new workers were trained mainly through individual apprenticeship (see *Table 4*).

The choice of the form of training for new workers depends on the character of the production involved, its structure, and the system of the organization of labour. For example, the team method predominates in the fuel, ferrous and non-ferrous metals, and building industries, because in these industries the team is a basic production unit. New workers are assigned to teams where they get a composite training. Here the keynote is mutual training (e.g. a boring-machine operator trains a cutter operator and vice versa). The system of training new workers on building projects has also changed. Workers study a number of related trades under a special programme. For example, a mason learns the trade of plasterer, and a plasterer those of paper-hanger and painter. On the other hand, individual training predominates in other industries.

Although both individual and team apprenticeships solve the problem of training skilled workers rapidly, which is of great importance to the state, they have a number of shortcomings that considerably weaken their advantages. The prime pedagogical principle of progressing from the simple to the complex, or from the easy to the difficult, makes it possible for the pupil to master knowledge consciously and thoroughly and to acquire the necessary skill. As a rule, this principle is not observed in team and individual training, because all the practical work is done under the supervision of an instructor during the latter's working hours and in the course of his normal work. Such training is subordinated to the normal production sequence which is determined by technology. Naturally, this interferes with the necessary system of training, because

Table 4. Training workers directly at factories in the Sverdlovsk Region

		1950						1956					
		Training of new personnel				Further training		Training of new personnel				Further training	
		Total		By individual apprenticeship				Total		By individual apprenticeship			
	Factory	N	%	N	%	N	%	N	%	N	%	N	%
1	2	3	4	5	6	7	8	9	10	11	12	13	14
1.	Urals Engineering Works	1,627	100	1,627	100	9,505	100	1,102	67·7	1,102	100·0	7,110	74·8
2.	Urals Electrical Apparatus Works	159	100	159	100	497	100	551	346·5	551	100·0	802	161·4
3.	Urals Footwear Factory	183	100	183	100	441	100	144	78·7	144	100·0	712	161·5
4.	Yegorshin Coal Trust	462	100	—	—	580	100	528	114·3	—	—	683	117·7
5.	Urals Chemical Machine-building Works	371	100	371	100	770	100	399	107·5	399	100·0	1,736	225·4
6.	Vakhrushev Coal Trust	681	100	—	—	871	100	682	100·1	—	—	951	109·2
7.	Sinarsk Pipe Works	242	100	120	49·5	1,664	100	228	94·2	136	59·6	1,323	79·5

(Table 4 continued).

		1958						1959					
		Training of new personnel				Further training		Training of new personnel				Further training	
		Total		By individual apprenticeship				Total		By individual apprenticeship			
	Factory	N	%	N	%	N	%	N	%	N	%	N	%
1	2	15	16	17	18	19	20	21	22	23	24	25	26
1.	Urals Engineering Works	1,664	102·2	1,664	100·0	9,436	99·3	1,587	97·5	1,587	100·0	10,950	115·0
2.	Urals Electrical Apparatus Works	644	405·0	664	100·0	1,147	230·8	510	320·0	328	64·0	2,214	446·0
3.	Urals Footwear Factory	169	92·3	169	100·0	669	158·5	267	145·0	267	100·0	483	109·5
4.	Yegorshin Coal Trust	560	121·2	47	8·3	841	145·0	525	113·5	124	23·6	608	105·0
5.	Urals Chemical Machine-building Works	319	85·0	319	100·0	2,105	273·3	429	115·7	429	100·0	2,007	209·0
6.	Vakhrushev Coal Trust	817	120·0	284	34·7	1,421	163·1	458	67·4	202	44·1	1,230	141·0
7.	Sinarsk Pipe Works	253	104·5	162	64·0	1,123	67·5	212	87·6	115	54·2	1,505	90·5

These statistics have been taken from the reports of enterprises in the Sverdlovsk Region. The figures are given as percentages of 1950. The proportion of individual training is given as a percentage of the given year.

the apprentice frequently does much more complicated work than he is called upon to do after he has completed his training. Another weak point in individual training is that the theoretical knowledge received by the apprentice is manifestly inadequate.

To a considerable extent, these shortcomings can be avoided by a proper organization of training. In this respect the experience of the Urals Heavy Tube Construction Trust of Sverdlovsk is relevant. There, young workers (apprentices) are formed into separate teams under the supervision of experienced instructors. They decide on the work to be done by each team, in accordance with the principle of proceeding from the simple to the complex, or from easy to difficult operations. Theoretical training proceeds simultaneously with production training. At each stage of production training, the apprentices study the appropriate section of the programme of the technology and organization of production.

At the Urals Carriage-building Works, personnel are trained in many trades simultaneously. Throughout the period of training, new workers are attached to the Technical Training Department, and receive state grants. The training programme conforms with the long-term personnel requirements of the various departments. Newly employed workers are given the opportunity of getting to know the plant, their department, and the nature of their future trade. Industrial and theoretical training is conducted in classes and production workshops under the supervision of experienced workers. The cardinal pedagogical principle calling for a system and proper sequence is observed. When necessary, the management extends the study workshops and their material facilities. This method of training workers reduces costs. For example, in 1958, the total cost of training a worker in workshops was 53 roubles 60 kopeks, while at vocational schools it came to nearly 600 roubles.

The training ends with the worker submitting a 'test piece' for which he receives a rating, and sitting for an examination on a theoretical course programme. After completion of their training, the Personnel Training Department assigns them to their regular work place. The plant has a large body of industrial training instructors drawn from among skilled workers, foremen, engineers, and technicians. The Personnel Training Department, which runs the training workshops, helps the instructors to improve the level of production and theoretical training and to apply tried and proved principles and methods of training. This is achieved primarily by linking up the entire process of training with production, and improving it in step with the expansion of the plant's own technical facilities.

The Urals Engineering Works has 1,005 instructors engaged in training new workers. Most of them are highly skilled workers, who have been training apprentices for a number of years. One of them is V. V. Ostatochnikov, a boring-machine operator of the highest grade, who has been working at the plant since 1940. He considerably exceeds the output norm and studies part-time at a technical school. One of his former pupils, A. P. Koshcheyev, operates a large boring machine, has qualified for the 5th rating, and studies at an evening institute. The Technical Training Department issues industrial training programmes and notes on methods for instructors. The plant has set up assembly, welding, cold-metal-working, and other trade sections that help to supervise and improve the training of new personnel and bring theory closer to practice. In this manner skilled workers are trained in the very process of production.

FURTHER TRAINING AND REFRESHER COURSES

While new skilled personnel are trained not only in production but also at vocational, general education, and other schools, advanced training can be obtained only in production. Its purposes are to deepen and broaden a worker's knowledge and skill within the limits of his trade, to save labour, and to encourage workers to make active efforts to improve technological processes and to further technical progress. Many ways of improving the qualifications of workers have taken shape at the enterprises in the Sverdlovsk Economic Area. These include training in a second and related trade, schools of advanced experience, production-technical courses, special-purpose courses, and schools and courses for foremen. Despite the diversity of forms (purpose, programme, and method of organization), there is one feature common to all. There is a direct link with the tasks of production, with the economy, and with the development of technology. It would be impossible to carry out the far-reaching technical tasks that our industry has been set without giving workers the opportunity of obtaining uninterrupted training and improving their qualifications. Special training in new technology has to be organized for workers, engineers, and technicians, in order to achieve the all-round mechanization and automation of production. A steadily increasing number of refresher courses, which are attended by millions of workers, is being set up within enterprises. In the Sverdlovsk Region, for example, more than 100,000 workers annually raise the level of their skill (see *Table 5*).

Table 5A. *Various forms of improving of workers' skills at enterprises and building projects in the Sverdlovsk Region*

	1957	1958	1959
Total number of workers who have improved their skills	112,915	126,524	147,004
(a) at schools of advanced work methods	26,251	25,797	27,479
(b) training for a second trade	11,175	14,261	18,252
(c) at special-purpose courses	28,665	38,454	41,380
(d) at production-technical courses	39,786	39,110	51,634
(e) at permanently functioning courses and at schools	2,405	2,430	2,008
(f) other forms of training	4,633	6,472	6,251

This table has been compiled on the basis of the summary reports submitted by the Statistical Department of Sverdlovsk Region.

Table 5B. *Growth of the qualifications of workers in Sverdlovsk Region*

	1950	1955	1957	1958	1959
		as a percentage of 1950			
Total number of workers who have improved their qualifications	100	105·1	123·6	128·5	155·0

Table 5 shows the breakdown of the different forms of industrial training. Of the total number of workers improving their skills, 22·9 per cent attend schools of advanced work methods, 8·2 per cent courses offering training in a second trade, 24·8 per cent special-purpose courses, 38·6 per cent production-technical courses, and 5·6 per cent other forms of industrial training.

In 1958-1959, the schools of advanced work methods at the ferrous metal enterprises in the Sverdlovsk region were attended by 15,049 workers, whose labour productivity, as a result, rose by an average of 3-10 per cent. The most skilled and experienced workers acted as instructors. For example, at the Urals Engineering Works 22 of the 116 workers in the steel-smelting department, and 44 of the 142 workers in the press and forge department, served as instructors at schools of advanced work methods. These figures are based on a questionnaire conducted by a team of authors and the Sverdlovsk Economic Council. In the Sverdlovsk Economic Area more than 2,500 skilled workers annually act as instructors at these schools.

After the workers of the Revdin Metal Goods and Metallurgical Works had completed the course offered by these schools, the output per square metre of hearth in the open-hearth furnace department increased by 4 per cent and the number of high-speed smelts by 18·8 per cent. A study of advanced work methods allowed a large number of workers to meet and overfulfil new output norms. For example, after completing one of these courses, a nail-machine operator, P. A. Bryakunov, increased his output from 98 to 123 per cent, and an automatic machine operator, A. I. Shashmurina, stepped up her output from 97 to 103 per cent of the norm.

At the Urals Heavy Engineering Plant, 3,908 workers studied advanced work methods at 484 schools in 1959. A scientific generalization of the most rational work methods, and the application of these methods in production, are part of the enterprise's plan of organizational and technical measures.

A particular operation became a bottleneck in the work of the Urals Cable Plant. Only four workers were able to fulfil the norm for this operation. After a school of advanced work methods was organized, the norm was exceeded by all the workers. This helped to increase the copper output by more than 12 per cent, and the section responsible for the above operation no longer acted as a brake on the plant's main output.

The growth in the cultural and technical level of the workers has led to the adoption of a more ambitious form of exchanging experience. Inter-factory schools have now become widespread in many industries. Scientists from institutions of higher learning and research institutes have lately begun to help in the work of these inter-factory schools, and the study of technical problems of development has been more fully combined with concrete production problems. These schools are doing much to accelerate technical progress and achieve a general rise in output. For example, timber industry enterprises, acting on recommendations made by these schools, have begun to use on a large scale the Druzhba benzine-motor saw. Trees are felled by one lumberjack without an assistant, hauled by the crown of the tree, carried along motor roads and narrow-gauge railways, and cut up by small composite teams. A school for the study of methods of felling timber by a single man was organized at the Travyansk Lumber Yards in Sverdlovsk Region. P. P. Leshchevsky, a benzine-motor-saw operator, was one of the first workers at the Alapayevsk Timber Trust to achieve a 20 per cent higher labour productivity over lumberjacks working in pairs. All the saw operators attending the school began to work singly. Inter-factory schools have been organized by the Krasnoyarsk Lumber Yards to

Q

study tractor-driver N. S. Samoilov's method of hauling timber by the crown of the tree which has helped to increase labour productivity.

The inter-factory schools at non-ferrous metals enterprises have now become a permanent means of spreading advanced work methods and new knowledge in the member plants. In 1959 alone, more than 30 inter-factory schools were set up at non-ferrous metals enterprises in the Sverdlovsk Region.

The transition to new, more progressive forms of labour organization, which help to bring about a considerable increase in output, is inseparably linked up with the learning of related trades, and depends on the whole system of technical training. Composite work teams are organized on the principle of interchangeability, whereby in a worker of one trade can replace a worker in another any time. At the North Urals Bauxite Mines, one of these teams, headed by M. Minzaripov, set a record in 1958, when in a single month it worked 304 linear metres of drift. The members of the team replace one another in various operations, and all of them have been trained in one, two, and even three related trades. The very organization of the work of a composite team helps its members to acquire a high degree of skill in both their main and a related trade. A boring-machine operator bores through rock and ore, carries out current repairs of his pneumatic drill, and performs other operations connected with his main trade. He may also act as a blasting operator, compute the charge, and light the fuse.

In building work, composite teams include people of various trades, who fulfil a definite round of jobs, consisting of the main and a number of auxiliary jobs. For example, the main job of a composite team of bricklayers is to lay bricks, but it also assembles prefabricated reinforced-concrete units for ceilings, partitions, and stairs, installs window and door frames, erects and dismantles scaffolding, and so on. Whenever necessary, the team carries out a number of other jobs, such as installing stoves, tiling, and so on. The labour productivity of a composite team is, as a rule, 50 per cent higher than that of a conventional team. Technical training in a second and related trade creates favourable conditions for organizing such teams. They have become widespread in the fuel industry, in mines producing for the ferrous and non-ferrous metals industry, and on building projects.

By combining trades, it is possible to make better use of machinery, to reduce the amount of time the equipment stands idle, and to lengthen the life of equipment. In addition, manpower is saved, labour productivity increased, and the continuity of production maintained. Work has been organized in this way in the rail and structural steel department of the Nizhniy Tagil Iron and Steel Plant. More than half the workers have been trained in a second trade. Because of the large quantity of intricate equipment, the chief mechanic's department had three teams of fitters: one for equipment maintenance, one for communication maintenance, and one for lubricating the equipment. As a result of training the workers in a second trade, it became possible to replace the three teams by one, and thereby establish its responsibility for the condition of the equipment. Machine operators were taught the trade of fitter with the result that the staff of fitters was reduced by 60. In the course of eight years of operation, the rail and structural steel mill in the steel-rolling department has doubled its labour productivity. Although the working-day was shortened to seven hours in 1958, the labour force was not increased.

Table 6. Training in related trades at some enterprises in the Sverdlovsk Region

Plant	Department	Number of workers questioned	Workers with					
			one trade	%	two trades	%	three or more trades	%
1. Nizhniy Tagil Iron and Steel Plant	Open-hearth	225	129	50·6	61	31·0	35	18·4
2. Sverdlovsk Tool Works	Machine	43	19	44·0	19	44·0	5	12·0
3. Verkh-Isetsk Plant	Open-hearth	116	69	59·6	39	33·6	8	6·9
4. Urals Machine-building Works	Forge	142	65	45·8	44	31·0	33	23·2

The statistics for this table are taken from a questionnaire conducted among workers by the authors and the Sverdlovsk Region.

In the four departments covered by the questionnaire used in the investigation reported in *Table 6*, it was found that more than half the workers had two or more trades. A considerable number of workers had three or more trades and a sound knowledge of the entire production cycle. The learning of related trades quite obviously promotes a fuller development of workers, because the sharp division of labour with highly specialized occupations disappears in the course of this training. For example, in learning to operate excavators, turbines, compressors, machine-tools, and milling machines, the worker at the same time studies not only the operation of these machines but also their repair and maintenance. Training is conducted in such a way as to enable the worker who is operating machines with mechanical or automatic regulation to correct minor faults by himself, and to help in current repairs and regular overhauls of equipment.

As a part of the long-term plan of introducing automation and mechanization at enterprises in the Sverdlovsk Region, new workers will be trained as fitters of electrical equipment and operators of hoist equipment. They will be taught to handle electric welding equipment. There will be also a larger number of builders, miners, metallurgists, and workers in the building materials industry who are qualified in two or more trades. Leading enterprises are resolutely breaking down the narrow forms of labour division, which were a common practice during the war years because of the influx of a large number of un-skilled workers. In that period, the new workers were employed on a disjointed technological basis. The older skilled workers were used chiefly as instructors, setters, and fitters. The situation has now under-gone a radical change and workers are receiving a comprehensive training. Material incentives are being introduced for workers mastering two or three related trades. Some very instructive experience has been gained in this field in the ferrous metals industry in the Sverdlovsk Region, and the Sverdlovsk Regional Trade Union Committee of Steel Industry Workers has worked out and introduced a system of incentives for workers who repair their own equipment. At the Pervouralsk and Sinarsk pipe plants, it has been decided to train all production workers in the trades of fitter, electrician, and welder, in order to remove the need for repair shops and reduce auxiliary staff. In 1958, a total of 14,261 workers were taught a second trade at enterprises in the Sverd-lovsk Economic Area, and in 1959 their number rose to 18,252 as against 11,175 in 1957. As a rule, workers were trained in a related trade at the factory under special training programmes. These pro-grammes, however are being considerably reduced, because workers can learn new trades by teaching each other during working hours. The programme of theoretical training is also being reduced, because workers acquire the necessary theoretical knowledge while learning a new trade.

SPECIAL COURSES OF TRAINING

Special-purpose courses are a widespread means of raising the quali-fications of workers. This is a very flexible form of training, which makes it possible to obtain quick responses to changing requirements of production. As a rule, the courses are organized to speed up instruction in the operation of new equipment, and of new technological and more economical processes. In 1958, in the Sverdlovsk Economic Area, these courses trained 38,454 workers, including 12,099 workers in the iron and steel industry, 5,623 workers in the engineering industry, and 3,442 workers in the non-ferrous metals industry, while in 1959 they were attended by 41,380 workers.

The introduction of automatic production lines at many factories has led to the setting up of courses for the study of automation. The curriculum of these courses covers electronic automation, the study of photocells, photorelays, and so on. The theoretical classes are held after working hours in classrooms. Many enterprises have originated technical centres equipped with numerous visual aids, in the workshops themselves. The Pervouralsk Pipe Works, for example, has 10 such centres and 13 stands with sets of visual aids. Each classroom has a technical library, drawing-boards, and other equipment. In the workshops of the Urals Engineering Works, there are 25 technical classrooms.

In 1959, the technical courses in the Sverdlovsk Economic Area were attended by 51,634 workers, including 1,359 at the Nizhniy Tagil Iron and Steel Plant, 1,344 at the Gorstroi Trust, 298 at the Urals Aluminium Works, 475 at the Turbine Motor Works, and 2,669 at the Urals Heavy Engineering Works. Instructors for these courses are drawn from among engineers and technicians. The permanent instructors in the network of courses at the Urals Heavy Engineering Works, for example, includes 146 engineers, at the Sinarsk Pipe Plant 70 engineers, and at the Urals Aluminium Works 80 engineers. In the Sverdlovsk Economic Area, as a whole, more than 6,000 highly qualified engineers and technicians combine their production work with the gratifying task of training workers.

Technical courses raise the qualifications of workers, and increase the number of workers with medium and high qualification ratings, which in its turn leads to an increase in the number of workers who are able to make suggestions for improvements in the machines and processes of production. Hundreds of workers have become excellent organizers and industrial administrators, thanks to the training received on these courses. G. S. Koptely, a foreman at the pipe-rolling department of the Sinarsk Pipe Works, attended a course at a factory school for foremen and, jointly with I. I. Chursinov, a foreman at the New Pipe Works, who had attended a similar course, started the movement for reducing the time during which equipment lay idle. P. N. Monashkov came to the Sinarsk Pipe Works after he was demobilized from the Soviet Army, and attended courses at a technical school, a school for foremen, a secondary school for young workers, and a polytechnical institute. He is only one of the many workers who have followed this path.

The reorganization of technical institutes was a major step taken in the Sverdlovsk Economic Area to improve the system of training and improving the qualifications of personnel. These institutes formerly served only the ferrous and non-ferrous metals industries. Now one institute serves enterprises in seven different branches of the administration, and the others serve the remaining eight branches. The Sverdlovsk Economic Area now has two centres which direct technical studies within enterprises and also serve to raise the qualifications of engineers, technicians, and workers in the leading trades in full-time courses. The content of the work of these institutes changed radically following the reorganization, in 1957, of the management of industry and construction. They were brought into closer contact with production and began the instruction of factory officials in methods of organizing industrial training for workers. Their engineers help enterprises to set up education centres. For example, the Degtyarsk Copper Mine was given assistance in setting up a first-class educational institution, which has now become a model for other enterprises. The example of the Degtyarsk Copper Mine was followed by the Vakhrshev Coal, Volchanskcoal, and Sverdlovsk Mining Construction Trusts, the Urals Electrical Equipment Works, the Kirovograd Copper Plant, and the Serov District Heat and Power Plant.

The higher standard in industrial training achieved after the Economic Councils were set up gave immediate results. In 1958, for example, the enterprises of the Sverdlovsk Economic Area trained 47,769 new workers and helped 126,524 workers to improve their qualifications. The corresponding figures for 1957 were 45,965 and 112,915, and in 1959 they were 49,460 and 147,004. The importance of this rapid advance in technical education for young people is now particularly great, because young men and women who have attended eight-year and eleven-year schools are taking jobs in industry. At the same time, a large number of senior pupils at secondary schools are getting training in production. According to a rough estimate, at least 60,000 pupils received training at enterprises in the Sverdlovsk Economic Area in 1964 alone.

It is not only a matter of quantity. Far-reaching qualitative changes are taking place in the system of vocational training. Young people with a high level of general education, but with little production experience or knowledge of a particular trade, are entering industry. There is now an urgent need for vocational training workshops, at least at the larger enterprises.

In our opinion, these workshops should have two independent parts: a production workshop providing vocational training, and a school for theoretical study. Enrolment should be confined to young people between the ages of 15 and 16, who have completed eight years of study at a secondary school. The training received by them at such a workshop would allow them to enter basic production. It would be expedient to attach a group of 10-12 pupils to each engineer-instructor. The workshop should operate on the same lines as any other production department of a factory. In so far as the training is highly specialized, it is necessary to provide these workshops with modern machines and tools, in order that the trainees will learn the most up-to-date techniques.

In the first year of training, the trainees should receive the rate of pay established for apprentices, and when they start normal work they will be paid according to the quantity of work and the existing norms and tariff rates. A part of the money realized from the sale of the products should be used to create a special fund for the payment of bonuses to outstanding trainees, for the purchase of equipment, and for the cultural and everyday needs of the trainees.

The trainees should be able, from the start, to experience satisfaction in their work and in the contribution they are making to society. It is therefore desirable, wherever possible, to fix norms for apprentices as soon as training begins. Gradually, as the trainees acquire production experience, these norms can be increased and brought up to the norm of an adult worker.

Such workshops are already being organized in the Sverdlovsk Economic Area, and an important role in getting them started is being played by the trainees themselves. The Communal Machine-building Plant, for example, now has a training workshop with five sections providing vocational training for pupils in the eighth to the eleventh years of Secondary School No. 36, in Sverdlovsk. Each section has its production programme, pupils' output norms, an emulation movement, and so on. This training workshop has been provided with modern turret lathes, automatic machine-tools, instruments, and apparatus. The production and theoretical training is conducted by highly skilled workers, engineers, and technicians under a curriculum and method devised by the Technical Training Institute. Similar workshops are being set up in Sverdlovsk at the Bearing Works, the Trade Machines Plant, and other enterprises.

Evening vocational schools, in which workers study part-time, are playing an important role in raising the cultural and technical standards of the working class. The setting up of evening departments at vocational schools brings these schools into closer contact with production. At the same time as they gain new experience in their own trades, the workers studying at these schools also learn the rudiments of engineering.

LONG-TERM TRAINING PROGRAMMES

n order to take advantage of the broad prospects that the Seven-Year Plan for 1959-1965 offers for promoting vocational training, a basic improvement has to be achieved in planning the work of the vocational schools. The existing practice of drawing up current and annual plans excludes most forms of long-term training. Moreover, it takes inadequate account of the prospects for developing industrial enterprises. This impedes the co-ordination of general education and technical training on the scale of an entire economic area. The Nizhniy Tagil Iron and Steel Works had drawn up and carried out a long-term (1959-1965) plan for raising the general education and technical standard of its workers. It has set itself the aim of becoming a model enterprise in mechanization and automation. To achieve this, the main body of workers must have a high standard of general and special training, including elements of engineering.

The drawing up of a long-term plant started with a calculation of the necessary minimum of general education required by the different trades. Account was taken of the changes in the division and character of labour brought about by the mechanization and automation of production processes. Such a minimum of general education was determined for 250 leading trades. For example, a blast-furnace operator should have at least seven or eight years of secondary education, while a worker operating an oxygen installation or the control panel of a rolling mill should have a full ten years of secondary education.

In deciding that a blast-furnace operator needs a minimum of ten years of secondary education, account was taken of the fact that he must have a thorough knowledge of the system of automatic control, of the thermal régime of a blast-furnace, and of the loading of the bunkers and he should also be able to service and operate a photoelectric pyrometer, ultra-sonic consumption-meters, and oxygen bath blowers.

Following the example of the Nizhniy Tagil Works, the Urals Engineering Works decided that a cupola furnace operator requires a full secondary school education on the grounds that he has to compute the furnace charge depending on the grade of pig iron, be familiar with its principal properties, and the influence that the materials of a charge have on the physical and mechanical properties of the grade of pig iron being produced. Furthermore, he has to know how various elements of the charge influence the smelting of the metal, and be able to understand the mechanism and features of the technological process.

Until recently, wage rate and classification tables mentioned only technical knowledge and practical skill without reference to the necessary level of general education of the worker. In drawing up their long-term plan for the training of workers, the Nizhniy Tagil metallurgists fixed the level of general education required. Such a plan enables each worker to see the prospects for his own advancement. Nine out of every ten workers in the plant were questioned individually with regard to their general education and technical skill. They were advised what form of training was most suitable for their age, general education, and technical knowledge. The aim of this plan, covering a period of seven years, is to give all workers the equivalent of seven or eight years of general education as the minimum, and to increase the number of workers having a full secondary or higher education. More than 300 engineers and technicians took part in this important project. As a result, a seven-year plan of cultural and technical growth became a part of the works' plan of technical development.

In the course of seven years, the number of workers who have completed a seven- or eight-year course, or a full secondary education, increased from 42 per cent in 1958, to 76 per cent in 1965. Implementation of this seven-year training plan is turning the Nizhniy Tagil Works into one of the country's largest universities of production training. Its foremen's school already has an enrolment of 940, as against 574 in the 1957-58 school year. In 1959, more than 10,000 workers had been trained in part-time courses at the plant, and at present they are training over 2,300 workers. Work teams and brigades undertake training as a unit, and these include workers who have not studied for as long as 10 or 20 years. For example, V. N. Azovtsev, a gas worker in the coke-chemical department, enrolled in the seventh-year class at a school for young workers, after a 15 years' break in his education. N. A. Tarasov, the leader of a team of fitters at the steel section rolling department, enrolled in a foremen's school after a 20 years' break.

A total of 65,200 workers will raise their level of education under the long-term (seven-year) training plan. Of these, 5,000 will complete seven or eight years of general education, 2,500 a full secondary education, 1,000 a technical course, 1,500 a course for foremen of communist labour, and 27,700 various vocational courses. An elected committee has been given the responsibility for this mass training programme and greater material and technical facilities have been made available.

Other enterprises in the area have followed the example of the Nizhniy Tagil metallurgists. In 1959, the Krasnogorsk District Heat and Power Plant, in the town of Kamensk-Uralsk, provided 75 per cent of its workers with some form of training. The Pervouralsk New Pipe Works now has a branch institute and a technical school on its premises, including a school for foremen, excellently equipped schools for young workers, and numerous courses. The long-term training plan of the Urals Heavy Engineering Works is given in *Table 7*.

These long-term training programmes are part of the nation-wide drive to raise the cultural and general educational level of all workers and peasants. A new type of worker, with a knowledge of the fundamentals of science and an ability to use modern machinery, is coming to the fore. This knowledge and ability lead to a continuous increase in the general productivity of labour. One of these workers is B. V. Kukharenko of the Verkh-Isetsk Plant. He came to the plant in 1947 as an apprentice. In 1951, he was called up for military service, and in 1954, when he was demobilized, he returned to the plant. He attended a part-time school for young workers and, at present, is a fifth-year student at the Urals Polytechnical Institute. 'The more technical knowledge I get,' he says, 'the more I begin to feel that labour is a source of satisfaction. I can understand my machine in all its aspects, know its strong and weak points, and make it obey my will.' Shirmanov, a fitter at the Urals Carriage-building Plant, had learned five trades and had already begun work on his output plan for the following year.

METHODS OF TRAINING

The Sverdlovsk Economic Area has issued special circulars on methods of training. Seminars have been held for full-time and part-time instructors to study the principles of training, to choose the most rational methods of instruction, to share experience, and to improve the teaching. Research into vocational training is used to help enterprises to eliminate duplication in various forms of training. This will save the state huge sums of money and will encourage workers to progress from one form of training to another. In our view, these forms of training should be as follows.

First, training in a new general trade. Second, special-purpose courses and schools of advanced methods of work to study the methods employed by those who have made improvements in production in both Soviet and foreign technology. Third, improvement of qualifications at schools for young workers and foremen of communist labour, and also

Table 7. Long-term plan for training workers at non-factory schools and at courses set up at the Urals Machine-building Works

	Year							
	1959	1960	1961	1962	1963	1964	1965	Total
Number studying at schools for young workers (SYW)	2,800	3,200	3,150	3,100	3,050	3,000	3,000	—
Number expected to complete SYW								
7 years of general education up to 1962, 8 years after 1963	200	300	325	350	350	375	400	2,300
10 and 11 classes	450	450	475	500	525	550	550	3,500
Number studying at technical schools	840	875	875	900	900	925	925	—
Number of graduates from technical schools	135	125	150	150	175	175	175	1,085
Number studying at evening and correspondence institutes	900	926	950	975	1,000	1,000	1,025	—
Number of graduates from institutes	100	100	110	125	150	150	175	910
Number of new workers trained	1,500	1,500	1,500	1,500	1,500	1,500	1,500	10,500
Improvement of qualification at factory courses (plan)								
Workers	7,090	7,200	7,250	7,300	7,300	7,350	7,350	50,840
Engineers and technicians	800	825	850	875	900	900	925	6,075
Total	7,890	8,025	8,100	8,175	8,200	8,250	8,275	56,915
Total number trained annually	10,275	10,500	10,660	10,800	10,900	11,000	11,075	75,210
Number continuing education	13,930	14,525	14,575	14,658	14,650	14,675	14,725	101,730

Appendix No. 1 to Order No. 553 issued at the Urals Machine-building Works on 16 November 1959.

at permanently functioning courses. Fourth, correspondence institutes and technical schools at enterprises.

All these forms of training must be strictly co-ordinated. Each stage should give the worker new knowledge and skill. Soviet factories, with their up-to-date equipment, are excellent laboratories for the vocational training of workers. Many of them have, or are setting up, well-equipped technical classrooms, for which provision is being made in the standard designs of factory departments now under construction.

Following the reorganization of the management of industry and construction in 1957, it became possible to promote certain exchanges of methods of technical training between various branches of industry. This has helped the Sverdlovsk Economic Area to raise the level of training in industries that formerly lagged behind. Long-term planning, and the fostering of the general education and technical skill of workers are closely linked up with the improvement of the existing forms of production training. Under present-day conditions, the content of many of these forms is undergoing a radical change.

Today, vocational training can only be successful if it combines basic, mutually supporting elements of instruction. These are, first, general polytechnical training, in which, as a result of the extension of automation, it is necessary to give a broader knowledge of the elements of hydraulics, pneumatic systems, electrical and radio systems, hoisting and transport machinery, and the basic methods of organizing labour and production; second, general vocational training with the emphasis on setting and computing, analytical and control functions; and third, production training within enterprises and improvement of workers' qualifications through the implementation and spread of advanced methods of work.

The co-ordination of these three elements of training requires a close link between general education and technical training in the course of production. Regrettably, in practice these two forms of training are frequently kept separate.

The Sverdlovsk Economic Area has adopted the line of strengthening the bonds between general education and technical training within the framework of the existing forms of training. In the 1959-60 school year, for instance, vocational training was introduced at 150 schools for young workers. At these schools, instruction is organized in such a way as to teach the pupils vocations in a broad field: the trades of fitter-assemblyman, the cold cutting of metals, the installation and maintenance of electrical equipment in industrial enterprises, building trades, steelmaking trades, and so on. Subjects such as technical drawing, the

fundamentals of metallurgy, modern advances in science and technology in various fields, labour organization, and the administration of
production have been added to the curriculum. At many schools for
young workers in the Sverdlovsk Economic Area, the curriculum is
designed to teach workers to handle the latest types of machinery within
the next three years. Young workers attending these schools will be
able to enrol in technical institutes and, at the same time, they will have
the knowledge to operate modern plant.

The schools for foremen are likewise being reorganized. They were
set up at heavy industry enterprises, and were attended by nearly
250,000 workers annually. To enrol in one of these schools, a worker
required not more than five or six years of general education, in conformity with the general educational level of the main body of workers
at that period. Today, because of the tasks facing Soviet industry in
automation and mechanization and because of the improving general
educational level of the workers, the tasks and the content of the work
of these schools are being fundamentally revised. Indeed, in the Sverdlovsk Economic Area alone, the new recruitment includes first and
second-year students of institutes, 11,000 graduates of general secondary
schools, and 6,000 graduates of secondary schools providing production
training. In other words, nearly 40 per cent of the new workers have had
a secondary education.

Under these conditions the term of training at the schools for foremen
in the Sverdlovsk Economic Area is; one year for students who have
completed a full secondary education; two years for students who have
completed 6 to 8 years of secondary education; and three years for
students who have completed 5 to 6 years of a secondary education. At
the Nizhniy Tagil Iron and Steel Plant, for example, the curricula of
the schools for foremen have been revised to include general subjects
and a course of lectures on literature, art, new technology, and other
subjects. A similar line has been taken up by the Seversky Iron and Steel
Plant, the New Pipe Works in Pervouralsk, the Alapayev Iron and
Steel Plant, and other enterprises. The schools for foremen are thus
becoming schools for foremen of communist labour.

CONCLUSIONS

Vocational training is an important means of raising the cultural and
technical standards of workers. In its development, the system of vocational training is giving workers a continuously increasing volume of

general and specialized knowledge. At present, some of the aspects of vocational training are directed towards giving new workers a knowledge of the fundamentals of their future trade, but in the near future, when every secondary school leaver entering industry will have a good grasp of these fundamentals, the system of vocational training will be designed to give workers the qualifications of engineers and technicians. Properly organized vocational training within enterprises, in combination with thorough general education, will be one of the major means of surmounting the existing differences between mental and physical work and of shaping the harmoniously developed and educated worker of communist society.

NOTE

1. All the factual information and the details of the system of the management of the economy given in this paper refer to the situation as it was in 1959. Prior to the setting up of regional economic councils in 1957, about half of all the industrial goods were produced by undertakings managed by federal agencies. In November 1962, nearly all local industry was placed under the control of the regional economic councils. These constituted the main form of state management of industry. They operated within their regions in accordance with federal and republic laws, the directions of the Communist Party and the Government, and the targets of the economic plan. Their most important task was to ensure the general fulfilment of state plans for the region concerned and for each industrial enterprise within it, with special priority for requirements of state importance and of co-operative and export deliveries. They took part in drawing up the economic plans, submitting their recommendations for the solution of major economic problems, and worked out appropriate economic relations between enterprises and the regions. In those republics where there were several economic regions (for example, the Russian Republic, the Ukraine, and Kazakhstan) there were also republic economic councils co-ordinating the work of the regional councils.

Legislation introduced in October 1965 displaced the regional economic councils as the main unit for the management of the economy. The system then introduced is described in Appendix II.

16

The socio-psychological study of automatic systems

D. A. OSHANIN

THE SOCIAL SCIENCES AND AUTOMATION

An important social aspect of the scientific and technological revolution of the mid-twentieth century is the close convergence of the functions of man and machine, and their interweaving into a single functional whole, which make it possible to speak of a 'man-machine' system. The basic, and most difficult, question in this connection is that of an optimum distribution of functions between the human and the machine factors in this system, taking strict account of the relative advantages and disadvantages of the two. This question cannot be satisfactorily resolved without invoking the social sciences, particularly individual psychology, social psychology, and sociology.[1] Their importance is the more evident when it is recognized how greatly technical potentialities have increased in recent years.

Until very recently, psychological studies have been, more often than not, of a narrowly applied nature, confined, in the last analysis, to recommending the best of a very limited number of technically possible variants of the different means for the control of machines. The situation is now quite different. In principle, practically any demand for adaptation of the machine to man is technologically feasible. Quantitatively and qualitatively our demands, in this respect, are determined only by our present knowledge of man's functional potentialities and limitations.

PSYCHOLOGICAL PROBLEMS

The problems confronting scientists in connection with studies of automatic systems fall into two groups. The first comprises problems involved in modelling mental processes. If we set ourselves the task of automating any action in the man-machine system, that has hitherto been performed by an operator, we must first discover how the operator performs the given action. Having established the principle of a man's work, is it not possible to transfer this principle to the machine by finding an acceptable technological equivalent for it?

The simplest problems of this kind are solved when we record on punched cards the control of certain machine-tools. The markings on the punched card are either computed, or are made, without any calculations, directly from the machining by a worker of a sample product. In the latter case, it is primarily important to establish the most rational structure of the operations performed by the human operator.

In other cases, an indispensable condition for transcribing human working functions is that they first must be formalized, i.e. a mathematical description of these actions must be given. An interesting example is the attempt made by A. A. Lyapunov and G. A. Shestopal to compile an algorithm for the operations of a railway station inspector.[2]

The translation of psychological functions into automatic performance by a modelling of the corresponding nervous mechanisms is a more complex, but also a much more promising and universal means. Naturally, at the pesent time, it is only possible to consider the application of this method to more or less elementary mental processes. For instance, initial attempts to have been made to model the mechanisms of perception and direct memorizing.

There are some problems we must note in discussing the modelling of nervous mechanisms and in stressing their immense significance for continued automation of production. In designing automatic systems, we must beware of the naïve anthropomorphism inherent in attempts to imitate uncritically and senselessly the functions that are specific and effective only for higher forms of living matter. Even where such imitation is feasible, which is rarely the case, it does not necessarily mean that this is the shortest and most rational way towards automation.

This is, incidentally, also the opinion of many of our automation specialists. 'An automatic system cannot precisely imitate processes occurring in living organisms', B. P. Petrov writes in this connection. 'Even closely similar processes can and must be reproduced in technology in different ways. Moreover, there is no need to strive to imitate precisely these processes.'[3] Technical simulation of the functions of living organisms, in the vast majority of cases, must have as its aim not complete analogy but only broadly conceived isomorphism.

Second, and of quite a different nature, are the tasks of psychologists in which the purpose is not to substitute man by machine but to combine or to co-ordinate the human and machine factors in the man-machine system. They have to find the optimum combination of man and machine in a single functional whole. Properly speaking, these are the tasks we already touched upon at the beginning of this article. In this case, we should be concerned not so much with analogies between man and machine, or with those functions of man which can be replaced by a machine, as with the specificity of the human factor. Some work methods are specific to man alone and, because of these, he remains to this day an irreplaceable, and the most important, component in the man-machine system.

It is apparent that, without understanding the peculiarity of man, or without taking into account his specific human potentialities and his human failings, it is impossible to solve finally the problem of the proper co-ordination of the work of men and machines, or of the optimum adaptation of the machine to man.

The problem of optimum distribution of functions between man and machine is often posed in a most abstract manner. Therefore, its suggested solution is reduced to postulating certain general and perfectly self-evident points: 'man must perform those functions in a system that do not lend themselves to automation'; 'man should not be assigned tasks that a machine can do better', etc. It is clear that no universal solution can be found to this problem, and that any meaningful recommendations in this respect will always be related to some particular man-machine system, or, at best, to a certain group or class of such systems.

The solution of the question about which functions of a system should be assigned to man always presents considerable difficulties, mainly because it must meet several different criteria, and not one alone. For instance, we consider that it is absolutely impermissible to put forward, as the sole or even the principal argument in this decision, the criterion of relative economic effectiveness of the use of people or automatic devices in systems. In assigning some particular work to an operator in the man-machine system, we must, in the first place, ensure maximum protection for his life and health, and, perhaps to no lesser degree, we should see that his work essentially befits his human dignity.

THE CHARACTER OF WORK WITH AUTOMATION

In the most general terms, the work of an operator in the man-machine system consists of the reception of information from the object (or process)

R

being controlled; the composition, on the basis of this information, of an idea about the subsequent state of the object; the adoption of a decision corresponding on the one hand to this idea, and on the other hand to the job to be done and to his experience; and finally, the operation of this decision by means of purposeful control of the action of the object (or process).

Both the reception of information by man and the processing thereof (assessment of the situation, the adoption of decisions) and the exertion of an appropriate influence on the object, constitute forms of mental activity comprising processes of sensation, perception, attention, thinking, etc. All these processes are subject to certain regularities. The degree to which these regularities are taken into account in organizing the work of an operator in a man-machine system will determine the productivity of his labour.

Let us take, as an example, the problem of coding information. The point is that man-machine systems, as a rule, are remote-controlled. In these systems, the operator cannot directly observe the controlled variables of the job. Information on the variations is supplied to him in a coded form, as a certain system of signals which plays the role of a symbolic language.

In view of the above, the signals received by the operator should be considered from two aspects: semantically, the signal is a symbolic carrier of information about something occurring outside and independently of him; in the sensory aspect, the signal, on the contrary, must be regarded in itself as a definite stimulus, as an object that must be noticed in due time, identified as such, distinguished from all other stimuli, both signal and non-signal, which may impinge on the operator from the surrounding medium.

The stimulus may take the form of a light, a colour, a sound, a number, a path traversed on a screen by a point, a figure or a sign, given a certain meaning by the designer of the system. It may be easily, or not so easily, correlated with the phenomenon which it must denote. In this sense, we speak of a semantically fortunate or unfortunate choice of stimulus, i.e. for the symbolic representation of a given phenomenon. Regardless of the content of the signal stimulus, it may prove to be more or less effective simply because of its sensory characteristics, i.e. as an object of perception. As such, it can be more or less effective, i.e. more or less easily attract the operator's attention; it can be more or less distinguishable, or cause a more or less rapid and precise reaction. What matters, in this context, is not only the sensory modality of the stimulator (i.e. whether it is visual, aural, or tactile) but also its sensory characteristics ('dimensions') within each modality (for instance, in the case of a visual stimulus, its colour, tone, brightness, density, size, and shape).

There is still much work to be done in the study of signal stimuli. Therefore, while it is true that problems of sensation and perception (especially visual and aural, which play the main role in man-machine systems) are among those which have been most thoroughly studied by psychologists, it is equally true that the results so far obtained lack the precision and universality that would make them directly applicable to the designing of automatic systems.

HUMAN LIMITATIONS

Another major task is the determination of the maximum volume of information that it is rational or permissible to supply to the operator in the man-machine system. It is known that human capacity, as a transmitting link in systems, is limited and bears no comparison with the potentialities of machines which are capable of making millions of binary decisions per second. Repeated experiments have shown that, if two identical signals follow each other in quick enough succession (not more than 250 microseconds apart), the reaction time (for instance that of pressing a push-button) to the second signal will be longer than to the first. The smaller the interval between the signals, the greater is the reaction time. If this interval, known as the 'refractory period' is ignored, then it may result in a slow and therefore ineffective reaction by the operator exactly at the most critical moment. To prevent this, it is clearly essential that immediately before the operator's decisive actions, his 'communication channels' should not be busy.

The analysis of a situation, the evaluation of the state of the controlled object, and the adoption, on the strength of this evaluation, of a decision about the immediate actions needed to influence the object are spread out in time and often require intense exercise of mental functions, such as attention and thinking. For the successful exercise of these functions, it is often essential that the operator should receive the information he needs, not in a single communication, but exactly in the required sequence during the operation.

In order to establish this sequence, it is necessary to know precisely how the human mind deals with information and in what sequence. Only then can the process of supplying information be correlated in time with the responses of the recipient. Until we can discover at least the basic features of the psychological content of the internal process of dealing with information, in the solution of various types of operational tasks in the man-machine systems, the problem of the optimum sequence for the supply of information will remain unsolved.

THE PERCEPTUAL FIELD OF AN OPERATOR

In connection with the simultaneous feeding of information, mention is often made of the so-called 'magical number 7 ± 2': at any given moment an operator cannot transmit more than 5 to 9 bits (binary digits) of information. Therefore, the simultaneous appearance on a display panel of a greater number of signal stimuli does not mean that all of them will be perceived by the operator at one and the same moment. Despite the simultaneous feeding of information, its reception and processing will take some time. Therefore for visual signals located in a certain plane the sequence of the reception of information, in every case, will be determined by the sequence of the visual scanning of these signals. The scanning route, to a very large extent, depends on the manner in which the signal stimuli are located in the plane (display panel).

The problem of arranging the structure of the operator's perceptual field is of considerable importance. It is known from experiment that the arrangement of signal stimuli in spatial structures makes it much easier to notice the deviation of each controlled variable from a given value, as well as to detect the development of technical faults in the feeding of information (for instance, the malfunctioning of one or more signal lights).

A present hopeful line of development seems to be an arrangement of light stimuli on, for example, an electric display, which would give, in a diagrammatic form, the information which an operator needs to carry out particular technological tasks. The concept of a structure in this case has nothing to do with the idealistic interpretation of 'wholeness', or 'homogeneity' of images, of the exponents of the Gestalt theory. We are concerned with material structures, objectively realized and acting physically upon our sensory organs.

The need to organize structurally the operator's perceptual field poses a multitude of complex and interesting problems. Experiments carried out in our laboratory by Hsui Lian-Tsang have shown, for example, that in performing operations which are scattered over the perceptual field and organized into structures, the operator's errors definitely predominate in certain links of these spatial structures, regardless of the specific content of the actions corresponding to these links.[4] It is evident, therefore, that there may be considerable significance in the topography of such 'weak', or 'unreliable' links of spatial structures in distributing the signals in displays, and, in particular, in the proper localization of the signals carrying information which is most important for the given process. Mention can be made, only in passing, of another no less important question, in connection with the spatial location of signals. This is the optimum and permissible density of the location of the signals and technological symbols on a plane. The density of disposition determines the angular distance to the signal which must determine the effectiveness of its perception, as well as the optimum dimensions of the display, the choice of distance from the diagram to the operator's desk, etc.

THE EFFECT OF STIMULI ON THE OPERATOR'S BEHAVIOUR

In investigations of the work of an operator in automatic systems, individual psychologists and social psychologists often reduce it to the traditional causal chain, INFORMATION-DECISION-ACTION. Any action of the operator is then expressed by the formula $y = f(x)$, where $x =$ certain information delivered to the operator which, after appropriate processing, is invariably transformed into reaction y. Such an abstract and extremely tentative conception of the operator's work, can have a certain meaning when applied to practical purposes. One, however, must always keep in mind that the substitution of this working scheme for actual reality can lead not only to oversimplification but may even give a totally distorted picture of the actual process of transmission of information in the man-machine system. When carried beyond certain limits it becomes a crudely mechanistic conception.

As a link in an automatic system, man is distinguished by exceptional reactivity. His behaviour in the system is continually affected by a multitude of stimuli which incessantly impinge on him, both externally and internally. The study of all these stimuli – which have practically no effect on the operation of a machine, but always to some degree or other determine the behaviour of man – and the establishment of their interdependence and the degree and nature of their influence on the process of transmission of information by man constitute, as we see it, the main core of the psychological problem involved in the investigation of the man-machine system. The importance of such research seems evident to us. In understanding of the extreme reactivity and complex causative factors of man's behaviour, and a strict account of all the factors that can exert a measurable influence on him, are equally necessary both for designing automatic systems and for the proper inclusion of man into them.

One of the clearest expressions of psychological oversimplification in the study of the man-machine system is the fact that the operator in it is usually regarded as some average, standard individual. If, in facing the task of adapting the machine to man, we are compelled to disregard the individuality of the concrete person who would actually have to operate the machine, it is nevertheless realized perfectly well that in reality there is not, nor can there be, such an 'average individual', a person devoid of any individual traits. Each operator always brings into the man-machine system his own individuality. This is made up from a complex of specific features, an unknown quantity which, to some degree or other, determines his reactions in the system. Because of this, the behaviour of the man-machine system, strictly speaking, always remains mathematically unpredictable.

It is hardly to be expected that technical progress, which minimizes the importance of concrete 'occupational aptitudes' in favour of such general qualities as broad polytechnical knowledge and a sense of responsibility for the equipment entrusted to the operator, would be especially favourable to the mass application of psycho-technical methods of occupational selection. We are convinced, however, that the problem of occupational selection retains its significance for certain categories of occupations. The most important are those which require the operator to carry out responsible tasks in conditions of acute pressure of time and strong emotional stress. They may involve a hazard to the life and health both of the operator himself and of other people. The work of an operator in man-machine systems often belongs in this occupational category.

Having made all these assertions, the last thing we want to imply is that we are in any way satisfied with the 'classic' psycho-technical techniques of occupational selection. Moreover, we categorically object to operationalism, or statistical fetishism, inherent in these techniques. Truly scientific techniques of occupational selection still await their development. It seems to us that such techniques, in the first place, should be applied to the most general individual differences that are inborn, essentially unchangeable ontogenetically, and resistant to educational influences. We have in mind the general, typological, specific features of higher nervous activity: the strength, balance, and mobility of the excitation and inhibition processes.[5]

It must be said that at present we already have a few accurate techniques for assessing some of these principal qualities. They are, for example, the techniques for measuring the strength of the nervous system[6] developed by a team under V. M. Teplov at the Laboratory of Psychophysiology, Institute of Psychology, Academy of Pedagogical Sciences of the Russian Federation.[7] Furthermore, individual 'occupational aptitudes' must be studied in all those cases where they still play the decisive role in the operator's work. Here too, however, the indispensable prerequisite for the development of scientific techniques of diagnosis and measurement is a thorough analysis of the psychological and physiological content of these complex characteristics.

At our laboratory, such an analysis was recently attempted by Yu. A. Kalikinsky, in relation to what he termed 'technical hearing' of specialists controlling internal combustion engines.[8] As a result of the work carried out by Kalikinsky it was established that, in this particular case, 'technical hearing' must be regarded as a special feature of human hearing. expressed in the following complex of specific sensory and perceptual functions of the aural analyser: (1) high sensory perception in a narrow zone of closely limited variables of the occupational acoustic field; (2) high sensory perception under the conditions of background noise of high intensity; (3) a highly developed function of separating the components of the noise complex at low component intensity; (4) a highly developed function of differentiating noise structures at low levels of intensity of the signal complexes. In a special educational experiment, Kalikinsky has also been able to demonstrate that the complex ability of the aural analyser can be developed by means of a special technique within a relatively short time.

The study of the operator's individual features is necessary not only for the purpose of occupational selection. It is a fact that individuals differ from each other not only in the quality of their work. They may carry out their jobs equally poorly or equally well, achieving the same result by different means. How can we then explain differences of this kind? Should we not look for deep typological differences between individuals as the factor underlying different methods of work?

An interesting treatment of this problem is given in the study by E. A. Klimov (Kazan). Klimov has studied the working methods of weavers who operate many looms. They differed among themselves in the degree of mobility of their nervous processes. His study has shown that 'sluggish' and 'agile' weavers, who are equally efficient, adopt different methods, and create their own individual style of work.

The main and most positive features of the style of 'agile' weavers, who are distinguished by high potential of the motor activity and easy switching of attention, are agility and manœuvrability. They have a typical variation in speed of reaction time depending on the urgency of the situation, as well as being able to correct some faults in their work.

The 'sluggish' weavers, being less capable than their 'agile' work-mates, make a point of working very evenly, without haste. They compensate for their lack of agility by being able to do a relatively greater amount of fault correction. Thus, through compensatory mechanisms, they create an original, objectively valuable method of work that enables them to achieve high efficiency. Klimov's conclusion is that it is necessary to take into account the specific typological features of the workers' nervous activity and, correspondingly, individualize the training process, primarily in those occupations where the time factor plays the decisive role. We may note in passing that the activities of most operators in man-machine systems belong to occupations of this type.

THE FUNCTIONAL CONDITION OF THE WORKER

Man's extreme reactivity, his sensitivity to various changes occurring both in the physical and social environment and within the organism, finds expression in changes in his functional condition. The functional condition is an extremely unstable and elusive factor, which always directly affects man's efficiency.

An individual always starts his work in some functional condition or other. The influence of this 'initial' functional state is such that, even with regard to persons whose individual specific features are well known to us, strictly speaking we can never predict with absolute assurance what will be the character of their reactions in any particular situation, and what will be their labour productivity.

Whereas it is true that, for all practical purposes, we cannot take into account the initial functional condition of the operator in the man-machine system, and on this basis make appropriate corrections in our predictions of the effectiveness of the behaviour of the system as a whole, it is equally true that, to a considerable extent, we can influence in the required direction the operator's initial state by properly organizing his surroundings.

Here we certainly approach what is one of the main resources of the scientific organization of labour. Today, of course, we know very little about the effect of separate factors on an individual's functional state and about the possibility of controlling the functional state through these factors. Wherever we succeed in establishing a regular relationship between them, we are at once able to draw direct practical conclusions. Suffice it to note an example of the changes that occur in the functional state of the visual analyser as a result of dark adaptation for the purpose of increasing the visual sensitivity of pilots before flights.

The initial functional state, i.e. the one in which the operator in an automatic system starts working, by no means remains unchangeable during the working process. On the contrary, it is subject to continuous variations occurring largely under the influence of, and as a result of, the working process itself. The transmission of information in the man-machine systems puts a great strain on the nervous system. It has to receive, identify, and differentiate signals, which often come to the operator in a continuous stream, to judge on this basis the consecutive conditions of the object being controlled, rapidly to take considered decisions, and then, on the basis of these decisions, to submit the object immediately to certain actions. All this places a constant strain on the mental processes. Under these conditions fatigue inevitably sets in after a while, and keeps increasing right to the end of the working day.

Fatigue exerts most varied effects on the performance of the operator. In particular, as a rule, it has a negative effect on the capacity of the analysers, reduces the receptive field,[9] and causes abrupt changes in the optimum characteristics of the signal stimuli, and in the processes of choice and decision. If his work lasts several hours, it may well happen that the demands presented to the operator, which are fully within his human capabilities in the first hours of work, may prove to be beyond these capabilities later in the day. This will result in abrupt deterioration of quality, errors, increasing number of rejects, etc., if not in accidents and breakdowns.

Therefore, we believe that one of the designer's main tasks is to design such systems, and to ensure such working conditions for man in these systems, as will reduce to a minimum and, if possible, fully eliminate the possibility of all these negative fatigue effects. This can be achieved, on the one hand, by taking special measures to preclude the possibility of human errors in the system. This can be done, for example, by duplicating the functions, or by extensive use of automatic devices, which control man and 'refuse' to obey his erroneous commands. On the other hand, the possible strain should be estimated not only for a person who is just starting work and is completely rested, but also for a relatively tired individual who has already worked for a few hours.

However, to prevent the occurrence and harmful consequences of possible functional changes due to fatigue, the designer of the system should, in all cases, know the factors that cause these changes and their exact manifestations. In this respect, the concepts of fatigue 'in general', or even of 'central', 'nervous', or 'psychic' fatigue are of little use to the designer. He needs information on the concrete manifestations of this or that specific form of fatigue, which is produced, or will be produced, by the operator's work in that kind of man-machine system with which the designer is concerned.

Finally it should be noted that, whereas on the one hand the transmission by man of a maximum amount of information results in rapid deterioration of his functional state, the man's state is no less adversely affected by prolonged exposure to situations in which he is necessarily cut off from all external impressions. Most convincing data in this respect have been obtained of late through experiments carried out in special chambers. This fact must also be borne in mind, especially with regard to such modern moving systems as space ships, for instance.

PERSONAL FACTORS AFFECTING THE OPERATOR'S FUNCTIONAL CONDITION

The operator's functional state varies not only as a result of the performance of technological operations, which in man-machine systems consist of transmitting information. Many other factors impinging on him from his working surroundings also affect his functional state. First among them are those we call 'environmental factors', which concern the setting of the task, or the conditions under which it must be carried out, which form part of the complex of demands that may be presented to the operator.

It is obvious, for example, that the operator's state can be seriously affected by the realization of the high responsibility for the task allotted to him in the man-machine system. It is exactly at decisive, critical moments occurring in the performance of responsible tasks, and there are very many such moments in the work of an operator on an automatic system, that his individual features are most distinctly revealed.

Soviet psychologists have systematically investigated the emotional states of athletes during important competitions. Whereas some of them at such critical moments are distinguished by a 'state of combat readiness', which seems to correspond to optimum excitation of nervous centres, others experience a strong nervous overexcitation which subjectively takes the form of 'pre-start fever' or 'start fever', while a third category experience a state of 'start apathy'.

All these emotional states are observed at the most critical moments in operators working within man-machine systems. For instance, there are known instances of a deep inhibition of the operators' nervous centres in emergency and near-emergency situations. Such states, strongly resembling the 'pre-start' or 'start fever' of athletes, were observed, for example, among men on duty at remote-control panels, railroad operators, etc. It is clearly important to investigate experimentally all the effects produced by such emotional states on the course of the mental processes, which play an especially important role in the transmission of information by man in man-machine systems. The changes such a study would reveal in the effectiveness of various mental functions, such as perception of signal stimuli of different modalities and sensory characteristics, loudness, brightness, colour, shape, etc., could then be taken directly into account by designers of automatic systems.

We often do not understand clearly enough how the perceptual functions of an operator can be affected by increased demands on the quality of his performance, even where no critical situations arise. Let us take such an example. According to I. P. Pavlov, the strength of reaction to an external stimulus, within certain limits, remains proportional to the physiological strength of the stimulus: a stronger reaction corresponds to a stronger stimulus and vice versa. One of the indices of the strength of a reaction is reaction time, which is Pavlov's law, known as the 'law of strength',[10] and this helps in the choice of a signal of optimum intensity, depending on the required reaction time.

The 'law of strength' has been repeatedly checked and confirmed, both with regard to simple psychological reactions and to the so-called reactions of choice, in which the person being tested must react only to some of the signal stimuli presented to him, or must give different reactions to different signal stimuli.

We have discovered some deviations from the 'law of strength'. A. E. Olshannikova demonstrated, during research carried out in our laboratory, that the 'law of strength' remains valid only so long as, in the oral instructions given to the person under test, prime importance is not attached to the demand that the reactions be without error. On the contrary, the law ceases to operate as soon as the experimenter begins to concentrate the attention of the persons under test on the need to avoid all errors. In the latter case, Olshannikova's subjects even displayed a certain paradoxical behaviour: the reaction time to weak stimuli was often shorter than reaction time to strong stimuli. This is most probably the case because the emphasis on absolute absence of error, by 'mobilizing the powers' of the subjects, heightens their nervous excitability, and, thereby, the more intense stimuli become retroactive and cause an inhibition process.

The work of the operator in the man-machine system, in most cases, is highly responsible and therefore he is under pressure to avoid errors. The question arises whether we should, in the light of Olshannikova's findings, take a new look at the expediency of abstract experimental studies of the effectiveness of sensory characteristics of signal stimuli in choosing optimum signals in man-machine systems. On the other hand, since these experiments show that the demand for accuracy, as a rule, invalidates the 'law of strength', the investigation of the speed of reaction in making decisions, under the conditions when absolute freedom from errors is required, could be used as a good test in respect to certain problems.

ENVIRONMENTAL FACTORS AFFECTING THE FUNCTIONAL STATE OF THE OPERATOR

Environmental factors play just as important a part as is played by adjustment factors in the processes by which the operator deals with information in man-machine systems. These factors consist of the different material stimuli acting upon the perceptual system during work, such as illumination, the colour of the walls of the working premises, temperature, atmospheric pressure, technological 'noise', and many other stimuli which suddenly or continuously impinge on the operator from the working environment. Much research, mostly physiological, in both this and other countries, has been done on the influence of these factors on labour productivity. But obviously much still remains to be done in this field.

In this connection we shall dwell briefly on the complex and contradictory role of stimuli which may be termed 'non-signal variables or signals'. We have in view the study carried out at our laboratory in Moscow by L. V. Filonov.

In using some object (a red lamp, for instance) as a stimulus, we usually attach a signal function to only one of its properties (such as a flash of red light). Besides this property, the object possesses a number of other clearly visible characteristics. The signal lamp had definite size, shape, and position. When it lights up, it glows for a definite time, and its brightness may remain constant, diminish, or increase, etc. All these characteristics of the signal stimulus, in themselves, carry no signal meaning. As distinct from the flash of red light, from the point of view of conveying useful information, they constitute non-signal variables. Obviously, when several signal stimuli are presented simultaneously or consecutively, they may differ either in respect to their signal characteristics (red, green, amber), or also in respect to non-signal characteristics (shape, size, brightness, saturation, etc.).

Inasmuch as, during the reception of information, the operator responds only to the signal variables of the stimulus, it would seem that the other, non-signal variables (size, position of the bulb, etc.), should have no effect on his reactions. It might also be assumed that the non-signal variables, being 'extra-stimuli', would cause some kind of reaction on the part of the operator, distracting his attention from the signal, thus hampering his decision and almost immediately having a negative effect on his reaction time. This does actually happen, though rarely. The non-signal variables, which carry no signal message, under certain conditions or after repetition, as it were merge or form a complex in the form of a halo round the signal variables. In this case, the existence of non-signal differences between the stimuli shortens the reaction time instead of increasing it. The dynamics of the transition of non-signal characteristics from a negative 'halo' to a positive 'signal halo' round the signal variable is extraordinarily complex and conforms to definite psychological regularities.

In general, the difference between the signal and the non-signal variables is extremely tentative. Filonov's work has shown, among other things, that in the case of variations which are classed as a signal, according to the technical instructions (variations in colour, for instance), the operator can spontaneously switch from these to some others and attach a signal function to them. One can easily perceive how environmental factors, such as strong and sudden extraneous stimuli, directly affect the functional state of the operator. Much less is known about the effect the functional state of the nervous system can in turn exert on the action of extraneous stimuli.

K. O. Santrosyan (Yerevan) has convincingly demonstrated by experiments that the same extraneous (aural) stimulus can, in one instance, raise, and in other instances lower, the thresholds of light and colour sensitivity, depending on the excitability of the visual analyser within the given interval of time. Yermolayeva-Tomina has demonstrated experimentally the different effects of extraneous aural (or visual) stimuli on visual (or aural) sensitivity, depending on the type of the nervous system. Whereas in individuals with a weak nervous system, an extraneous stimulus lowers sensitivity, in persons with a strong nervous system, it has the reverse effect. This is explained by the appearance of

260   D. A. OSHANIN: *Socio-psychological study of automatic systems*

negative induction, on the one hand, and by the formation of a strong dominant focus in the visual area of the cortex, on the other hand. However, this occurs only some time after the presentation of the extraneous stimulus, whereas at the moment of its appearance, the reverse is the case. This is probably due to the different nature of orientational activity in individuals with strong and weak nervous systems.

NOTES AND REFERENCES

1. Psychological and psychophysiological terms employed in this paper are discussed in *Psychology in the Soviet Union*, edited by Brian Simon, London, 1957.
2. A. A. Lyapunov and G. A. Shestopal, Algorithmic description of control processes, *Matematicheskoe Prosveshchenie*, 1957, issue 2, pp. 93-95.
3. B. P. Petrov, Main trends in the development of automatic regulation and control theory, Soviet Academy of Sciences session on scientific problems of industrial automation, Moscow, 1957, p. 7.
4. Author's paper on the dissertation by Hsui Lian Tsang, Efficiency of signal structures on an information display panel and special features of their mastery, Moscow, 1962, pp. 9-12.
5. Simon, op. cit., p. 17.
6. Simon, op. cit., p. 39.
7. *Typological peculiarities of the higher nervous activity of man*, edited by B. M. Teplov, Vols. I, II, and III, Moscow, 1956-1963.
8. Yu. A. Kalikinsky, Certain peculiarities on the hearing of experts in the technical testing of internal combustion engines, *Voprosy Psikhologii*, 1961, No. 5, pp. 121. 131.
9. Simon, op. cit., p. 15.
10. I. P. Pavlov, *Collected Works*, Moscow, 1951, Vol. III, Book II.

17

Social factors in the emotional attitude towards work

N. F. NAUMOVA

INTRODUCTION

Soviet sociologists, when studying the problem of turning work into a prime vital need, are guided by the fact that the distinguishing features of labour are the economic, social, and ideological relations between people engaged in the process of social production. These relations determine not only the economic but also the social, moral, and psychological significance for the individual of a particular social form of labour.

The social value of work for the individual depends on the position he occupies in a given socio-economic system. It is clear, for example, that the activities of two people, one of whom is selling his labour and the other hiring it, have different social values. The differences in the social values of labour, however, do not consist solely in the distinction between command and subordination; they are based on the great variety of forms of the social division of labour.

The moral value of work depends on the extent to which labour in a given social system fosters man's spiritual development or, on the contrary, turns him into a moral cripple. One social form of labour puts man objectively, regardless of his desire or will, in the position of a 'competitor', and makes his relations with the other members of society hostile. Conversely, another form draws man just as inevitably into a system of relations of collectivism and mutual assistance. It is clear that the objectively existing differences in human relations in a social group call into existence different moral values.

The psychological value of labour depends on the extent to which it contributes to the development of man's thought and his capacities for creative endeavour. Equally important is the question whether the given work evokes in the individual positive or negative feelings and emotions.

There are two aspects to the problem of turning work into a prime vital necessity. The first, or the objective aspect of the problem, is the tendency to change the social forms and content of labour, converting it from compulsory, monotonous work into free, versatile activity, including all those forms of activity of man in society such as material production, science, arts, and management. The other, or the subjective aspect, is the inner, psychological attitude of the individual towards his job.

In spite of the great importance of the objective aspect, we must not ignore the study of man's subjective attitude to his work, because it is satisfaction in work that is the main, and for some people the only condition for an optimistic view of life.

The twentieth century is the age of a great scientific and technical revolution, which exerts a strong influence on all aspects of social life. There are many people who tend to overestimate the possibilities of technology and the degree to which it affects the most complex aspects of the human personality. Sociologists sometimes make this error. They attempt to explain the particular features of people's attitude towards labour, under different social systems, by the specific features of the technical aids to their work, or by the technical features of their labour. We very often come across a statement to the effect that the worker's attitude towards his labours depends, first and foremost, on the degree to which his job is of technical interest to him, i.e. on the nature of the equipment and technology at his disposal and on the level of his skill.

There is no doubt that there does exist a certain connection between the two phenomena, the attitude towards labour and the technical vocational factor. This connection is refracted through the specific features of the society in which the given technical facilities function. Therefore, even the most careful examination of the conditions and technical content of labour, if it does not draw upon an analysis of people's social relations in the process of production, at best can give only a description of labour, and at worst gives a distortion of its essence.

The joy of creative endeavour is a natural, inborn human feeling. Every human being possesses the desire to create things, to alter and to remake the surrounding world. The actual implementation of this desire, however, has turned into a curse for many people who 'hate work like the plague'. The reason for this is that social labour has from time immemorial existed for the individual not only as a means of earning a living, but also as a means of exploitation: the slaveowner exploited his slave, the feudal lord exploited his serf, and so on. For thousands of years, these two aspects of labour had been indissolubly united. To earn one's living always meant to go into servitude and to work for someone else. A disgust with labour came into being as a natural psychological result of this social nature of labour. Hence, the first, and decisive, step towards the transformation of work into a prime vital need must be the elimination of exploitation, and the creation of those social conditions in which the products belong to the worker and to the worker and to society, but not to the private employer, regardless of whether it is one person or a group of people. The implementation of this measure implies a change of the social structure, and of the social system as a whole.

Do technical facilities play any part in the formation of attitudes to work? They undoubtedly do. The technical nature of labour and the worker's skill have a certain influence upon his attitude towards his work, but this influence is not the decisive factor. It merely intensifies or weakens the effect of the basic, socio-economic factor.

In our time, the development of technology, and first and foremost of automation, presents the essential technical prerequisite for turning work into a prime vital need, and for an organic merging of mental and physical labour. This prerequisite, which is of great importance *per se*, cannot yield the desired results if the social system does not create another, decisive prerequisite, which not only wipes out the compulsory social division of labour, and creates conditions for the thorough development of the individual.

A COMPARISON OF THE METHODS USED IN ANALYSING THE EFFECT OF THE SOCIAL FACTOR ON ATTITUDES TO WORK

One of the methods which may be used for examining the part played by the social factor in the formation of attitudes to work is a comparison of these attitudes among groups of workers with similar technical and occupational backgrounds under different social systems. In making such a comparison use has been made of some of the results of an investigation conducted by André Andrieux and Jean Lignon, two French sociologists, of fifty-eight workers of different occupations, age groups, sex, and levels of skill,[1] and of a similar investigation that we conducted at the V. V. Kuibyshev Plant in Moscow of a comparable group of Soviet workers.

Since the initial group of French workers was rather small, we deemed

s

it necessary to question a hundred and sixteen workers, summarizing the results in two groups of 58, and taking care strictly to keep to the correlation of the answers that are given in the larger group.

It should be borne in mind that in a comparative study of field data,[2] a methodological difficulty arises which may be difficult to overcome. A comparison is only possible provided that the questions in the questionnaire have the same meaning, or make the same sense to all those who make up the different groups under comparison. If the groups to be compared live under different social systems, questions verbally identical may prove to have a different meaning, or convey a different sense. Consequently, specially composed questions having the same meaning or conveying the same sense may turn out to be verbally different, which makes comparison very difficult. The identity of the questions cannot be established with sufficient accuracy, and the possibility of arbitrary interpretation arises.

Therefore we chose to use identical questions, being well aware that this may harm the precision of comparison. In order to avoid the inaccuracy exceeding acceptable limits, we had to reject some questions which may possess an altogether different sense under Soviet conditions. Among these questions were those like: 'Do you consider it right for a married woman to work at a factory?' A member of a socialist society takes it for granted that a woman may and should work at a factory, just as she may be engaged in all other branches of social production, or hold a leading position in industry, in the realm of science, or culture etc. This question would have sounded rather strange in Soviet conditions.

COMPARISON OF RESULTS FROM DIFFERENT METHODS OF ANALYSIS

The French sociologists arrived at the conclusion, after talking with those who were questioned and analysing the questionnaires, that most of the workers did not like their work, had no interest in it, and regarded it as just a means of making a living. The Soviet questionnaire gives us grounds to maintain that, in spite of the very wide technical range of the jobs done by the workers questioned, most of them like their work. The initial data shown in the French questionnaire require important corrections since, as Andrieux and Lignon have stressed, the answer 'Yes' does not always imply that the worker is actually fond of his work. 'The worker may say that he likes his work, but a talk with him may reveal that he is only interested in earning wages,' they write. 'He likes the fact that he isn't unemployed, that he has a job, i.e. that he can make a living, but he isn't fond of his work as such.'[3]

Do you like your work? (Question A)

French Questionnaire				Soviet Questionnaire			
Number of people asked	Yes	No	Indefinite answers	Number of people asked	Yes	No	Indefinite answers
58	17	36	5	58	52	5	1

In the talks with Soviet workers such a 'calculated love' of work was voiced by only one worker, who said: 'I like my job when I can make good money at it.' The main question (Do you like your work?) was supplemented by two follow-up questions, which were designed to bring out the actual attitude, though perhaps not always one realized by the workers, towards their work, and thus adjust the answers to the first question. To the first follow-up question, B – 'Do you ever think about your work during your spare time?'—the answers were:

French Questionnaire				Soviet Questionnaire			
Yes	No	Only when I come up against difficulties	No answer	Yes	No	Only when I come up against difficulties	No answer
6	35	13	4	43	9	6	—

To the second question, C – 'If you do, with what feelings do you think about it?'—the answers were as follows:

French Questionnaire		Soviet Questionnaire		
With anxiety, concern, bitterness — with bad feelings	With mixed feelings	With anxiety and concern	With mixed feelings	With good feelings
13	6	8	6	35

Out of the 58 French workers, 35 'completely shed any thought about their work as soon as they leave their work place . . .', 13 think

of it with anxiety, bitterness, and bad feelings, and only 6 think of their
work with 'mixed feelings'.[4] Out of 58 Soviet workers, 43 thought about
their work during their spare time; among them 35 did so 'with good
feelings', 'in a good mood', or 'with a feeling of profound respect and
joy'.

Unfortunately, the French authors do not give a table of the answers
to the second question: 'What time of the day is the most pleasant and
what time is the most unpleasant for you?' Drawing on some indirect
data, we may establish that, if we exclude the workers who said 'No'
to the main question, even those who 'like' their work consider 'morning
to be the worst time of the day, because I have to get up and go to
work', and the best 'the evening, when I leave my work'.

The following table contains the answers received from Soviet
workers to the question: 'What time of day is the most pleasant for
you?' (Question D).

Time of day	N
Morning	12
Evening (when I can have my rest)	18
Evening (because I had done a good day's work)	6
Working time	17
Indefinite answers	5

Many representatives of the French school of the sociology of work
consider that the main cause of the workers' negative attitude towards
their work is the fact that technical developments have broken jobs
down into narrow, repetitive operations. This had made work so dull and
monotonous that it is of no interest to man under any social conditions,
In analysing the French questionnaires, one cannot help noticing that
the opinion of the workers themselves about the reason for their dislike of their work differs from the sociologists' opinion on this issue.

It is striking that the great majority of the workers put social factors
in first place. It is even not the monotonous nature of their work that
they consider to be the most disagreeable factor, but the feeling of
dependence and subordination which accompanies it. This sense of
dependence is not due to technical reasons, of course, but to the economic
and social structure of the enterprise and society. The socio-economic
aspects of labour strike the worker as much more important than the
technical and professional aspects.

In the Soviet questionnaire we do not see such marked social trends
in the answers to question E, as we do in the French questionnaire.

This indicates that Soviet workers do not experience any feeling of social dependence. That is why they mention, first and foremost, other factors, which seem to be socially neutral at first, such as organization

French Questionnaire

What do you dislike most at your enterprise?' (Question E)

Objects of criticism	N
Noise	1
Bad safety provisions	1
Mean exploitation of workers	1
Work outside my trade	1
Primitive level of workers	1
A feeling of being shut off from the others	2
Unhygienic conditions, cloak rooms	2
Long working hours	2
Poor work organization	2
Tempo of operations	3
Nobody takes any notice of you	3
The work itself	7
Everything as a whole	7
Bad relations between workers	8
The monotony of work	13
Labour conditions, dirt	13
Subordination and dependence	42

(The number of answers is larger than the number of workers questioned, because many workers indicated more than one reason for their dislike.)

Soviet Questionnaire

'*What do you dislike most at your enterprise?'* (Question E)

Object of criticism	N
Noise	3
Dirt	4
Crowded premises	9
Canteen	3
Organization of labour	8
Discipline	4
Unhygienic conditions, cloak rooms	9
Night shifts	3
Indefinite answers	6
'I like everything'	9

of labour, and workers' discipline. Actually, the very fact that we find these issues mentioned as objects of criticism in the Soviet questionnaire shows that the Soviet worker does not consider himself to be simply the object of certain favourable or unfavourable circumstances. He feels himself to be master of the enterprise, and is anxious to do away with those defects that are a handicap to him personally, and also those that interfere with the smooth operation of the entire enterprise. There are social motives in the Soviet workers' answers to question A as well.

What is the social process by which the worker sees the reason for liking his work? At first sight it may seem that the main thing for him is that his work should be varied. This term is the one that is used most frequently in answer to the question 'Do you like your work, and why?' But in reading the whole questionnaire carefully we find that the workers themselves consider the word 'varied' to be inadequate, superficial, and unconvincing (especially in those cases where their work is not at all varied). The worker tries to analyse more profoundly his own attitude towards his work, and here a social motive comes to the fore. The commonest form of answers are of the type: 'I like my work because it's useful to our society', or 'I like my work because it is to the benefit of the whole of our people'. A twenty-two-year-old woman coil-winder writes in the questionnaire about her work: 'I can't say that my work is very interesting, but I am quite satisfied with it, since all our work is a contribution to the building of communism'.

Such statements by the workers show that civic sentiment, the sense of duty and the recognition that every worker's labour is essential for our society permit them to turn uninteresting work into something that is of interest to them.

The fact that the link between 'interesting work' and 'work that is liked' has proved to be not so indissoluble as some sociologists consider it to be also confirms the decisive part played by the social factor in forming man's attitude towards his work.

Soviet Questionnaire
'*Is your work interesting?*' (Question F)

Yes	No
44	14

The number of workers who are fond of their work (see answers to question A) does not coincide with the number of those who consider their work to be interesting. There are 8 more of the former. If this is examined objectively, then the difference is even greater, since, in our opinion, only 20 out of the 58 workers investigated have technically interesting work. The other 38 workers perform rather monotonous operations. Nevertheless 33 of them have come to like their jobs, and find something interesting and attractive in them. This 'something' is our society's need for every person's work.

Marxist sociologists maintain that the elimination of exploitation and the building of a communist social structure are the decisive prerequisites for turning work into a prime vital need, but they do not consider them to be the only essential prerequisites. In order to make work not merely a source of satisfaction, but also of great pleasure, it is necessary to establish effective social control over some of the most important processes of social development. The process now taking place in Soviet society, which involves increasing numbers of people in management and state administration, is of great importance in this respect. The direct participation of all members of society in management and administration, whereby everyone is involved not only in production but also in social and political activity, creates the decisive prerequisite for removing the old, morally crippling division of labour.

On the other hand, this participation is of immense educational importance. When every individual takes upon himself a real responsibility for the fate of the development of society, and ceases merely to carry out a fixed 'partial' production function, this is bound to give rise to a high sense of responsibility and civic duty.

It is also essential to set up an appropriate system of education and training. This system must form a creative individual, who is not only capable of creative activity but who is, at the same time, incapable of doing non-creative work. Such an individual will be able to introduce a creative element into any kind of work, and thereby neutralize the harmful effects of whatever 'partial' labour remains in existence.

NOTES AND REFERENCES

1. See A. Andrieux et J. Lignon, *L'ouvrier d'aujourd'hui. Sur les changements dans la condition et la conscience ouvrière*, Paris, 1960.

2. In studying the inner world of man, it is the objective method, i.e. investigation of man's actual conditions of existence, that must play the main part. The subjective method, i.e. a study of what man thinks of himself, should also be employed.

3. A. Andrieux et J. Lignon, op. cit., pp. 45-46.

4. ibid., pp. 71, 73.

18

The relationship between type of work and personality

N. G. VALENTINOVA

INTRODUCTION: CLASSIFICATION OF
WORKERS INVESTIGATED

This investigation is concerned with the influence of the degree of mechanization of labour on some personality traits in the worker. The primary data were obtained from interviews with and observations of 457 workers in the largest enterprises in Gorky region. The basic criterion in this investigation is the extent of mechanization. All the workers were selected by the stratified sample method and divided into five main groups: workers who are engaged in (a) manual labour, which does not involve the use of any machinery, (b) manual labour involving the use of machinery, (c) the operation of machines, (d) work on automatic machine or conveyor lines, and (e) maintenance and setting. *Table 1* represents the distribution of the sample by enterprises in the Gorky region.

Table 1. Distribution of sample by enterprises

Enterprises	a	b	c	d	e	Total	Engineers and technicians
Car Works	10	62	82	14	55	223	25
Krasnoye Sormovo	18	33	18	7	7	83	10
Machine Tool Works	2	4	20	–	7	33	–
Engine Works	1	3	16	1	7	28	–
Krasnaya Etna	3	1	9	15	6	34	–
Balakhna Works	10	14	8	2	9	43	–
Others	–	5	–	3	6	14	21
Total	44	122	153	42	97	458	56

The sample was composed of 73 per cent men and 27 per cent women. Distribution by standard of education is shown in *Table 2*.

MANUAL WORKERS, GROUP (A)

The first group includes workers engaged in manual labour unaided by any machinery. Despite the growing rate of mechanization of labour-consuming processes, this group is still quite numerous. It includes auxiliary unskilled workers engaged in the manual loading, handling, carrying, and storing of raw materials and products, as well as in the

Table 2. Distribution of sample by standard of education

Education	a	b	c	d	e
1. Up to 4th year	16	10	18	6	10
2. Up to 7th year (general)	11	30	34	9	22
3. Up to 7th year (vocational)	4	10	23	1	1
4. 7th to 9th year (general)	7	14	18	10	20
5. 7th to 9th year (vocational)	1	6	8	1	–
6. 10th year	5	34	37	9	25
7. Secondary vocational	–	18	11	5	18
8. Incomplete higher	–	–	2	1	1
9. Higher	–	–	2	–	–
10. Total	44	122	153	42	97

cleaning of premises. Most of the respondents of this group (44) are employed at the Car Works and the Krasnoye Sormovo Works. Nearly all of them have had from 4 to 7 years of education.

The labour of the workers of this group requires physical strength, stamina, and good health, but does not require any special training. The psychological characteristic of this kind of work is the need for intense and regular exertions of effort which, in turn, has an effect on the general psychological state and development of personality.

Prolonged observations at the enterprises, and especially the Railway Workshop of the Sormovo Works and the Accessory Workshop of the Car Works, led to the conclusion that this kind of labour gives rise to the following traits. The need for the correct location of an object requires a fine sense of co-ordination which, in turn, implies quickness and accuracy of perception and spatial orientation, as well as concentration of attention. The need for rapid movement with both hands requires well-developed co-ordination of motion. The need to ensure a smooth flow of articles, without delay to fellow-workers requires a sense of rhythm. Such work is sometimes dangerous (e.g. a loader's work), and it requires emotional stability and concentration.

This work does not satisfy everyone, especially young people with some education, for whom it is usually a temporary stage in life. It gives no mental satisfaction to young workers and therefore does not suit them, though they are fully aware of its importance for production and for society.

Changes in the character of the work of this group will affect the psychology of the workers. Arduous manual labour is to be eliminated by means of introduction of new equipment. This applies above all to labour-consuming operations such as handling, loading, and unloading. For example, the use of containers, with cranes and automatic loaders, is an important factor in the mechanization of many kinds of labour.

With the development of integrated mechanization and especially automation, loading and unloading will cease to be independent operations. The mechanization of these operations is difficult because loading and unloading devices have to meet a variety of complex requirements. Mechanization and automation will raise the problem of the retraining of a large number of workers now engaged in arduous manual labour. Some experience in such retraining has been accumulated at the enterprises under study, and especially at the Sormovo Works.

Manual workers can be quickly trained to operate machinery requiring special skills. For a young worker, it is easier to learn a new trade. Characteristically, the transition from manual to mechanized labour is an especially easy process among workers with secondary education. Though more difficult, this transition is quite possible for elderly workers with a low standard of general skill. Examples of the transition of workers from manual to mechanized work have been studied. One of these is I. K. Kedrov, a 44-year-old worker at the Krasnoye Sormovo Works, who has been employed for 27 years. He stated 'the work did not satisfy me because it was hard, and besides, the strain was uneven. I was transferred to this department, where I am working on mechanical and hydraulic presses. I had a month's training. Everything was necessary and useful in this training, but I felt that lack of schooling just pulled me down. Now my pay has not increased much, but my new work is much easier and much more interesting.'

In many respects such descriptions are useful, especially for assessing the difficulties which will arise in the retraining of middle-aged and elderly workers, who were previously engaged in manual labour and lack an adequate educational background. Special forms of education are necessary in such cases, and the search for these forms is now in progress.

MANUAL WORKERS WORKING WITH MACHINERY, GROUP (B)

The conditions and character of the work of the second group are similar to those of the first group. Arduous manual labour also predominates here. The group includes workers feeding machinery by hand, loader-operators using conveyors, unloaders, slingers, crane-loaders, transfer operators, in short all who are engaged in work with machinery but do not actually operate it. This is the most numerous group (122).

Comparing this group, in terms of educational background, with the previous one, we can draw one clear conclusion: the work requires a higher level of education and a wider range of knowledge. This group was investigated mainly at the Accessory Workshop of the Car Works. The respondents emphasized, and this has been confirmed by observations, that a positive factor in their work is the association with, and partial knowledge of, the work performed by more highly skilled workers engaged in operation, maintenance, and adjustment. Team work at fixed locations is a feature which distinguishes this group from the previous one.

The development of mechanization enhances the importance of this group, but as the operation of machinery becomes automated to an increasing extent, so its numerical strength will diminish. Owing to the current rapid rate of mechanization of labour-consuming processes, the number of machine operators will steadily grow. The required skills in this group will rise accordingly.

MACHINE OPERATORS, GROUP (C)

The third group comprises those engaged in mechanized work, which makes it possible to perform operations with the minimum of manual effort. The group includes machine-, loom-, and machine-tool operators; conveyor workers constitute a special subgroup. Whereas the work of press operators, machine-tool operators and conveyor workers is somewhat monotonous, the work of polishers and universal machine operators is very complicated and requires knowledge and ingenuity. Under conditions of mechanization, the importance of these occupations rises, while the development of automation decreases the number of those engaged in them.

Let us consider in greater detail (i) the differentiated work of press operators, (ii) conveyor operations, and (iii) the work of universal machine operators. Subgroup 1 was analysed at the Accessory Workshop of the Car Works. The worker's motor functions are of considerable importance in operating machine-tools. Whereas physical strength took priority when the level of mechanization was lower; agility, accuracy, speed, and quickness of reaction are at a premium here. Sensory functions and, in particular, accuracy of perception are also important, as are intellectual operations. For example, an assembly fitter's work can be described psychologically by subdividing it into the following operations: planning the work, preliminary operations (the selection of tools, preparation of parts, etc.), carrying out the work and checking one's own work and passing it.

The same subgroup includes a press operator's work. He operates small presses and drilling and other machine-tools and his work can be differentiated into three operations: 'feed', 'press', 'remove'. The speed and accuracy of the operator's movements and the continuity of his attention are extremely important. Some press operators perform from 13,000 to 15,000 uniform movements a day, which leads to fatigue. Though some machine-tools are being automated rapidly and successfully, this kind of work has not yet disappeared, for a number of economic and technological reasons.

Acceptance of the uniformity and monotony of their work is typical of many workers in this subgroup. A familiar repetitive routine permits them to think, while working, about their home affairs, etc. N. Kholezova (age: 43; education: 5th year of school; previously lived in a village) has been working at the Accessory Workshop for seven years. Her work may be reduced to putting a part into a press, pushing the button, and removing the part. Asked whether she liked her job, she answered that she did. Asked whether she could think during her work about something else she replied: 'I know all these operations very well and I can go through them without as much as a glance. While working, I can think about things at home and, if I am in a good mood and everything is all right, the work runs smoothly.'

G. Burova (age: 31; education: 5th year; length of service: 9 years), asked whether she liked her occupation, said: 'I like it because I am working at the same place and I am used to this work. Yes, I do the same work every day, but this does not seem monotonous or tiresome to me, and I don't want to move to another job.'

Y. Shurnina (age: 44; education: 4th year; length of service: 20 years) described her attitude to her work in this way: 'I get tired of noise, but not of monotonous work. I wouldn't like to exchange my job for another one. I am used to this place, I like this work and I have asked the foreman to leave me where I am and not to transfer me to another job.'

The subgroup consists mostly of elderly women with education not above the 6th or 7th years, and with a long working record. Those who have been working for long in the same occupation note that, when they first began the work, it seemed monotonous. The longer they worked, the more they liked it because they could think about something else: home, family, etc. All of them, without exception, note that the work runs more quickly if the primary products passed on to them are of good quality, if they are in a good mood, if they have good relations with their fellow-workers in the team, etc., i.e. if there is a positive emotional atmosphere. During the work, they can think about something else as long as it runs smoothly but, as soon as any difficulty arises, they have to concentrate on the work. The subgroup includes only women. Men find more interesting and diversified work. In general, men do not favour monotonous work and leave it at the first opportunity.

The subgroup of conveyor workers involves unskilled labour which will also be eliminated, though perhaps somewhat later than arduous manual labour (in the second decade from now). One of the major problems confronting industrial psychologists in a study of conveyor production is the monotony of the labour process. However, the opinion that the monotony of conveyor work is an unmixed evil, affecting all workers in the same way, is hardly valid. Soviet industrial psychologists must concentrate on the selection of workers according to their abilities and interests, i.e. on occupational selection. In order to find out which workers are suitable for conveyor work, we have studied it at the enterprises in question. A poll among conveyor workers has shown that there are two different types of worker: some prefer to do repetitive work while others quickly get tired of it and feel depressed. Those who can think about something else adjust themselves to this work. Others regard it as something imposed on them and the work holds their attention to such a small degree that the slightest distraction affects productivity or increases rejects. A worker who can easily adjust himself to conveyor work does not detest it, and sometimes gets so used to one operation that, when asked whether he would like to transfer to another operation, will reply: 'I like this operation because I can think about something else as I work.' Other workers answered that, on the contrary, they would like to be transferred to some other operation.

Here are some characteristic answers of the first type. 'After I have got used to the work, my hands do it without bothering my head.'

'When one dreams of something, work runs more smoothly.' 'My thoughts wander elsewhere, but my eyes look on.' Such workers easily do uniform work and are not irritated by it.

The answers of the second type were as follows: 'Whenever I think about something else, even for a moment, I can't keep up the pace.' 'I can think about something else, but this interferes with the work. As soon as I do it, the part is botched.' 'There are some who can work singing, which I never do. The work goes all wrong, especially when I feel depressed.'

A conveyor worker must time his movements to the pace set by his neighbour, or by the conveyor belt. Individual differences are important in this respect as well. Here is a conveyor worker's opinion: 'Conveyor work is much worse. I don't like to depend on others. When I like my work, I am satisfied, but from this work I get no satisfaction at all.'

There are also entirely different estimations. 'In conveyor work, one feels much better, more cheerful, and one tries to keep up with the others.' 'It's better with conveyor work: no one lags behind.'

The following experiment was carried out to determine the effect of a set pace on the operator. Several workers were required to work to a metronome set first at 40, then 60, and later 84 strokes per minute. At each stroke a worker had to put a plate on the rod. The respondents showed their different attitudes to the set pace. Here are some favourable attitudes. 'It's better with the metronome: the rhythm is pleasant.' 'It's nice to keep pace with the strokes. Work is easier, as if someone pushes it on.' 'The work is so much easier.' 'These strokes are very useful: you feel just when you have to make a move.'

There was also a negative attitude to the pace thus set. 'It's better without the metronome: I have to keep pace and without it I go at it as slowly or fast as I can.'

There are good grounds for supposing that, if a worker is unable to perform monotonous work at a set pace, he will never be satisfied with conveyor work. Moreover, his dissatisfaction, accumulating for many years, may cause him to deteriorate.

Those who are not suited psychologically to conveyor work are usually transferred to separate operations. Quite often among the best conveyor workers there are some who do not like the work but keep at it because of high pay. Psychologically unsuitable work affects them, and there is frequent occurrence of unstable types in this group. Since effects of this kind show only after a few years, a preliminary psychotechnical and medical selection of prospective conveyor workers is quite vital.

The description of conveyor work would be incomplete if mental factors of a higher order were neglected. Our purpose was to investigate how highly automated motor functions release attention for mental activity not related to the aim of the operation performed: we term this process the 'vacuum'.

Investigations have made it possible to identify three groups by their reactions to monotony. The workers of the first group have adjusted themselves to monotony; they think it soothing, convenient, calling for no attention and concentration, and use the vacuum for thinking about something else.

Those of the second group dislike the work and regard it as temporary. They find an outlet in studies and in the improvement of their skills, and their future prospects make it easier for them to put up with the strain.

The workers of the third group make a creative use of the vacuum for the improvement of production as a whole, or mental rehearsal of their study assignment (this applies to students at schools for young workers).

Psychologically, the workers in the first and third groups have much in common, and they differ from those in the second group as they are able to fill the vacuum with thoughts not directly connected with their work. The first and third groups differ, as, in the third group, the vacuum is a creative factor conducive to the development of personality. The third group suggests the possibility of solving the problem of the monotony of standardized simple tasks. Creative experiment makes it possible not only to overcome the monotony of such work, but also to use it for the development of personality.

Extensive work is in progress in the Soviet Union to study the mechanization and automation of technological processes in conveyor work. Conditions are favourable since standardized work paves the way for mechanized and automated devices. Some specific difficulties are also involved in this process. Though, in general, conveyor work has been widely used in assembly, there are cases when automation cannot be introduced so easily.

In the introduction of complex mechanization and automation of conveyor work, technical thought in the Soviet Union favours changes in technology wherever they make it possible to abolish conveyor work. At the same time, research is in progress to improve conveyor work. Measures are being taken to eliminate the harmful effects of conveyor work by choosing scientifically appropriate conditions of work and rest for different types of conveyor work, and by using what is known as 'second signal system'[1] conditioned-reflex stimulation. Such stimulation for conveyor production is expressed in various patterns of personal and social interests, which would decrease the harmful consequences of localized cerebral excitation and inhibition in standardized simple tasks. Work is thus made more intelligent and interesting and hence easier.

At Soviet enterprises using conveyor work, the forms of 'second signal system' conditioned-reflex stimulation include various material incentives and opportunities for the operator to improve his skill or to change over to another operation. Other major factors are the organization of conveyor work in teams, rationalizing and invention, change-over to different operations, a larger number of operations per worker, improved hygienic and aesthetic conditions of work, including ventilation, lighting, the painting of walls, flowers and plants in the workshops, broadcasting of music during work, etc.

WORKERS EMPLOYED ON AUTOMATIC MACHINERY, GROUP (D)

The fourth group includes workers operating automatic machine-tools and lines, automatic machine-tool operators, press operators, control desk operators at power stations, etc. The proportion of such employees is not yet high. However, their role in production will be rapidly increasing with the progress of automation. The elements of manual work are of less importance in this group, while technical knowledge is decisive. This group was investigated at the Cold Upsetting Workshop of the Krasnaya Etna Works and the Gauge Workshop of the Krasnoye Sormovo Works.

The investigation has revealed the required physiological and psychological functions of the operator. For example, an automatic machine-tool operator has to run 2 to 4 machine-tools, which requires a wide span of attention and quickness of reaction. Observations were made at the Cold Upsetting Workshop of the Krasnaya Etna Works to discover the most complicated operations and the physical and mental qualities required for them. The shift foreman reported that 40 persons were engaged in his shift, 20 of them operating automatic machine-tools. The shift is a good friendly team, and all its members study a great deal. As a result of automation, three separate operations have been combined, and are now performed with one machine-tool (manufacturing of blanks, shaping of hexahedral heads, and threading).

Standardized production involves the following requirements. The operator must know the operational instructions for his machine-tool, be able to regulate the speeds, avoid wastage of material, co-ordinate his movements to the pace of the machine-tool, check the quality of the output, control the rate of output, and set the machine-tool.

The corresponding psycho-physical qualities are: visual co-ordination, a spatial sense, accuracy in small manual operations, accuracy of tactile perception, a sense of rhythm, quickness and accuracy of visual perception, concentration, motor co-ordination, etc.

It was found that the operation of one machine-tool, or several, may be reduced to purely routine attention. The operators' mental energies are not absorbed by their work. They are not depressed by its monotony, and, since it is easy, are satisfied with it. 'Now we can meet and talk, while before we had just to stick to the press, seeing nothing around us until lunchtime, when we could meet our workmates.' 'I used to operate a press without an automatic feed. I just pressed the treadle, lifted the part with one hand and took it away with the other. This went on for several years. My back ached and I was bored. Now parts are fed into our presses automatically and the work is much easier. It is monotonous, but I like the work because I needn't think about it.'

In this group it is worth while to single out a subgroup consisting of the best-trained and most enterprising highly skilled operators. As a rule they combine the functions of machine-tool operators and machine-tool setters. They deal with complex equipment and quite often they have to introduce various technological improvements and eliminate faults. As a rule, they work as fitters, lathe operators, milling-machine operators, etc. They are the initiators of the introduction of the latest equipment. Dealing with complex devices, instruments, and installations, they have a wide range of scientific and technological knowledge. They are interested in engineering, in the broadest sense of the word, and they can analyse some technical problems in terms of different sciences, such as physics, chemistry, or electrodynamics. Naturally most of these operatives want to extend and improve their knowledge. They combine their work with studies at secondary, technical, and higher schools.

This is what N. I. Kirilov, an operator on an automatic line, at the Zavolzhye Engine Works, writes about his occupation. 'It is very interesting to work on an automatic line. The operator has to control all operations. In general, the equipment is the best available and therefore very interesting. The automatic line is important for production. It raises the productivity of labour, improves the quality, and brings down the costs.'

The automation of production and the introduction of the latest

T

equipment makes work attractive and varied. Variety is a major element of creative work. Several trades can be combined and thus something new learned. Among the factors fostering the operator's interest in engineering work and studies, mention should be made of the influence of well-organized teams running, for example, automatic lines (such as the automatic line for the treatment of chassis bodies at the Gorky Car Works, and the automatic line for the treatment of cylinder heads at the Zavolzhye Engine Works). These lines are run by small teams of 6 to 7 workers each. They value the trust which has been placed in them: running an automatic line is a responsible job.

If the production processes have been automated and mechanized to a considerable extent, and high levels of skill and extensive knowledge are at a premium, many workers want to improve their skills, and their interest in modern equipment may well develop into an urge to study this equipment thoroughly. This kind of worker is the prototype of the citizen for whom creative labour is a primary need and a source of pleasure.

However, the personnel servicing automatic machine-tools and automatic lines also includes a subgroup (mainly women with a fairly low level of education and training) engaged in the simplest functions of observation, regulation, feeding, and removing products. Examples are the automatic line of presses in the Accessory Workshop and the Automatic Machine-Tool Workshop of the Gorky Car Works. The operators find their work easier and more pleasant. However, their operations are rather primitive. They have no proper scientific-technological background which would enable them to study the new equipment, including machine-tools, systems, units, and devices. They can learn only separate technological operations. Nevertheless, many of them run several machine-tools (the Gauge Workshop of the Krasnaya Etna Works) and this stimulates their interest in work and production in general. They are satisfied with their occupation.

Among the respondents of this subgroup 69 per cent consider that their work is interesting, and 84 per cent that their occupation is interesting.

Another factor deserves attention. It has been indicated above that an automatic line is run as a rule by a small but well-knit team of 6 to 7 operators. The team running the cylinder head automatic line at the Zavolzhye Engine Works is a case in point. The team leader works as setter, machine-tool operator, and maintenance fitter. Other members of the team can also work in several capacities and replace each other, if necessary. The atmosphere of friendliness, mutual assistance, and responsibility is characteristic of the team. It should be noted that mental operations predominate in the work of this group. This is what a worker of the Zavolzhye Engine Works (age: 24; education: secondary) has to say on this point: 'I regard setting as a mental operation. We must also keep an eye on the instruments and react quickly to the readings. The knowledge I got at school stands me in good stead now.'

As the stock of automatic machine-tools is augmented, and their performance improves, the number of automatic machine-tool operators (not engaged in setting and maintenance) will relatively decrease. The amount of maintenance and setting work will increase at the same time. After some training, automatic machine-tool operators will be able to work as setters and maintenance men. The combination in one person of the functions of operator, setter, and, partially, maintenance man is already current in many enterprises.

The experience of managers of automated enterprises indicates that the work, and especially manual work in automated workshops, will tend to become easier. Even today, mental activity accounts for a far larger proportion of work in automated production. Obviously, in the automated workshops of the future, manual work will be reduced to a minimum, and mental work will be much easier because the machine-tools will be more 'intelligent' and easy to control.

Special mention should be made of the personnel (workers, technicians, and engineers) operating various automatic control desks. The role of this group, and its proportion, in production will rise with the development of automation, automatic control, remote control, and industrial television. A poll taken among the control-desk personnel furnishes interesting data on the work of this group. The consensus of opinion seems to indicate that, apart from the control instruments, the operator must be acquainted with the technology of production, since he is responsible for the quality of the finished products and rhythmic scheduling of production. Psychologically, a sound knowledge of the technology helps the control-desk operator to overcome fatigue caused by constant strain. The more experienced the operator, and the better his knowledge of production, the easier it is for him to put right any failure, and the greater is his self-confidence.

The work of this group includes mainly mental operations. The need for the operator to possess a sound knowledge of production to work successfully at the automatic control desk implies a certain measure of specialization. This is likely to continue in the future, and it will not be easy to transfer the control-desk operators to other jobs in the same branch (let alone other branches) without additional special training.

T*

FITTERS AND SETTERS, GROUP (E)

The fifth group comprises fitters and setters, i.e. personnel engaged in preparing and adjusting equipment for the performance of certain operations. Mechanization and automation rapidly increase the numbers in this group. Among the 97 workers investigated, 10 have had 4 years of education; 23: up to 7 years; 20: 7, 8, or 9 years; 25: 10 years; 18 have had secondary technical education; and 1 incomplete higher education. Thus the contingent consists mostly of persons with secondary and secondary technical education: 70 per cent have had at least 7 years at school.

This group was investigated at the Krasnoye Sormovo and Krasnaya Etna Works. In the Cold Upsetting Workshop of the Krasnaya Etna Works, an automatic machine-tool operator adjusts 2 or 3 machine-tools. He controls the operation of the line, and whenever a failure occurs he works as a setter (which incidentally also requires a wide span, and a concentration, of attention). The line produces mainly screws and bolts. The process consists of three stages: the manufacturing of blanks, shaping of the hexahedral head, and finally threading, all of which are performed automatically (except feeding). The operator has to operate several machine-tools, and secure a uniform rate of production and the required quality of output, which calls for constant attention, accuracy of visual co-ordination and perception, and sense of rhythm. The operator must also know how to repair and adjust the machine-tools, which involves some intellectual skill.

CONCLUSION

An analysis of the effect of different types of work on the personality of the operator suggests the general conclusion that the study of the evolution of labour in connection with technological progress is of exceptional importance for determining ways of forming those mental characteristics that are conducive to the harmonious development of personality.

NOTE

1. The 'second signal system' is a special form of higher nervous activity possessed only by mankind. It is a system of reflex links in their physiological expression; a system of links and reactions which are generated by words. See I. P. Pavlov, *Conditioned Reflex*; I. P. Pavlov, *Lectures on the Cerebral Hemispheres*. (There is an explanation of the 'second signal system' in Simon, *Psychology in the Soviet Union*, London, 1957, p. 74ff.).

The Soviet education system

The basic principles of the Soviet education system are a single educational programme, free education at all stages, co-education, and instruction in the pupil's native language.

Before the educational reform of 1958, the vast majority of Soviet children attended general schools of three types: primary four-year schools (7 to 11 years); incomplete secondary schools (7 to 14 years); and complete secondary schools (7 to 17 years). In isolated rural areas, primary schools were the only ones available, but, by 1958, most children were able to continue their education up to 14 years of age. In the urban areas, children were able to attend school for a complete secondary education and to qualify for the 'certificate of maturity'. Many of the children who had completed their general secondary education at 14 years of age went on to vocational schools for a period of from two to five years at specialized secondary schools, labour reserve or trade schools, and schools for young workers.

Since 1958, the general educational school has the following structure: primary school (forms 1 to 4) from 7 to 10 years; eight-year labour polytechnical schools (forms 1 to 8) from 7 to 16 years; secondary labour polytechnical school with industrial training (forms 1 to 10) from 7 to 17 or 18 years. In addition, there are secondary evening schools (forms 9 and 10) for young people already at work. Eight years of education is compulsory throughout the country. The term 'polytechnical' in the labour polytechnical schools means that the pupils are taught the general principles of productive work, but they are not trained to be technical experts. Local conditions determine the type of school available. In small villages with only a few children, for example, only primary schools are provided. The commonest type of school is the eight-year labour polytechnical school, which may exist either separately or as part of a ten-year school. Ten-year schools can exist separately with only the ninth and tenth forms. On completion of the ten-year secondary school, the pupil receives a matriculation certificate (attestat zrelosti) which entitles him to enter an institute or university. On completion of the eight-year school, the pupil can continue his general education in a ten-year school or enter a special production school (for from one to three years) or a technical college (from three to four years), which provide a full secondary professional education. A diploma of a technical college also confers the right to enter an institute or university. There are also boarding-schools with forms 1 to 8 and forms 1 to 10, and special schools for gifted children in the fields of physics and mathematics, music, ballet, and the circus, which provide their pupils with a secondary education and professional training.

The management of the Soviet economy

The management of the Soviet economy is controlled by the Government of the Soviet Union and by the Governments of the Union Republics. Changes were made in the system of management in October 1965. Before October 1965, the Soviet Supreme Economic Council, under the Soviet Council of Ministers, was the highest state body supervising industry and construction throughout the country. It was set up at the beginning of 1963, and was accountable to the Soviet Government and worked under its guidance. The Council issued orders and regulations which were obligatory for all state bodies irrespective of their position within the hierarchy. It was responsible for the direction of the work of state agencies concerned with the management of particular branches of industry or with industry and construction as a whole, also for the practical solution of current problems of the state direction of the economy. The Supreme Council was also responsible for the co-ordination of the work of the Soviet State Planning Committee, the Soviet Economic Council, the Soviet State Committee for Construction, and the state industry and production committees of the Soviet Union.

Since October 1965, there are the following organizations under the Soviet Council of Ministers, which is the highest body responsible for the management of industry:

1. The Soviet State Planning Committee (Gosplan) is a governmental body, responsible for working out the principal trends and problems of the economic development of the country, for drawing up national economic plans and for checking their fulfilment. It fixes the scale and rate of economic development, the proportional development for the different branches of the economy, and the structure of the national economy as a whole.

2. The Soviet State Committee for Science and Technology determines the principal trends of technical progress. It is responsible for the organization of the planning of research on scientific and technical problems and supervises the application of scientific and technical developments to the national economy.

3. The Soviet State Committee for Material and Technical Supplies organizes supplies for industrial enterprises.

4. The Soviet State Committee for Construction (Gosstroi) directs all the affairs concerned with construction.

5. The direct management of industrial enterprises is carried out by the Ministries for the relevant branches of industry in accordance with the principle of management of the economy on an industry basis.

Soviet wage rates and grades of skill

Industrial wages are fixed in accordance with the skill grades and wage rates which take into account the nature, difficulty, and amount of work performed. This means that the rate of wages is calculated on the basis of the grade allocated to the worker in accordance with his skill. In 1959, a six-grade wage-rate system was introduced for workers in engineering and metalworking industries, with ratios of 1:1·8 to 2, which replaced the previous seven-, eight-, and nine-grade systems, in many of which the rates of the highest grade were 2·5 to 3·5 times higher than the rates of the lowest grade.

Grades	I	II	III	IV	V	VI
Wage-rate ratios	1·0	1·13	1·29	1·48	1·72	2·0
Relative increase of ratios (percentage)	–	13·0	14·0	14·7	16·2	16·3

The system introduced in 1959 considerably reduced the differential between the highest and lowest grades, but retained the material incentive to raise the standard of skill. With the introduction of the new system, a considerable increase was made in the monthly rates of the lowest grade; for industry as a whole, these are at present 40 to 45 roubles, and the actual minimum wage is 60 to 65 roubles when various bonuses and supplementary payments are taken into account.

This adjustment of the wage system and regrading were accompanied by a reduction in the proportion of lower-paid grades with wages below 60 roubles a month; in the coal industry the number of these was reduced from 12·6 per cent to 2·2 per cent, or by 5·7 times, and in the oil industry from 16·5 per cent to 7·1 per cent, or by 2·3 times. In the electrical engineering industry the number of low-paid workers (with wages of less than 60 roubles a month) was reduced from 7 per cent to 3·6 per cent. The number of medium-paid workers (with wages of from 60 to 140 roubles a month) increased from 80·4 per cent to 85·4 per cent, while the number of highly paid workers (with wages exceeding 140 roubles a month) fell from 12·6 per cent to 11 per cent. These facts indicate a tendency for the differential in the wages of the lower- and higher-skilled workers to decrease, concurrently with a simultaneous rise in the actual minimum wage.

NOTE

1. For fuller details see A. S. Shkurko, 'The industrial wage system in the U.S.S.R.' *International Labour Review*, Vol. XC, No. 4, pp. 352-364, 1964.

Bibliography

WORKS BY INDIVIDUAL AUTHORS

Place of publication, unless otherwise stated, is Moscow.

AGEYEV, S. S., *The development of talent in the process of work*, Baku, 1961.

ARKHANGELSKY, L. M., *Work and morality*, Sverdlovsk, 1961.

BREYEV, B. D., *Technical progress and the composition of manpower*, 1963.

CHISTYAKOV, M. I., *Advancement of cultural and technical standards of working people in the Soviet Union*, 1962.

DANIELYAN, N., *Distinctions between intellectual and physical labour*, Yerevan, 1958.

DAVIDOV, YU. N., *Labour and freedom*, 1962.

DRACHEV, V. K., *Work and leisure*, Simferopol, 1963.

FEIGIN, Y. G. (Ed), *The problems of placing labour during the comprehensive construction of communism*, 1960.

FOMINA, V. A. and BELOZERTSEV, V. I., *Characteristic features of the development of the socialist mode of production*, 1962.

GUDOZHNIK, V. K., *Communism and automation of production*, 1963.

KAIDALOV, D. P., *Communism, work, and man*, 1960.

KAMAYEV, V. D. and LENSKAYA, S. A., *The role of automation in the construction of communism in the Soviet Union*, 1963.

KATS, Y. D., *Essays on labour statistics*, 1959.

KOGAN, L. N., *Work and beauty*, 1963.

KORNIYENKO, V. P., *Social division of labour during the transition to communism*, 1963.

KOSTOMAROV, G. D. (Ed.), *Sources of communist labour*, 1963.

KOTOV, F. I., *Labour problems during the seven-year plan*, 1960.

KOZLOVA, O. V., *Advancement of the cultural and technical standards of the working class in the Soviet Union*, 1959.

KUDRYAVTSEV, A. S. (Ed.), *Labour economics in the Soviet Union*, 1961.

KUZNETSOV, A. D., *Labour resources in the Soviet Union and their utilization*, 1960.

LAPTIN, M. N., *Lenin on material and moral incentives to work*, 1962.

LENIN, V. I., A great beginning, *Works*, 4th edition (Russian), vol. 29.

—— The role and functions of the trade unions under the new economic policy, *Works*, 4th edition (Russian), vol. 33.

—— The immediate tasks of the Soviet Government, *Works*, 5th edition (Russian), vol. 36.

LEVIN, I. M., *Work and wages planning at industrial enterprises*, 1958.

LITVYAKOV, P. P. and TYAPKIN, N. K., *Work for society and its productivity*, 1961.

MARKOV, N. V., *Physical and intellectual work under communism*, 1962.

MARX, K., The poverty of philosophy, *Works*, 2nd edition (Russian), vol. 4.

—— Economic and philosophical manuscripts, 1844.

—— Marx and Engels earlier works, 1956.

MAXIMOV, M. I. (Ed.), *Romanticism of work*, 1963.

MERKULOV, A. P., *Work and automation*, 1963.

MOSYAGIN, S. I., *Technical progress and development of forms of communist work*, 1963.

NIKOLSKY, V. S., *Organization of work and wages in coal mines*, 1957.

NOTKIN, A. I., *Material and technical basis of socialism*, 1954.

OKLADNOI, G. M., *Advancement of cultural and technical standards of the working class*, Kharkov, 1958.

Advancement of cultural and technical standards of the collective farms, Kharkov, 1958.

OSIPOV, A. P. and others, *Soviet worker and automation*, 1960.

PATRUSHEV, V. D., *Intensive labour under socialism*, 1963.

PETROV, A. S., *Work and creation of the masses*, 1962.

PLATONOV, R. P. and SILIVANCHIK, P. P., *Communism and the harmonious development of the individual*, Minsk, 1963.

PRUDENSKY, A. G. (Ed.), *Working time reserves in Siberian industry*, Novosibirsk, 1961.

SONIN, M. Y., *Reproduction of manpower in the Soviet Union and the labour balance*, 1959.

STRUMILIN, S. G., *Problems of socialism and communism*, 1961.

Problems of labour economics, 1957.

SUKHOMLINSKY, V. A., *Work and aesthetic education*, 1962.

TERPIGOREV, A. M., *Work and self-education*, 1959.

VOLKOV, F. M., *Extended reproduction of skilled manpower in the Soviet Union*, 1961.

VOLKOV, Y. E. (Ed.), *Soviet worker*, Sverdlovsk, 1963.

YANTSOV, A. I. (Ed.), *School and work*, 1963.

YOVCHUK, M. T. and others (Ed.), *Soviet working class*, 1961.
YOYRYSH, A. I., *Work and communism*, 1961.
ZHEZHELENKO, V. P. and others, *Machinery, labour, and man*, 1963.
ZVORYKIN, A. A., *The creation of the material and technical basis of communism*, 1959.

OSIPOV, G. V. (Ed.), *Sociology in the U.S.S.R.*, 2 vols, 1965.

The following papers from the present volume have now appeared in substantially the same form in the above Russian collection:

2. Smirnov, G. L. (Vol. I, p. 344).
3. Osipov, A. P. (Vol. II, p. 10)
5. Aleshina, F. Yu. (Vol. II, p. 348).
7. Zdravomyslov, A. G. & Yadov, V. A. (Vol. II, p. 189).
9. Semyonov, V. S. (Vol. I, p. 416).
10. Yeremeyev, B. I. (Vol. II, p. 75).
11. Yovchuk, M. T. (Vol. II, p. 28).
13. Kogan, L. N. (Vol. II, p. 57).
16. Oshanin, D. A. (Vol. II, p. 116).
17. Naumova, N. F. (Vol. II, p. 139).
18. Valentinova, N. G. (Vol. II, p. 99).

COLLECTED ARTICLES

Certain problems of work and health, 1962.
Communist attitude to work, 1963.
For communist work, 1962.
From socialism to communism, 1962.
Growth of the creative activity of the working class in the Soviet Union, 1963.
Labour economics, 1957.
Labour problems; transactions of the Institute of Labour, 1958.
Labour problems in the Soviet Union, 1958.
Manpower resources in the Soviet Union, 1961.
Philosophical problems of cybernetics, 1961.
Problems of labour planning, 1962.
Problems of labour productivity in the period of communist construction, 1962.
Socio-economic problems of technical progress, 1961.
Standard bearers of communist work, 1961.

Technical progress and labour problems during the transition to Communism, 1962.

Work for society, in the period of the comprehensive construction of communism, 1963.

ARTICLES

All have appeared in *Problems of Philosophy – Voprosy Filosofii*

BOBNEVA, M. I., Man and machinery, 1961, No. 4.

ITELSON, A. B., Cybernetics and problems of the psychology of work, 1962, No. 4.

KOGAN, G. P. and FAINBURG, Z. I., The changing nature of work and the development of man, 1963, No. 3.

KURYLEV, A. K., The development of the individual under communism, 1961, No. 11.

LEONTYEV, A. N. and PANOV, D. Y., Human psychology and technical progress, 1962, No. 8.

MANEVICH, E. L., The elimination of distinctions between intellectual and physical work in the period of the comprehensive construction of communism, 1961, No. 9.

MASLOV, P. P., Division of labour and the development of the individual, 1962, No. 10.

NOVOSELOV, N. S., Division of labour under communism does not preclude the possibility of changing work and the development of the individual, 1963, No. 3.

OSHANIN, D. A. and PANOV, D. Y., Man and automatic control systems, 1961, No. 5.

STRUMILIN, S. G., Communism and division of labour, 1963, No. 3.

Notes on Contributors

FAINA YUDOVNA ALESHINA (born 1923, died 1962), M.Sc. Econ.; former research associate of the Institute of Labour.

SERGEI TIMOFEYEVICH GURYANOV (born 1928), a post-graduate student of the Institute of Philosophy; a sociologist with a special interest in the sociology of religion.

ARON IOSIFOVICH KATZENELINBOIGEN (born 1927), M.Sc. Econ.; Research Associate of the Institute of Economics of the Soviet Academy of Sciences; an economist working in problems of the economic effectiveness of mechanization and automation, and on the problems of the organization of labour.

LEV NAUMOVICH KOGAN (born 1923), D.Phil.; lecturer in the Department of Philosophy, the Urals State University, Sverdlovsk; engaged in work on the problems of the sociology of labour; publications: *The October Revolution and the development of the creative activity of the masses*, Sverdlovsk (1957), and *Labour and beauty*, Moscow (1963).

MOTEL KHAIKOVICH LIBERMAN (born 1912) an engineer in the Department of Labour and Wages in Sverdlovsk, now working on economic problems of the material stimulation of labour.

ALEXANDER NIKIFOROVICH MASLIN (born 1906), Dr.Sc. (Phil.); professor, head of the Culture Section, Institute of Philosophy; historian of philosophy, working on problems of cultural revolution and social culture.

NINA FYODOROVNA NAUMOVA (born 1930), Candidate of Philosophical Sciences; Scientific Associate of the Institute of Philosophy of the Soviet Academy of Sciences; a philosopher working on the social effects of technical progress.

DMITRI ALEXANDROVICH OSHANIN (born 1907), M.Sc. Ped.; Head of the Laboratory of Industrial Psychology, Institute of Psychology, Soviet Academy of Pedagogical Sciences; working on the problems of the psychology of labour and machine design.

ALEXANDER PAVLOVICH OSIPOV (born 1918), Candidate of Historical Sciences; reader in the Library Institute; engaged on research into social problems of the occupational structure.

GENNADY VASILEVICH OSIPOV (born 1929), D.Phil.; Professor of Sociology; Director of the Concrete Sociological Research Section of the Institute of Philosophy, Soviet Academy of Sciences.

VLADIMIR VASILYEVICH PETROV (born 1910), head of the Department of Labour and Wages in Sverdlovsk; an economist now studying the social aspects of industrial training.

VADIM SERGEYEVICH SEMYONOV (born 1927), M.Sc. (Philosophy); a senior research associate of the Institute of Philosophy, specializing in the problems of class and class relations.

VLADIMIR NIKOLAYEVICH SHUBKIN (born 1923), Candidate of Economics; Senior Scientific Associate of the Institute of Economics and the Organization of Industrial Production of the Siberian branch of the Soviet Academy of Sciences; a specialist in economics and sociology, investigating statistical and mathematical methods in sociology.

GEORGII LUKICH SMIRNOV (born 1921), M.Sc. (Phil.); social philosopher; member of the editorial board of *Kommunist*; main research interest is the composition of the Soviet working class.

STANISLAV GUSTAVOVICH STRUMILIN (born 1877), Academician, eminent Soviet economist and sociologist, statistician, and historian; working on problems of planning, economics of labour, and statistics; major publications: *Planning in the Soviet Union* (1957), *Problems of the economics of labour* (1957), *Statistical and economic essays* (1954), *Building Communism* (1959).

NATALIA GRIGORIEVNA VALENTINOVA (born 1930), a research associate of the Institute of Philosophy of the Soviet Academy of Sciences; a social psychologist.

VLADIMIR ALEXANDROVICH YADOV (born 1929), graduate of the department of philosophy, Leningrad University, Candidate of Science; Assistant Professor, Head of Laboratory of Sociological Research, Leningrad University; engaged in research in the sociology of labour and social psychology.

BORIS IVANOVICH YEREMEYEV (born 1927), sociologist; research assistant in the Institute of Philosophy, Soviet Academy of Sciences; engaged in research into sociological aspects of technical developments.

MIKHAIL TRIFONOVICH YOVCHUK (born 1906), Alternate Member of the Soviet Academy of Sciences; specialist in the history of philosophy; head of the department of the History of World Philosophy, the Institute of Philosophy, Soviet Academy of Sciences; author of several papers on the history of philosophy and sociology.

ANDREI GRIGORYEVICH ZDRAVOMYSLOV (born 1928), graduate of the department of philosophy, Leningrad University, Candidate of Science; Assistant Head of Laboratory of Sociological Research, Leningrad University; engaged in research in the sociology of labour.

ANATOLII ALEKSEYEVICH ZVORYKIN (born 1901), Doctor of Economics; Professor; Vice-President of the International UNESCO Commission on the 'History of the Scientific and Cultural Development of Humanity'; Associate of the Institute of Philosophy, Soviet Academy of Sciences; economist and sociologist; author of a series of articles and books on economics, the organization and planning of production, and now working on the problem of the social consequences of mechanization and automation of production.